Stalingrad to Kursk

Triumph of the Red Army

Geoffrey Jukes

Pen & Sword
MILITARY

First published in Great Britain in 2011 by
Pen & Sword Military
an imprint of
Pen & Sword Books Ltd
47 Church Street
Barnsley
South Yorkshire
S70 2AS

Copyright © Geoffrey Jukes, 2011

ISBN 978 1 84884 062 1

The right of Geoffrey Jukes to be identified as Author of this Work has
been asserted by him in accordance with the Copyright, Designs and
Patents Act 1988.

A CIP catalogue record for this book is available from the British Library.

Typeset in Ehrhardt by Phoenix Typesetting, Auldgirth, Dumfriesshire

Printed and bound in England by the MPG Books Group

Pen & Sword Books Ltd incorporates the Imprints of Pen & Sword
Aviation, Pen & Sword Maritime, Pen & Sword Military, Wharncliffe
Local History, Pen and Sword Select, Pen and Sword Military Classics,
Leo Cooper, Remember When, Seaforth Publishing and Frontline
Publishing.

For a complete list of Pen & Sword titles please contact
PEN & SWORD BOOKS LIMITED
47 Church Street, Barnsley, South Yorkshire, S70 2AS, England
E-mail: enquiries@pen-and-sword.co.uk
Website: www.pen-and-sword.co.uk

Contents

Maps

GERMAN CONQUESTS
Sept. 1939 - April 1941

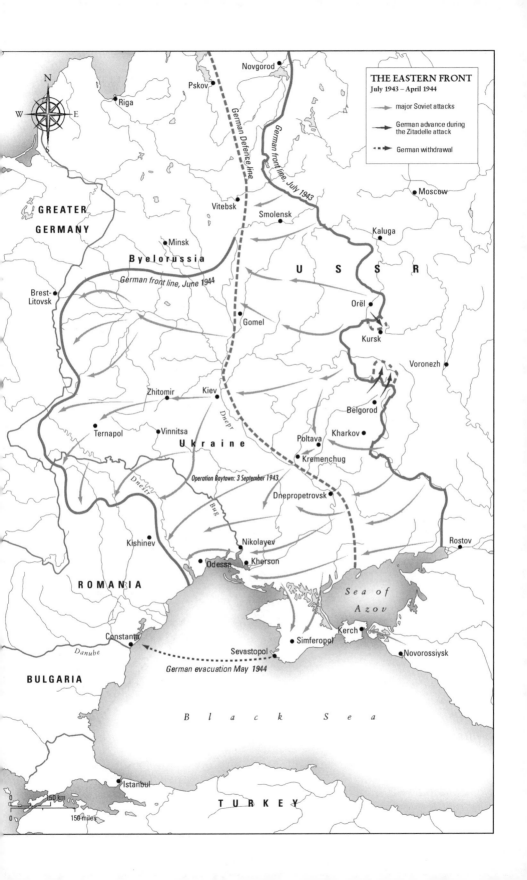

THE EASTERN FRONT
July 1943 – April 1944

major Soviet attacks

German advance during
the Zitadelle attack

German withdrawal

Novgorod

Pskov

Riga

Moscow

German Defence line

German front line, July 1943

Vitebsk

Smolensk

Kaluga

GREATER
GERMANY

Minsk

Byelorussia

U   S   S   R

German front line, June 1944

Orël

Brest-
Litovsk

Gomel

Kursk

Voronezh

Zhitomir

Kiev

Belgorod

Ternopol

Vinnitsa

Dnepr

Ukraine

Poltava

Kharkov

Kremenchug

Operation Baytown: 3 September 1943

Dnestr

Bug

Dnepropetrovsk

Kishinev

Nikolayev

Rostov

Odessa

Kherson

ROMANIA

Sea of
Azov

Constanța

Danube

Sevastopol

German evacuation May 1944

Kerch

Simferopol

Novorossiysk

BULGARIA

Black   Sea

Istanbul

0   150 km

0   150 miles

TURKEY

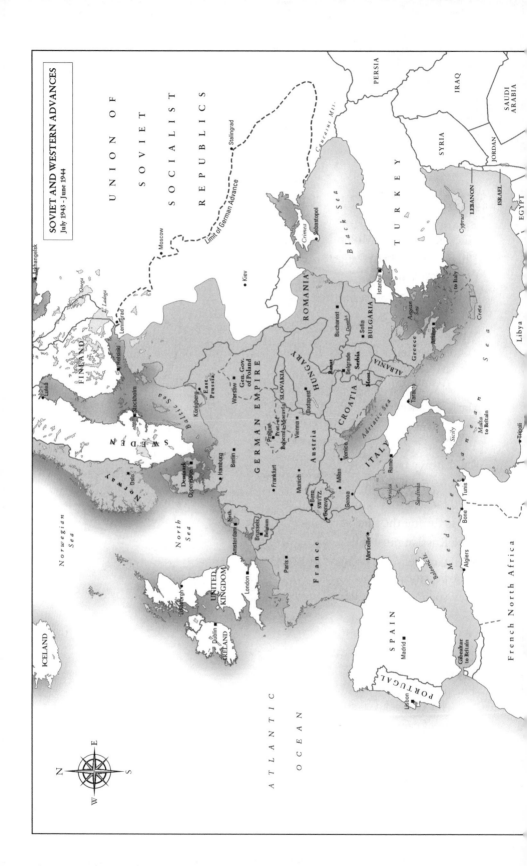

List of Plates

Following Stalin's 'scorched earth' order, retreating Soviet troops removed what they could and destroyed what they could not.

Moscow women digging anti-tank ditches, October 1941.

Barricades and a barrage balloon at the Bolshoi Theatre, Moscow.

To boost morale the traditional 7 November revolution anniversary parade was held as usual in 1941, but most of the participants marched on to the front line.

Even the local horses found the mud too much . . .

At last the snow came and the mud froze.

Germans not dressed for winter surrendering to Russians who were.

Soviet mobile forces in the Moscow counter-offensive consisted largely of skiers.

Abandoned German equipment outside Moscow.

Chuikov's leadership of the 62nd Army's defence of Stalingrad was inspired and inspiring.

The defenders of Stalingrad linked buildings by trenches.

Paulus, promoted to field-marshal by Hitler but captured at Stalingrad.

Manstein, generally considered the most gifted of the German generals.

Pavel Sudoplatov, the NKVD controller of Agent Max for most of the war.

Guderian, the moving spirit behind the creation of 'Blitzkrieg'.

A long chain of German prisoners.

Model, a master of defensive fighting, whose particular skills were more and more in demand as the war progressed.

Preparing to fire 'Katyusha' multiple-rocket launchers.

Wrecking German supply trains was an important element in partisan warfare . . . and hanging was a regular German riposte.

Soviet tanks and infantry advancing to the Dnepr.

New tanks for old: wrecked tanks awaiting the furnaces.

The 'Big Three' at Tehran, November 1943.

The Germans who did get to Moscow. Some 57,000 of them were paraded through the streets in June 1944.

Introduction

Any author who ventures to add yet another book to the masses already written about the Soviet-German war of 1941–45 can reasonably be required to explain why. Hasn't the subject been done to death already?

Not quite. In the Soviet period, evaluation by both Soviet and non-Soviet analysts of the Soviet armed forces' performance in the Second World War passed through a number of phases, and was by no means always primarily concerned with depicting what had actually happened. During Stalin's lifetime such analysis as appeared in the Soviet Union tended to treat the entire war as an episode in his biography, admitting no errors, attributing all successes to his personal genius, all setbacks to German perfidy and incompetent or treacherous Soviet generals, some of whom were shot as scapegoats, and even presenting the long retreats to Leningrad, Moscow, the Volga and the Caucasus as 'active defence', deliberately luring the Germans on, the better to destroy them, as Kutuzov had lured Napoleon in 1812. Allied delays in opening a Second Front in France were castigated, and often attributed to Anglo–American plans to see not only Germany but also the Soviet Union weakened as much as possible (citing remarks to that effect made in July 1941 by US Senator (and from April 1945 President) Truman, and noting Churchill's long record of hostility to Communism), and the role of Allied aid under Lend-Lease was generally unacknowledged in public statements. The only information Stalin gave the Soviet public about the human cost of victory was to say in an interview in 1946 that the Soviet war dead numbered 7 million. This was a hideous understatement; after his death figures of 20 million, and later of 'over 20 million' were widely cited, but work on the first official assessment intended for publication began only in the Soviet Union's last years, and the results were not published until 1993. They placed the total number of dead at 26.7 million (about 8.7 million military and 18 million civilian), almost four times Stalin's figure; even so, they have been widely criticised by some Russian analysts as underestimated. They are also incomplete, in that they give detailed figures of military losses for only 43 of the Red Army's 73 major

1

'operations', and, even in some of those that the work does deal with, there are detectable gaps, though the principal author has stated that the losses in these and in the thirty operations not covered are nevertheless included in the totals for the whole war.

Although millions of survivors from the disasters of 1941–42 knew otherwise, Stalin's official fictions were maintained until two years after his death. Not until 1955 did it begin to be publicly admitted that the long retreats had not been voluntary, and comprehensive 'de-Stalinisation', including substantial criticism of his record as war leader, was initiated by Khrushchev only at the 20th Communist Party Congress in February 1956, almost eleven years after the war's end. A number of prominent generals joined in it, explaining the early disasters primarily in terms of Stalin's drastic pre-war purge of the military leadership and his erroneous wartime decisions, especially in the first months. Most of the allegations were true, but the post-Stalin political leaders and quite a few of the generals were mainly concerned to divert attention from their own misdeeds and shortcomings in the preparation for, and the conduct of, the war, including some for which Stalin was not solely or even partly responsible.

There were, however, a few honourable exceptions. The wartime naval Commander-in-Chief, Admiral Kuznetsov, wrote in his memoirs: 'we found many other mistakes, so we won't write them all off as "Stalin's wrong assessment of the situation". He made his mistakes, and we made ours.'[1] Then Zhukov, the most outstanding of the Soviet wartime generals, admitted in his memoirs that 'neither the People's Commissar Minister, then Marshal Timoshenko nor I, nor my predecessors as Chief of General Staff . . . nor the leading General Staff personnel reckoned on the enemy concentrating such a mass of armoured and motorised forces, and throwing them in on the very first day in compact groups on all strategic axes'.[2]

Hardly any of the political or other military leaders were prepared to admit as much as these two, and Soviet censorship served them faithfully. The memoirs containing Admiral Kuznetsov's admission were not published until the brief period of 'thaw' in 1965, and Zhukov's took even longer to appear. The passage cited above was among many the censors deleted from his manuscript, and was not published until 1992, in the twelfth (and first post-Soviet) edition of his memoirs.

From the mid-1950s onwards a flood of military memoirs and historical studies appeared, but all were subject to censorship, and many more were self-censored by their authors. Common to those that dealt with broader issues than the authors' personal experiences were tendencies to exaggerate German and understate Soviet numbers of troops and weapons, and continuing complaints about Anglo-American delays in opening a Second Front in northern France. Lend-Lease was more frequently mentioned than before, but usually only to play down its importance or complain of its late arrival or inadequacy, and in particular to present the major victories at Moscow and Stalingrad as achieved without it. The Supreme Command archives remained closed, obliging both Soviet and Western analysts to rely largely on Soviet official histories, captured German documentation and what could be read in or between the lines of published Soviet accounts.

After Khrushchev was deposed in 1964, Stalin's image as war leader was at least partially rehabilitated, with the censored memoirs of his principal military subordinates, Marshals Zhukov, Vasilevsky, Rokossovsky and Konev in particular, praising his control of every aspect of the war effort, his organisational abilities, extraordinary memory and the growth in his knowledge and ability in the conduct of military strategy as the war progressed (not forgetting to mention his increasing willingness to take their advice). Soviet censorship removed critical passages from some of these works, and these reappeared only in post-Soviet editions, but the positive elements in the evaluations of Stalin were written by the authors, rather than inserted by the censors. Post-Soviet releases of archival evidence mostly confirm the marshals' accounts of the growth in Stalin's abilities and their influence on his decision-making from mid-1942 onwards. This was particularly the case with Zhukov and Vasilevsky; their roles in devising the strategy that resulted in the major victories at Stalingrad and Kursk will be described later.

During the 1980s Gorbachev's policy of 'glasnost' produced some disclosures; for example, the public was finally allowed to know that almost 3 million Soviet soldiers had surrendered, deserted or defected in the first six months of the war, and that it was not, as the Soviet Union had claimed for over 40 years, the Germans who had shot 21,000 captive Polish officers, civilian officials and priests in Belorussia in 1941, but Soviet NKVD (Interior Ministry) troops in 1940, on Stalin's direct orders. Also in this period revisionist accounts of the war began appearing; some were balanced and sober, others less so, but all questioned aspects of the previous successive, changeable, but always between changes unchallengeable, versions of the Soviet 'official line'. The image that line had sought to present was of a country inadequately prepared by Stalin for war, but able to overcome the initial disasters caused by his errors and German perfidy through the heroic efforts of the army and people, united, inspired, organised and led throughout by the Communist Party, and by its triumph exhibiting the superiority not merely of Soviet over German military prowess, but of the Soviet Communist socio–political and economic order over that of capitalism. That the USSR's principal allies were leading capitalist powers was conveniently ignored, and if the losses they incurred were mentioned at all, their much lower levels compared to those of the Red Army were usually cited only as evidence of how little fighting they had actually done, and how marginally they had contributed to victory.

The floodgates opened far more fully after the Soviet Union was dissolved at the end of 1991. Access to archives became easier; publications included a 15-volume selection of Supreme Command orders and reports from 'Fronts' (army groups) and armies, covering most aspects of the military effort; new journals such as *Military-Historical Archive* appeared, to compete with the long-established *Military-Historical Journal*; the memoirs of Marshals Zhukov and Rokossovsky were republished with the passages Soviet censorship had deleted restored in italics; large numbers of books about them and other leading generals such as Konev and Timoshenko came out; and several books about Intelligence, espionage and counter–espionage were published, including memoirs by at least two former NKVD (predecessor of the KGB) generals. In consequence, much more is now known about the reasons for many of the actions of the Soviet Supreme High Command (the Stavka, consisting of Stalin and his principal military and political subordinates), while increased access by Russian and foreign scholars not only to the archives but to survivors of the war has resulted in some outstanding descriptions of just what it was like to be a Soviet soldier defending Moscow, Leningrad or Stalingrad, or taking part in the succession of major offensives that began at Stalingrad in November 1942 and became almost continuous after the defensive battle of the Kursk salient in July 1943, to end at Berlin and Prague in May 1945.[3]

However, the availability of this additional information, and the end of most of the Soviet-era manipulation of public discourse, has engendered a number of new controversies among both Russian and foreign analysts of the war, and the questions raised include:

1. To what extent did Stalin's purge of the military in 1937–38 really 'decapitate' the Red Army and bring about the disasters of 1941?
2. Why was Stalin so convinced that Hitler would not attack the Soviet

Union while the British remained undefeated, that until the very last moment he apparently ignored all warnings about the imminence of invasion, and even after it had begun, continued to maintain, until the official declaration of war arrived, that it was a 'provocation' by German generals, undertaken without Hitler's knowledge?

3. Why did Stalin believe that if Germany did nevertheless invade, its main objectives would be not the 'political' targets of Leningrad, Moscow and Kiev, but the 'economic' targets of Ukrainian coal, iron ore and grain, and Caucasian oil?

4. Did the German invasion pre-empt by only 15 days a Soviet attack on Germany, scheduled to begin on 6 July 1941, and aimed at taking over not only Germany but all of German-occupied Europe, as Victor Suvorov has claimed?

5. Was the attempt, in the first weeks of invasion, to use the Bulgarian ambassador to convey peace proposals that offered the Germans substantial territorial concessions a genuine panic-induced offer or, as Soviet sources subsequently asserted, simply an attempt to 'disinform' the Germans and gain time?

6. Was Operation 'Mars', against the German Army Group Centre in November–December 1942, a diversion, intended only to prevent it sending troops south to counter the Soviet counter-offensives at Stalingrad (Operations 'Uranus' and 'Saturn'), as Zhukov's and other Soviet-period accounts maintained, or was it meant to be either the main assault of the 1942–43 winter campaign as David Glantz has claimed,[4] or as Aleksey Isayev contends,[5] of equal status with 'Uranus', and, as both argue, subsequently ignored or played down only because it was a disastrous failure?

7. What are the most likely reasons for the improvement in Soviet Intelligence about German intentions between mid-February 1943, when a major German counter-offensive took them completely by surprise, and 8 April, when Zhukov was (rightly, as it proved) so sure of German intentions that he proposed, and Stalin agreed, to base the Soviet strategy for the summer campaign entirely around the German plans?

8. Was the tank battle at Prokhorovka on 12 July 1943, during the Battle of Kursk, the biggest tank battle ever; and was it, as Soviet-era accounts unanimously claimed, a Soviet victory so decisive that it forced Hitler to abandon the entire German summer offensive on the very next day?

9. How important were Lend–Lease supplies to the Soviet war effort?
10. Need the price of Soviet victory have been so high, namely more lives lost than the combined total for all the other major belligerents on both sides?

In what follows I shall try to answer these questions. Since much depends on the balance of forces at various times in the war, some points about the differences in meaning of the military terms used by the two sides should be noted now.

The terms company, battalion, regiment and division meant roughly the same in the Wehrmacht and Red Army, but Soviet units, especially in the first two years of the war, were often kept in the line until reduced almost to nothing before being withdrawn to reserve, and during the entire war were less likely than German ones to be made up to strength in the course of an operation.[6] The Germans did not have brigades; the Soviets had them mostly in tank, motorised and airborne forces, and they were approximately equivalent to a German regiment. Neither army had the rank of brigadier; a Soviet brigade was usually commanded by a colonel, though sometimes by a major-general. Both armies had the rank of 'colonel-general', unfamiliar to Western readers. In the Wehrmacht a colonel-general (*Generaloberst*) was the second highest rank; in the Red Army general (*polkovnik*) was the third highest, corresponding to a British or American lieutenant-general.

Although Soviet forces usually outnumbered German, the discrepancies were by no means always as large as might be suggested by comparing the numbers of divisions engaged, because the war establishment of a German infantry division (16,859 in 1941) was considerably larger than the Soviet equivalent, the 'rifle' division (14,483, further reduced to 12,795 in 1942, and to about 9,000 in 1943), and at least until mid-1943 Soviet divisions were far more likely to be at low strength than German ones. The Red Army also maintained a number of horse cavalry units that were called divisions, but their strength was usually only 3,000, numerically at best a reinforced regiment.

At the higher levels the differences in usage of terms increased considerably. As generally in Western armies, a corps in the Wehrmacht was a formation comprising several divisions. That was initially also true of the Red Army, but from 1940 the term acquired a special association with mechanised forces, the Soviet counterparts to panzer and motorised infantry (from 1943 'panzer-grenadier') divisions. The Red Army had formed its first two mechanised corps in 1932, and two more in 1934, but defence head Voroshilov had prevented further expansion and in November 1939 had them abolished in favour of much smaller tank brigades, broadly equivalent to German regiments. In April 1940 Marshal Timoshenko replaced Voroshilov as People's Commissar (Minister) for Defence, and when the panzers, having to some extent demonstrated their value in the rapid defeat of Poland in 1939, displayed it even more convincingly in the conquests of the Low Countries and France in 1940, and Yugoslavia and Greece in 1941, he persuaded Stalin to decree an immediate start to forming 'several' mechanised corps, each with 1,000–1,200 tanks.[7]

Timoshenko ordered the formation of eight such corps, each consisting of one motorised infantry and two tank divisions. But that process began only in August 1940 and was not completed before the war began. For example, Rokossovsky, commanding the 9th Mechanised Corps on the day of the invasion, noted that while it had almost all its personnel, it did not have a single one of the vehicles the mobilisation plan specified for transporting its infantry, and only 30 per cent of its tanks. Moreover, the tanks' engines were so worn out that he had had to limit their hours of use for crew training.[8] Of the six mechanised corps thrust into catastrophically unsuccessful counter-attacks in the first week of invasion, only one was at full strength in men and equipment. No German corps, mechanised or not, ever went into action in a similarly incomplete or mechanically unsatisfactory state.

After the original mechanised corps had been disbanded or destroyed, the Soviet use of the term corps diverged totally from German or Western practice. In 1942–43 a Soviet mechanised corps was not quite equal to a German panzer division, and a tank corps was even more inferior, as Table 1 shows.

Table 1. Relative strengths of German and Soviet mobile units

	German Division		*Soviet Corps*	
	Panzer	*Motorised Infantry**	*Tank*	*Mechanised*
Men:	16,932	14,029	7,800	15,018
Tanks and SP Guns:	200	–	68	204
Other vehicles:	2,147	2,415	871	1,693
Field Guns:	58	56	24	36
Anti-Tank Guns:	101	73	12	36
Anti-Aircraft Guns:	63	–	20	36
Mortars:	54	108	52	148

*Retitled panzer-grenadier from 1943.

A Soviet mechanised corps was broadly reckoned as superior to a German motorised infantry division and roughly equal to a panzer division; a tank corps was considered equivalent to only half of a panzer division.[9] Later, as Soviet officers acquired experience in handling larger formations, bigger corps were reinstituted; for example, a Guards cavalry corps and a Guards rifle corps, each of three divisions, took part in the final battle for Berlin in 1945. But the reintroduction of corps of this size was by no means general; in that same battle there were also twenty of the smaller tank and mechanised corps.[10]

The next higher levels, army and army group (in Soviet parlance 'Front'), exhibited even greater differences in the two sides' practices. For example, the total German invading force comprised only three Army Groups, North, Centre and South. Army Group North had two armies plus one panzer group, Centre had two armies and two panzer groups, South had three German and two Romanian armies, and one panzer group (all the panzer groups were later retitled panzer armies). The Soviet counterpart to an army group was a Front. Initially the invaders were faced by four such 'Fronts', the North-West, West, South-West and South, with eleven armies between them, but as the Germans advanced out of the relatively narrow border area and the front line became progressively longer, additional Fronts were created, so that by the end of 1941 there were nine. This did not mean a doubling of the active army, but rather a reduction of the number of troops in a Front, prompted by the demonstrated inability of most Soviet generals at that time to control very large numbers of men successfully; the four original Fronts had between 440,000 (North-West) and 864,600 (South-West) troops under command, the nine successors between 244,000 (Bryansk) and 558,000 (Western). Zhukov had two Fronts (Western and Kalinin) under his command during the defensive battle and counter-offensive at Moscow in late 1941 and early 1942, and in the counter-offensive he had 941,600 troops, but no other Soviet general was entrusted with anything like that many until much later in the war. The 1,134,800 troops engaged in the Stalingrad counter-offensive (Operation 'Uranus') in November 1942 were divided between three Fronts, and until 1944 the largest number entrusted to any Front commander other than Zhukov was 738,000, in Rokossovsky's Central Front at Kursk in mid-1943. The largest Fronts in the entire war were the 1st Belorussian (Zhukov, 1.1 million) and the 1st Ukrainian (Konev, 1.2 million), both engaged in the Vistula-Oder operation in January 1945. Individual German army group commanders had controlled larger numbers than those from the first days of the war.

An initial Soviet attempt to put larger numbers of troops under single control by creating 'Directions', each under a Commander-in-Chief in charge of several Fronts, was abandoned by mid-1942; of the four nominees two (Voroshilov and Budenny) proved failures, and were dismissed within three months, a third (Timoshenko) performed successfully until the spring of 1942, but then, with Stalin's support, and overruling objections by the Chief of the General Staff Shaposhnikov and by Zhukov, initiated an attempted offensive in Ukraine that turned out disastrously. The fourth Commander-in-Chief, Zhukov, proved consistently successful, but his opposition to Stalin's insistence on mounting an over-ambitious general offensive in early 1942 led to the dictator abolishing his post and leaving him temporarily in command of only one Front. However, his role as a 'Stavka representative' (see below) saw him regularly in control of two or even three Fronts during 1942–44.

All posts of Commanders-in-Chief of 'Directions' were replaced from mid-1942 by 'Stavka representatives'. These were normally based in Moscow, but Stalin would dispatch them to the front line to coordinate the preparation and conduct of specific operations, especially those involving more than one Front. Most regularly employed in this role were Zhukov and Vasilevsky, each of whom at various times controlled three Fronts. The Stavka representatives had considerable powers over the individual Front commanders, but Stalin maintained close control over them, requiring each to send him a report on the day's events every day before midnight.[11]

However, months of disaster would precede the introduction of the system of Stavka representatives. The first weeks of the war were notable mainly for chaos, mass panic, surrenders, desertions, defections and attempted counter-strokes, most of which were catastrophic failures. It may now be appropriate to consider the circumstances that led to the invasion, and the early stages of it, with particular attention paid to matters suppressed or glossed over in Soviet-era accounts.

Chapter One

Descent into Conflict

Pre-war relations between the Soviet Union and Germany had fluctuated from close cooperation to latent and overt antagonism. After signing the Treaty of Rapallo with Weimar Germany in 1922, the Soviet Union for 11 years actively assisted the Reichswehr to circumvent the bans that the Versailles Treaty had placed on German possession of tanks or military aircraft, by allowing it to establish secret training schools, for aircraft pilots and observers at Lipetsk in 1925, for tank crews at Kazan and for chemical warfare at Tomsk in 1926. At all three schools Soviet officers trained alongside Germans, but the installations were all closed within six months of Hitler's appointment as Reichskanzler in January 1933, in reaction to overtly anti-Soviet pronouncements and actions by the new Nazi regime.[12] The numbers of Germans who underwent some training in the USSR were not large, but included several who became prominent in the Second World War, including for example in 1929 Colonels Keitel and Brauchitsch and Major Model, and in 1932 Lieutenant-Colonel Manstein,[13] all of whom would become field marshals during the war. Interaction between the two armies had been profound enough that as late as 1935 Colonel Koestring, the German military attaché in Moscow, observed, after attending Soviet manoeuvres, 'all these commanders and leaders are our pupils'.[14] But by 1939 many of them would have been removed, imprisoned or shot, and any lessons they had absorbed from the Germans would have to be relearned in the coming war.

The post-First World War German and Soviet armed forces had both come into existence as a result of regime change engendered by defeat in war. Initially both depended heavily on officers from the previous regime's armies – the Reichswehr recruited the most capable for the very limited numbers of posts permitted under the Versailles Treaty, and the new Soviet government relied heavily on the skills and experience of former Tsarist officers (the so-called *voyenspetsy*, 'military specialists') to win the Russian Civil War of 1918–20. But once that war was over, their paths began to diverge. The Reichswehr and later Wehrmacht as far as possible maintained continuity with the customs and traditions of the

Kaisers' armies, particularly in officer education, but by 1931 most ex-Tsarist officers had been dismissed from the 'Workers' and Peasants' Red Army', and education of officers was neglected during Voroshilov's head-ship of the defence structure (1925–40). For example, the highest-grade institution for training senior officers, the General Staff Academy, was not established until the summer of 1936,[15] and the purge of 1937–38 removed many of those who attended its first courses, as well as several of those who taught them. After Timoshenko replaced Voroshilov as the People's Commissar (Minister) for Defence in May 1940, he instituted assemblies during that summer of officers commanding regiments (mostly colonels), where it was found that 200 of the 225 participants had had no formal training other than in courses for junior lieutenants – in other words, they had been taught how to command a platoon, but not a company or a battalion, let alone a regiment. The other 25 had completed courses at military training schools (when they were lieutenants or at most captains), but none had attended a Military Academy.[16] The average standard of Soviet officers in 1941 therefore compared poorly with their German counterparts, even before the effects of the purges of the Soviet military in 1937–39 are taken into account.

Some post-Soviet accounts have maintained that the abandonment of Tsarist military methods and standards of training was largely respons-ible for the early disasters, but this ignores historical reality. From the end of the Napoleonic Wars in 1815 to the Bolshevik seizure of power in November 1917 Russia fought successful wars only against mostly small and uniformly technologically inferior opponents in the Caucasus, Central Asia and the Far East. Its three wars against industrially advanced powers – Britain and France in the Crimean War of 1854–56, modernising Japan in 1904–05, and Germany in 1914–17 – all ended in humiliating defeats. Its most successful strategic-scale operation of the First World War, Brusilov's 1916 offensive, had been achieved against Austro-Hungarian, not German, forces and its gains did not survive the German intervention that followed Romania's entry into the war.

It was these wars that Stalin had in mind when in 1931, in the early stages of industrialisation, he referred to Russia's being defeated in the past because of its 'backwardness', and his invocation during the war of inspirational figures of past Russian military glory included none more recent than Suvorov, who died in 1800, and Kutuzov, who died in 1814. Probably the most that can be said is that the General Staff's overall main-tenance of good standards throughout the Second World War owed much to four former Tsarist officers, Tukhachevsky and Yegorov (both shot in the 'purges'), who headed it for most of the 1930s, and Shaposhnikov and Vasilevsky, its heads for most of the period 1938–45. But where the field forces and their commanders were concerned, the results obtained against major opponents by Russia's pre-revolutionary army in its last hundred years of existence do not seem to have offered much that merited perpetuating.

After Hitler came to power, Stalin began seeking allies to contain Germany's resurgent militarism, and intensified his efforts in 1938, after Hitler first annexed Austria in March, then in September created a crisis over the alleged oppression of the predominantly German population of Czechoslovak Sudetenland, and threatened to invade it. Stalin brought 76 divisions and smaller formations equivalent to another 14 up to full strength, arranged with the head of the Czechoslovak Air Force to send 700 aircraft to Czech airfields, and on 25 September 1938 had the French military attaché notified of the steps he had taken, clearly in hopes of encouraging similar action by France and Britain, as he was not prepared to be the only one to stand up to Hitler. Besides, Soviet ground forces could reach Czechoslovakia only through Poland or Romania, and heavy British and French pressure on both countries, especially on Poland, would have been needed to obtain acquiescence to such transit.

A group of German generals, horrified at the risk of war Hitler was courting, plotted to overthrow him, and in August sent an emissary to London to urge Chamberlain's government not to give in to him. Chamberlain was notified within two days of the emissary's arrival and was informed of the content of his message, but both the British and French governments doubted the German generals' ability to mount a successful coup, and both feared Communism more than Nazism. In both countries, still emerging from the Great Depression, the Communist parties were attracting far more voter support than their Nazi/Fascist counterparts, and, in a mirror image of Stalin's own views of British and French intentions, both governments suspected that the Soviet Union was trying to drag them into a war with Germany. They were also sceptical about the Red Army's capabilities, following Stalin's purge of its leaders in 1937–38, in which 3 of the 5 marshals, 15 of the 16 army commanders, 60 of the 67 corps commanders, and all 17 of the most senior political officers had been court-martialled and shot, and thousands of other officers executed or imprisoned. So the only pressure Britain and France applied was on Czechoslovakia; their ambassadors woke President Benes in the middle of the night, and told him to cede the Sudetenland.[17] Had the Chamberlain and Daladier governments done what the German generals requested, either Hitler would have been deposed or the Second World War would have broken out in October 1938. In the latter event Germany's 51 divisions (only two of them armoured, with a third in process of formation) would have faced 38 Czech, 65 French and about 90 Soviet divisions in a war on three fronts, coupled with at the least a British naval blockade, air raids and financial pressure. The German generals might then have succeeded in disposing of Hitler and negotiating peace within a few weeks. Instead, a meeting, to which neither Stalin nor any Czechoslovak delegation was invited, resulted on 29 September in the notorious Munich Agreement, by which the British and French prime ministers and the Italian dictator gave Hitler everything he had demanded, proving his apprehensive generals wrong, convincing some of them and many of their colleagues that he was a genius at obtaining results by merely threatening military action, and raising his domestic prestige to levels that made his removal unthinkable for the foreseeable future.

For Stalin, who believed (not without some justification) that what the British and French governments really wanted was to point German ambitions eastward, the lesson of Munich was 'if you can't beat 'em, join 'em'. As a dual signal to Germany, he replaced his Jewish Foreign Minister Litvinov, who favoured cooperation with the UK and France to restrain Germany, with Molotov, who was more anti-Western, less anti-German and not Jewish (though his wife was), and began the switch in policy that culminated in the Molotov–Ribbentrop Pact, a non-aggression treaty with secret clauses delineating the signatories' respective spheres of influence in Eastern Europe. The pact was signed on 23 August 1939; nine days later Germany invaded Poland, and the USSR followed suit on 17 September, the invaders abolishing the Polish state and dividing it between them. Over the next 20 months Germany invaded eight more countries (Denmark, Norway, Luxembourg, Belgium, Holland, France, Yugoslavia and Greece), and the USSR five (annexing Lithuania, Latvia and Estonia completely, and taking territory from Romania and Finland). The political quasi-alliance was complemented by agreements under which the Soviet Union supplied oil, grain and minerals to Germany, and provided facilities in the Murmansk area, including a naval base, intended for use by German submarines. In the event they did not use it, though a supply ship was stationed there for some months, but in September 1939 Germany's prestigious transatlantic liner *Bremen* succeeded in evading the Anglo-French naval blockade when returning from New York by heading for Murmansk, and stayed there until March 1940 before slipping down the Norwegian coast to

Hamburg. But perhaps the most blatant case of Soviet aid to the German war effort at sea occurred in July and August 1940, when the disguised commerce raider *Komet* was provided with Soviet pilots and the services of an icebreaker to transit via the Northern Sea Route to the Pacific, where it sank several Allied merchant ships before returning home via the Cape of Good Hope.

The outbreak of the Second World War was soon followed by economic measures against Germany, in particular the British imposition of an economic blockade. Restrictions on British and French trade with the Soviet Union also ensued, especially in the provision of modern equipment, as requirements for their own war efforts took priority over exports. This situation created a mutual interest between the two dictatorships, for the Soviet Union to provide Germany with raw materials, food and oil, German deliveries in return including items as such as lathes, optical equipment and armour plating. The first economic agreement was signed on 21 August, two days before the Molotov–Ribbentrop Pact. Under a second agreement, signed in February 1940, the Soviet Union undertook to deliver in 12 months a million tonnes of foodstuffs, 900,000 tonnes of oil, 500,000 tonnes of iron ore and 300,000 tonnes of scrap iron and steel, 100,000 tonnes each of chrome ore and of cotton, plus smaller but significant amounts of precious metals such as platinum. In addition, it helped in two ways to reduce the effects of the British blockade, first by providing a 50 per cent reduction in charges for rail transits between Germany and Iran, Afghanistan or Japanese-occupied Korea and Manchukuo, and secondly by making some purchases on Germany's behalf in countries where dealing with Germany was embargoed.[18] How much these goods and services contributed to Germany's war effort may be debatable, but they certainly diminished the effects of the Anglo-French blockade.

Communist dogma of the time held that the capitalist world would ultimately attempt to avert its inevitable doom by uniting to attack the Soviet Union, but Germany's invasion of Poland and the consequent British and French declarations of war appeared to postpone this indefinitely. It seemed that this would enable the Soviet Union to digest the territories the Molotov–Ribbentrop Pact had allowed it to swallow, and to build up its strength while the major capitalist powers weakened theirs by fighting each other. For Stalin this appeared a splendid outcome; not only had he apparently succeeded in postponing the inevitable war indefinitely, he had weakened the Soviet Union's potential attackers and divided the capitalist world, turned German military power away towards the west, where he expected it to be bogged down for several years, as it had been in 1914–18, and acquired a buffer zone to protect the Soviet heartland of Russia, Belorussia and Ukraine. At a meeting on 7 September 1939 Dimitrov, of the Communist International (Comintern), noted Stalin's satisfaction that 'A war is on between two groups of capitalist countries . . . we see nothing wrong in their having a good fight and weakening each other.'[19]

However, after eight months of inactivity in the west, Hitler's armed forces shattered Stalin's expectations by achieving in just six weeks the conquest of France that the Kaiser's armies had sought vainly for over four years, and forcing the British off the continent. They remained in the war and brusquely rejected Hitler's peace offer, but they could not successfully reinvade mainland Europe single-handed, so Hitler could now direct the bulk of the German army and the Luftwaffe towards the objective he had defined over a decade earlier in his book, *Mein Kampf* (*'My Struggle'*), of gaining *Lebensraum* ('living space') for the German people by expansion to the east. At the end of July 1940, one month after the French surrender and only a week after issuing the Directive for the planned invasion of the United Kingdom (Operation 'Sealion'), he ordered the army staff to begin at once making plans for invading the Soviet Union within the next 12 months.[20]

Despite the Molotov–Ribbentrop Pact, Stalin still saw Germany as a threat, and his preoccupation with creating a buffer zone prompted him to attack Finland in the 'Winter War' (December 1939–March 1940) after it rejected his offer of territory in Karelia in exchange for an eastward move of the border (then only about 21 miles from Leningrad) in the Karelian Isthmus, cession of some small islands in the Gulf of Finland, and provision of land for naval and air bases from which to control access to it. It was an historic irony that when war did come, his series of aggressive westward moves merely gave him borders with the Germans, who in 1941 overran his new 'buffer zones' in a matter of days, while the outstanding performance of the vastly outnumbered Finnish Army reinforced future enemies' and allies' already low opinions of Soviet military competence – enough in Hitler's case for him to stake everything in 1941 on a campaign meant to produce complete victory in only five months. American military forecasts in 1941 held that Moscow would fall within a month and a British prognosis gave it only six weeks, and on 31 May, after the evidence of German preparations to invade the Soviet Union had become overwhelming, London instructed its commanders-in-chief in the Middle East to make plans for seizing Mosul and its important airfield in northern Iraq to use as a base for future bombing raids aimed at destroying the oil wells, storage tanks, refineries and pipelines at Baku in Soviet Transcaucasus before their anticipated swift capture by the Germans.[21]

The final German plan for the invasion (Operation 'Barbarossa') was contained in Führer Directive 21, issued on 18 December 1940. Its basic concept was one that had already proved successful in the previous campaigns: deep penetrations by pincer movements of armoured and motorised infantry divisions would encircle enemy forces between them and the bulk of the army, the footslogging infantry with mostly horse-drawn equipment, including their artillery, following up behind.[22] The invading forces' front line was divided by the marshes of the Pripyat River, the largest wetland area in Europe, in southern Belorussia and north-west Ukraine, covering about 240 kilometres (150 miles) from north to south, and twice that distance from west to east, and there Stalin compounded his major error of reluctance to credit even the possibility of invasion with yet another, a misreading of what the Germans' primary objectives would be if they did nevertheless invade.

The 1940 Soviet General Staff appraisal had correctly assessed those objectives as primarily military and political rather than economic, and therefore anticipated that the major German assault would come north of the Pripyat marshes, with Army Group North aiming at Leningrad and Army Group Centre at Moscow, and only Army Group South moving south of the marshes, heading for Kiev. These cities were not the objectives as such; the General Staff's judgement was (rightly) based on the view that the Germans expected their political, industrial and symbolic importance would force the Red Army to stand and defend them, being destroyed in the process, rather than try to preserve itself by retreat as its predecessors had done at Moscow in 1812.

Stalin, however, believed that Germany's main purpose in invading would be economic, to satisfy her driving need for resources for fighting a prolonged war, specifically Ukrainian coal, iron ore and grain, and the oil of Transcaucasus. He therefore rejected the General Staff's assessment, held that the main German drive would come south of the marshes, and insisted on having more forces deployed there than in the north.[23] Consequently, of the 153 Soviet divisions deployed at the borders in mid-1941, 83 were south of the marshes and 70 north of them. The German deployment was the obverse of this, with 76 divisions to the north and 41 (plus 14 Romanian) south of the marshes. The disparity in the deployment of tank and motorised infantry divisions was even greater. The

Germans had 21 such divisions north of the marshes, only 8 south of them, whereas the Soviets deployed 24 to the north and 30 to the south. The shortest distance from the Baltic coast to the northern edge of the marshes is about 250 miles, that from their southern edge to the Black Sea coast 375 miles, 50 per cent greater. So the German spearheads, the mobile forces, were distributed at an average of about 19 kilometres (12 miles) of front per division north of the marshes and 75 kilometres (47 miles) south of them, whereas the corresponding figures for the Soviet mobile forces were 16.6 and 20 kilometres (10.4 and 12.5 miles). In short, the Germans concentrated their most potent units with a ratio of force to space in the north almost four times that in the south, whereas the Red Army distributed them almost evenly, but with a slightly higher density in the south. Had both sides' mobile forces been of equal fighting value the balance between them would therefore have favoured the Soviets slightly in the north and overwhelmingly in the south. However, they were then by no means equal. In an interview long after the war Molotov would say, 'before the war Stalin considered that we could only meet the Germans on an equal basis in 1943'.[24]

Hitler would briefly espouse Stalin's reasoning about objectives in August 1941, and in 1942, after the Soviet winter victories and the American entry into the war made prolonged hostilities inevitable, it would totally define the aims of the German summer offensive, but Operation 'Barbarossa' itself was a plan for a short war. The invading forces were expected to destroy the Red Army in a single campaign lasting about five months, and Directive 21 did not specifically mention the economic prizes, clearly because after the expected rapid victory they would be there for the taking. Soviet Intelligence, still recovering from Stalin's purge of 1937–39 that had destroyed most of its networks and eliminated many of its best operatives, provided several warnings but no convincing correctives for the excessive economic rationalism that Stalin ascribed to Hitler; in fact the then head of GRU (Military Intelligence), Lieutenant-General F.I. Golikov either accepted Stalin's view or at least pandered to it, in a notorious assessment made in March 1941 (discussed below), and in 1965 admitted, 'I distorted the Intelligence to please Stalin, because I feared him'.[25] That was hardly surprising. Golikov's eight predecessors as Head of Military Intelligence had been arrested during the purges of 1937–39, and all bar one of them had been shot.[26] However, the post-Soviet release of archive material has shown that the much-maligned Beria – from November 1938 head of the NKVD (People's Commissariat of the Interior), the alternative source of secret

Intelligence, and also responsible for the Border Guards – displayed considerably more intestinal fortitude than Golikov. Although Stalin had had his two immediate predecessors, Yagoda and Yezhov, deposed and shot, Beria risked his leader's displeasure by regularly sending him detailed Border Guards' reports about German military preparations along the western frontiers. Beria not only survived, but was given increased wartime status and responsibilities by Stalin, including overseeing the Soviet atomic bomb programme, so Golikov's caution was perhaps excessive – but at least he survived to die a natural death in 1980, whereas Stalin's successors had Beria shot on trumped-up charges in 1953.

Although Stalin saw war with Germany as ultimately inevitable, he hoped, as he later told Churchill, to postpone it at least until 1942. Several events in the weeks preceding the invasion complicated the Soviet threat-assessment process, but the factor that created the greatest problems for the General Staff was Stalin's strongly held belief that Hitler would not undertake a two-front war, and therefore would not attack while the British remained unconquered and scornful of his peace proposals. On 5 May 1941, in a speech to newly commissioned officers, Stalin said that the Red Army had become able to do more than 'defend socialism', it had acquired the capacity to mount offensives (against whom he did not specify, but probably did not need to), and this speech is prominent among the sources cited by Victor Suvorov to support his argument (discussed later) that Hitler's invasion pre-empted a planned Soviet full-scale attack on Germany by only 15 days. In his speech Stalin also referred to Germany as being 'weak' in the First World War because it had had to fight on two fronts, the implication being that it would not voluntarily do so again.

The British several times warned Stalin of Germany's preparations to invade the Soviet Union, but he rejected these as attempts by a desperate government, headed by the dedicatedly anti-Communist Churchill, to relieve the pressure on itself by dragging the USSR into the war. Several Soviet Intelligence 'residents' in German-occupied European countries also provided warnings, but he dismissed them as more British 'plants'. He seems to have believed sincerely that Hitler would not voluntarily undertake a two-front war, because he said so on several occasions. Undoubtedly he was encouraged in that belief by the German deception campaign, which included assurances that German army and air force units were being sent to the east only to be out of range of British bombers while they trained for the invasion of England.

It has been claimed that the deception campaign also included at least two letters from Hitler, in December 1940 and May 1941, in which he assured Stalin 'on my honour as a chief of state' that he had no intention of attacking the Soviet Union. No archival evidence has been found for either, but in post-war interviews Zhukov mentioned being shown both letters by Stalin, and indirect evidence of the second's existence is provided by (1) its date, 14 May, (2) an apology in it for 'the method I have chosen for delivering it to you as quickly as possible', and (3) the surprise landing at Moscow Central Airport on 15 May 1941 of a German Ju52 transport aircraft, which was refuelled and allowed to depart, even though permission for its flight had not been sought beforehand, and several senior Air Defence Force officers were reprimanded for failing to have it intercepted.[27] Both letters are said to have explained the presence of German forces in the east by the need to be beyond the range of British bombers. But the weaknesses in that justification raise several questions to which as yet no answers have been found.

First, did not the Soviet embassy or its Intelligence 'resident' in London (who had, as was found out after the war, several excellent clandestine sources in MI6, Bletchley Park and the Foreign Office) notify Moscow that from late October 1940 the British had observed the fleet of invasion barges being dispersed, Bletchley had deciphered 'Enigma' messages indicating the nominal postponement but actual abandonment of the invasion, and that as far back as 31 October 1940 the Defence Committee, chaired by Churchill, had assessed the future likelihood of invasion as 'relatively remote'?[28]

Secondly, although officially Operation 'Sealion' was only postponed until the spring of 1941, it was widely known in Germany and occupied Europe that it had been abandoned after the Luftwaffe's defeat in the Battle of Britain; this was reported to Moscow in April 1941 by the GRU 'residents' in German-occupied Paris and Prague. Nor was it any secret that in Hitler's ideal world, as described in *Mein Kampf*, Germany would rule the Eurasian 'heartland', including additional *Lebensraum* taken from Russia and Ukraine, while the British Empire ruled most of the rest; certainly he had made a public peace offer to the British after the fall of France, and embarked on preparations to invade only after its rejection.

How serious Hitler was about 'Sealion' can never be known, because the Luftwaffe proved unable to achieve the essential precondition of air superiority over at least the Channel and southern England, and its heavy losses, especially of aircrew, made it very unlikely that it would wish to try again. However, at a meeting with his generals as early as 31 July 1940

Hitler had described Russia as 'the factor on which Britain is relying the most', and remarked that 'with Russia smashed, Britain's last hope would be shattered',[29] indicating that two weeks before the Battle of Britain even officially began ('Eagle Day', 13 August) he believed he could put the United Kingdom out of the war without needing to invade it, by invading the Soviet Union instead – and had already ordered the Wehrmacht to begin planning to do so.

On 10 May 1941 Hitler's deputy, Rudolf Hess, flew to Scotland. Given Churchill's long anti-Communist record, the flight could have only one purpose: to try to persuade the British to make peace with Germany and even join the war against the Soviet Union. Lord Beaverbrook, whom Churchill sent to interrogate Hess, and later to Moscow, confirmed in 1964, in his last public speech, that such had indeed been Hess's mission, and that Stalin had claimed to believe Hitler had sent him.[30] Given the twin realities of Churchill's anti-Communism and of Hitler's attempts during the 1930s to achieve an alliance or at least an 'understanding' with the British, if Stalin really believed what he said to Beaverbrook, would he not have put at least the frontier Military Districts on combat alert? That he did not do so suggests that, despite what he said later, he never seriously believed it, accepted that the British had rejected Hess's proposals out of hand, and interpreted their determination to continue the war as fortification for his belief that Hitler would not attack the Soviet Union.

Churchill's warnings were mainly based on Bletchley Park's deciphering of German messages, but the British believed the Germans had so thoroughly penetrated Soviet security that to tell them what the source was would be tantamount to informing the Germans that their most secret messages were being read. Hence important information was passed to the Soviets only in paraphrased form and with no indication of its source other than vague hints about a spy in the German High Command. Only after the war did it emerge that the precaution had been unnecessary, because, first, the Germans had not penetrated Soviet security, and secondly, Stalin knew what the source was because at least one producer (Cairncross) and some recipients (including Philby and Blunt) of deciphered Ultra material had been Soviet agents since well before the war.

In mid-May the People's Commissar for Defence Marshal Timoshenko and the Chief of General Staff Army General Zhukov came to see Stalin, gave him details of German deployments along the border, and concluded that Germany 'has the ability to pre-empt us in deployment and strike a surprise blow. To avert this . . . I consider it necessary to on no account cede the initiative in action to the German command, to pre-empt the enemy in deploying and to attack the German army at the moment when it will be in the deployment stage and not yet able to organise a front and cooperation between the arms of service.'[31] In short, they proposed attacking first.

Stalin's reaction was blunt: 'Have you gone out of your minds?'[32] They cited his apparent endorsement of offensive action in his speech of 5 May to the newly commissioned officers; he replied that he had said that only to 'encourage the lads' and counteract the widespread feeling that the German army was invincible, and he warned that 'heads would roll' if any pre-emptive action was taken. In 1965 Zhukov conceded that the forward deployments needed for a pre-emptive attack would probably have resulted in an even bigger disaster: 'I think the Soviet Union would have likely been beaten if we had deployed all our forces at the frontiers, as in their plans the German forces had precisely in mind destroying them at the beginning of the war.'[33] The additional forces brought forward would have fallen into German encirclements along with those already deployed along the borders, and would have fared no better against German attacks that were on a far larger scale and faster moving than the Soviet generals, himself included, had anticipated.[34]

So Stalin was almost certainly right in vetoing any attempt at pre-emption in mid–May. He did not state his reasons for doing so, but his alleged receipt of Hitler's 14 May letter may have been among them. However, Timoshenko and Zhukov were disingenuous in trying to exploit his recent reference to the Red Army's alleged capacity to undertake offensives. They must both have been well aware that such statements about the army's ability to undertake offensives, and boastful songs and slogans about 'beating the enemy on his own territory' for 'little loss of blood', did not match the reality of hastily expanded forces in the midst of reorganisation, with equipment that was largely obsolete and often unserviceable because it was badly maintained, raw pilots with few flying hours for lack of aviation fuel, tank drivers with very little driving experience (Soviet tank driver-mechanics averaged 5 to 10 hours' driving practice, their German counterparts 50), nominally motorised infantry with hardly any vehicles, one-sixth of officers' posts unfilled, and many of the remainder filled by underqualified reservists. But at that time, as Zhukov admitted, neither Stalin nor his generals, himself included, foresaw the intensity of the initial German assaults, nor the panic flights, huge encirclements, mass surrenders, desertions and defections that resulted.

Several additional factors have been advanced to explain Stalin's persistence in the belief that Hitler would avoid a two-front war. They included an expectation that invasion would be preceded either by demands for territorial concessions or for increased deliveries of oil, minerals and grain, or by an ultimatum, in each case giving some time to negotiate and prepare. But Hitler's record provided no basis for any such belief. The Rhineland, Austria and Czechoslovakia before the war, Poland, Denmark, Norway, Belgium, Netherlands, Luxembourg, France, Yugoslavia and Greece during it, had all been invaded without prior warning or ultimatum. One of his earliest acts as Reichskanzler had been to conclude in January 1934 a non-aggression pact with Poland, and in a speech at the Berlin Sportspalast during the Munich crisis in September 1938 he had declared that the Sudetenland was 'the last territorial claim I have to make in Europe'. Stalin, having also invaded countries he had undertaken not to, had no reason to believe Hitler would be more punctilious than himself, nor more likely to keep his word in the Soviet than in the Czechoslovak and Polish cases.

A consequence of the 1937–38 purges was that the survivors hesitated to challenge any views they knew Stalin held strongly. For example, as noted above, on 20 March 1941 Golikov, head of GRU, produced an assessment detailing a host of indicators of German preparations for imminent invasion, but summarised them as providing no evidence of any such intent.[35] And when Stalin rejected the General Staff's assessment that the main German thrust would come north of the marshes, Timoshenko and Zhukov meekly accepted his view and deployed their forces accordingly. Zhukov would later write: 'I shall not conceal that it seemed to us then that on questions of war and defence Stalin knew not less but more than us, probed deeper and saw further. Only when we came up against the difficulties of war did we realise that our opinion about Stalin's outstanding knowledge and military leadership qualities was mistaken'. This passage was another of those removed from his manuscript by Soviet censors, to reappear only in editions published after the Soviet Union had ceased to exist.[36]

The deceptive German claims that the troops were being sent eastward simply to be out of range of British bombers while training to invade the British Isles could have been checked on the ground. The Soviet embassy and Intelligence 'resident' in Berlin and agents in Germany, Belgium, Holland and France could observe, and report, that from March to July 1941 the main British air effort was against German shipping, entailing daylight bombing and mine-laying along the Belgian, Dutch and German coasts; otherwise there was only area bombing of some inland cities by night. Neither effort was specifically directed at barracks, airfields, training grounds or the armaments industry, even on the few nights per month when visibility might permit attempts at more precise bombing. Nor was it then particularly large-scale; the first British four-engine bombers came into service only in early 1941, and the first 'thousand bomber' raid did not take place until May 1942. So Stalin should have known that the German explanation was totally false, as British bombing posed no specific threat to the troops in their previous locations. If he was not told that, it was a serious failure of Intelligence and/or diplomacy, but there is nothing in the public domain to suggest that he even asked the necessary questions.

His persistence in the conviction that Germany had lost the First World War by fighting on two fronts is hardest of all to explain. In 1914, when Stalin was already active in the Communist Party that aimed to overthrow the Tsarist regime, the German Great General Staff sought to avoid a two-front war by overcoming France during the six weeks it expected Russia would need for mobilisation. Having failed in that, it then fought the unwanted two-front war, and in 1917 came close to winning it. In February the Russian front and regime collapsed, thereby creating the power vacuum that enabled the Communists, Stalin included, to seize power just nine months later, and in the summer the French army experienced large-scale mutinies. Then, after having fought a two-front war very successfully for 30 months, Germany lost the ensuing one-front war in less than 20 months. As a member of Lenin's government, which accepted the humiliating Treaty of Brest-Litovsk, Stalin must have known that Germany was anything but weak at that time: the Germans presented the treaty with the very short time limits for acceptance characteristic of an ultimatum, and non-compliance would have led to the occupation of St Petersburg by German forces that were already less than 80 miles from the city and were interrupting their advance only to accept massive Russian surrenders.

It is possible Stalin had accepted the contention of some post-1918 German authors, that if the many divisions kept in Russia and Ukraine to enforce a 'victor's peace' had instead been sent to the Western Front, Germany could have won the land campaign in 1918 and thereby secured from the maritime powers of the UK and the USA, which it could not invade, acceptance of a negotiated compromise to end the war. But there is no evidence that he ever mentioned this to anyone.

His persistence in the belief is made even more curious by the fact that the circumstances of mid-1941 favoured Germany far more than did those of 1914–18. There was no Western Front, no possibility that the British could single-handedly recreate one, and no likelihood that the USA would go beyond providing strong material support for the British war effort to itself entering a European land war. That situation changed only in December, and then only because Hitler unnecessarily declared war on the United States four days after the Japanese attacked Pearl Harbor. It seems not only that Stalin ignored these factors, but also that none of his closest military advisers, most of whom had fought in the First World War, witnessing the successive German victories and the moral collapse they caused, dared draw his attention to them.

It has also been suggested that Stalin's reluctance to face reality was because he realised how much harm his purge of the senior military had done, and he hoped to postpone a showdown with Germany until that had been corrected. This seems unlikely for three reasons. First, post-Soviet research has found that the purge was less sweeping than hitherto thought (this is discussed below). Secondly, the object of the purge was to cement Stalin's domination of the military, the only nation-wide organisation capable of challenging the rule of the Communist Party, which he had already subordinated to himself by eliminating all possible rivals. If he accepted that this would weaken the armed forces' ability to defend the country, he could do so only by assuming that they would not be required to fight in the near future, and there is no evidence that he ever acknowledged he had weakened them. Thirdly, it would in any case be against human nature for a leader, especially a dictator who had suppressed all opposition, to see himself as a destroyer of his country rather than as its saviour.

In fact his purge of the officer corps was less devastating than has been widely assumed. Statements by Voroshilov that 40,000 officers had been removed in 1937–38 were for long taken as definitive of the purge, whereas in fact that figure was for all dismissals, including those on the grounds of age, ill-health, death, incompetence, corruption, abuse of office or habitual drunkenness, and by no means all of those dismissed for political reasons were arrested. A report in 1938 by E.A. Shchadenko, then Head of the Red Army's Command Personnel Directorate, responsible for officer selection and appointments, stated that from 1 March 1937 to 1 March 1938 17,413 officers had been dismissed on political grounds, of whom 5,329 (30.6 per cent) had been arrested and charged. On a later occasion Shchadenko complained that 12,000 lieutenants had been dismissed but only 2,000 arrested, and said that 'we should either arrest everyone we dismiss or not demand dismissal of people whom we are not going to arrest'.[37] In April 1940 Shchadenko reported to Voroshilov on officer discharges each year since 1935. The figures were as follows:

Table 2. Discharges, Arrests and Reinstatements of Officers, 1935–39

Year	Total Discharged	Arrested	Reinstated
1935	6,198	0	0
1936	5,677	0	0
1937	18,658	4,474	206
1938	16,362	5,032	1,225
1939	1,878	73	26

So in 1937–39 a total of 36,898 officers were dismissed; 9,579 (26 per cent) of them were arrested, and 1,457 (3.9 per cent of all dismissed, 15.2 per cent of those arrested) were reinstated during 1939. In addition 19,106 were dismissed on political grounds but not arrested, 14,968 of them for being 'connected with conspirators', and the other 4,138 under Voroshilov's June 1938 Directive that officers of 'unreliable nationalities' (e.g. Polish, German, Romanian, Latvian, Lithuanian, Estonian, Finnish and Korean) were to be discharged immediately.[38] By the end of 1939 no fewer than 7,486 (50 per cent) of the former and 1,919 (46.3 per cent) of the latter had been reinstated.[39]

Detailed figures for arrests in the air force have not been published, but dismissals from it for all causes in 1937–39 totalled 5,616. Applying the same criteria as for the army, the author of a detailed and painstaking study[40] concluded that one-third of dismissed air force officers, about 1,590, were arrested. Dismissals and arrests in the navy were included in the army totals for 1937, but figures for the other two years are not available. Nor are there any data in respect of warrant and non-commissioned officers, privates and seamen. However, Robert Conquest's unsourced claim that 'at least 20,000 Political Officers were arrested or killed'[41] is contradicted by two authoritative sources. First, in 1937 Voroshilov (then the People's Commissar for Defence) gave the total of Political Officers in the armed forces as 22,000;[42] if Conquest's claim was correct, 10 out of every 11 of them would have been removed, and certainly nothing remotely resembling that happened. Shchadenko's 1940 report noted that altogether 5,953 (27 per cent of 22,000) Political Officers had been dismissed during 1937–39, and that 876 (39.9 per cent) of the 2,194 dismissed in 1937 had been arrested.[43] Granted the gaps mentioned, known dismissals of officers for 'political' reasons from the army and air force in 1937–38 and the navy in 1937 totalled 29,345, of whom 11,169 (38 per cent) were arrested. Figures for the (relatively small) navy for 1938 would probably take the total of dismissals to around 30,000 and of arrests to about 12,000. In November 1938 Lavrenti Beria replaced Nikolai Yezhov as People's Commissar for the Interior (NKVD) and immediately instituted a reviewing process. By mid–March 1940 as many as 12,461 of the officers dismissed on political grounds had been cleared and restored to rank,[44] and about 7,000 more had been rehabilitated by the time the Germans invaded. Between them these two waves of reinstatements account for almost two-thirds of the number of dismissals cited by Shchadenko.

The thorough study mentioned earlier listed in an appendix all those the author succeeded in identifying as having been shot, died in prison or committed suicide. He noted:

> If we speak of the Marshals, Fleet Flag Officers (= our Admirals of the Fleet and full Admirals), Army Commanders and Army Commissars of 1st and 2nd Rank (= our full Generals), then as far as I know, all are listed. In looking at the Corps level (= our Lieutenant-Generals) there may be some individual additions. Rather more additions may be made . . . at Division and especially Brigade level (= Major-Generals and Brigadiers), and even more at Regimental (= Colonels) level. As for other categories of senior (Lieutenant-Colonels, Majors) and especially of middle-rank (Captains, Lieutenants) officers shot in 1937–38, great additional work stands ahead. I have listed only those I succeeded in finding up to summer 1997. Especial difficulties lie ahead in finding those executed 'for politics' among junior commanders (= warrant officers and NCOs), Red Army and Red Navy men (= privates, and ordinary seamen).[45]

His admittedly incomplete list contains 1,763 names, including 91 retired officers who were among the founders of the Red Army, and seven widows (including the widows of two and divorced wife of one of the three executed marshals), two wives and two sons of other executed officers. These numbers were not nearly as large as suggested by previous studies, and granted the incompleteness of the list, they represent only a small proportion of the officer establishment, which totalled 106,247 in 1936 and 373,910 in 1941 (not counting officer cadets commissioned during either year).[46] From Shchadenko's 1940 figures it is possible to construct

approximate totals for the army officer establishment in the five years
from 1935 to 1939.

Table 3. Total Red Army officer establishment, 1935–39

Year	Dismissals	As per cent of total	Total establishment
1935	6,198	4.9 per cent	126,490
1936	5,677	4.2 per cent	135,167
1937	18,658	13.1 per cent	142,427
1938	16,362	9.2 per cent	177,848
1939	1,878	0.7 per cent	268,286

These figures show that from 1935 to 1939 the requirement for officers
more than doubled, a direct consequence of the Soviet introduction of
universal conscription on the day Germany invaded Poland. The totals of
dismissals are, of course, not cumulative; they would be offset by the
annual output from officer training schools, and by the reinstatements.
Nevertheless, the replacement of one officer in eight in 1937 and of one
in eleven in 1938 by someone less experienced, at a time when the armed
forces were about to be vastly and rapidly expanded, did not make for
efficiency.

Granted that the numbers purged were small in relation to the number
of posts, that does not mean the armed forces were not seriously damaged.
First, the purge impacted particularly heavily on the senior ranks: those
executed included all 11 Deputy People's Commissars of Defence, 98 of
the 108 members of the Supreme Military Council, 3 of the 5 marshals,
13 of the 15 army commanders, 8 of the 9 full admirals, 50 of the 57 corps
commanders and 154 of the 186 division commanders. Among the political officers purged were all 16 army commissars, 25 of 28 corps and 58
of 64 divisional commissars.[47] Several accounts of the period refer to
disastrous declines in military discipline, through lower ranks coming to
see all their superiors as potential 'enemies of the people', officers themselves losing trust in one another and lacking the self-confidence needed
to assert their authority, and some using denunciations to settle old scores.
Secondly, the vacancies that the purge created at the very top of the military hierarchy were filled by hasty promotions, some of which took the
promotees far above their 'ceiling'. Three significant examples of this
were the generals who in 1941 commanded the first forces to face the
invaders, the Baltic, Belorussian and Kiev Special Military Districts,
which became the North-West, West and South-West Fronts (army
groups) on the outbreak of war. Of these Zhukov said in 1957: 'Baltic

Front was commanded by academy instructor F.I. Kuznetsov, who had never commanded anything except a regiment. Western Front was commanded by Pavlov, who before that had commanded a mechanised regiment and a tank brigade. South-West Front was commanded by Kirponos, who apart from a training school, had never commanded anything.'[48]

This is somewhat unfair to Kirponos, who commanded a division in the 1939–40 'Winter War' with Finland. Nevertheless, Zhukov's point was valid. The peacetime rule of thumb for commanders of battalions or above was that posts at each level should on average be held for four years before promotion was considered, but three months after the Winter War ended Kirponos was promoted from commanding just under 15,000 men to heading first Leningrad, then Kiev, Special Military Districts,[49] the latter having four armies and eight mechanised corps, which in the first fortnight of the invasion totalled 58 divisions, 3 brigades and 14 'fortified regions' (fixed defences manned by garrison troops), with altogether 864,600 troops.[50] He had by-passed the command levels of corps and army, which would between them have given him eight years' additional experience, and by the end of September his Front was encircled, with the Germans claiming 665,000 captured. Kirponos was perhaps fortunate to be killed in action, as Stalin made scapegoats of Pavlov and his principal subordinates, who were court-martialled and shot after presiding over a comparable disaster at Western Front. Kuznetsov was the luckiest of the three, in that he survived the war. However, he was demoted to command of an army after less than four weeks, and apart from two weeks in command of the newly created Central Front in July–August, was never again given control of a Front.

The problems facing promotees such as Kuznetsov, Pavlov and Kirponos were compounded by the fact that their predecessors, shot as alleged anti-Soviet conspirators, were suspected of having appointed like-minded officers to senior positions on their staffs, and most of those were also replaced, thus burdening the novice commanders of the most important frontier Military Districts with staff officers whom they did not know, and whose experience was often as limited as their own.

However, it is by no means certain that the Red Army would have initially fared substantially better in 1941 if there had been no purges. Marshal Konev's post-war remark that among the most senior victims 'only Tukhachevsky and Uborevich were modern' was perhaps harsh, but the unpurged armies of all Germany's previous antagonists had been overcome in campaigns lasting from a few days to a few weeks, and his stricture certainly applies to the subsequent brief performance as field commanders of the few surviving members of the pre-war top echelon. Nor, as some Russian analysts claim, would the army necessarily have performed better if Tukhachevsky had survived. First, the doctrine of 'beating the enemy on his own territory' by instant counter-offensives against any invader dated from his appointment as deputy chairman of the Revolutionary Military Council and Head of Red Army armament in 1931, after which General A.A. Svechin's more balanced book *Strategy* was banned. Secondly, Tukhachevsky believed that if Germany did invade, its objective would be to seize the food and mineral resources of Ukraine, so the Red Army's strongest forces should be deployed south of the Pripyat marshes. While in prison awaiting trial and execution, he wrote a long analysis showing he still adhered to those views.[51] It will be seen later that attempts to implement these beliefs, which Stalin shared and imposed on the General Staff, played a considerable role in the series of disasters that marked the first months of the invasion. Perhaps Tukhachevsky would have changed his mind about the distribution of forces had he lived until 1941, but his belief in instant counter-offensives by mobile formations would surely have been confirmed by German successes with 'Blitzkrieg' during 1939–41. His development of a theory of 'deep operations', based on very large formations of tanks and mechanised infantry, was probably his main contribution to Soviet military thought, but this could not come into its own until the second half of 1943, and when it did so it owed as much to the study and adoption of German methods as to any theoretical prescriptions.

Of the surviving members of the old cohort of marshals, Kulik proved so incompetent that in March 1942 Stalin demoted him to major-general. Similarly, Stalin had to remove Voroshilov from command at Leningrad in September 1941, and Budenny at Moscow in October. In both cases the fall of the city appeared imminent, and in both cases it was Georgi Zhukov who replaced them; he was the first of a group of younger generals, all in their early to mid-40s but regular Red Army officers since Civil War days, who soon rose to command Fronts, and by 1945 were all marshals or (4-star) army generals.

The organisational problems confronting the Red Army in 1941 substantially pre-dated the purges, and the origin of some of them can be traced back to the reforms introduced in 1924–28 by Mikhail Frunze. Because of the infant Soviet Union's acute economic problems, the need to release labour for industry and agriculture, and the lack of any imminent external military threat, full-time armed forces manpower was reduced during those years from 5.5 million to 562,000. Forces that size could train only about 300,000 conscripts a year, less than one-third of the annual 'contingent' reaching call-up age. Though the force size was gradually almost trebled to 1.5 million by 1935, and then almost trebled again to over 4.2 million by mid-1941, reservists recently trained under the revised programmes instituted by Timoshenko in mid-1940 were inevitably only a tiny proportion of those mobilised for the war. Because of the speed of the initial German advance, many failed to reach their units at all, while others found themselves thrown into battle before they had completed even the most basic training; and, of course, a substantial proportion of those just becoming old enough to conscript were also lost, because they lived on territory that the Germans overran in the first few weeks and occupied for up to three years.

The position with officers was no better. On the eve of invasion the existing forces were 36,000 (9.6 per cent) short of their officer establishment; the mobilisation plan needed 55,000 more reservist officers than were actually available,[52] and, like the rank and file, most officers had only received the limited training that the war with Finland had shown to be seriously deficient.

Perhaps at least as much damage as was caused by the purges resulted from the very rapid expansion of the armed forces between 1939 and 1941.[53] As noted above, the reduction in officer numbers caused by dismissals coincided with a rise in demand caused by expansion, and consequently promotions skyrocketed, from 26,021 in 1937 to 124,509 in 1938 and 198,450 in 1939 (i.e. in each of the latter years over half of all officers received a promotion). At the end of 1940 two-thirds of officers (246,626 of 373,910) had held their current posts for less than 12 months; including appointments made during the first half of 1941, on the day of invasion about three-quarters of all Red Army officers had held their posts for less than 18 months, and between 30 and 40 per cent of middle-ranking officers were undertrained reservists.[54] While the forces' manpower had almost trebled, output from officer-cadet schools had only doubled.[55] The creation of masses of new units following the introduction on 1 September 1939 of universal conscription, which more than doubled the numbers annually conscripted, meant accelerated promotion at all levels from platoon commander upwards; inevitably some turned out to be over-promoted, but even many who eventually proved themselves competent had not held their new posts long enough to master them before the invasion.

However, a number of promising senior officers either were not purged at all or served time in prison then were reinstated. Four in particular, all then in their mid-40s, would become Stalin's principal military subordinates. First to emerge, and destined to become the most prominent, was G.K. Zhukov, who, by writing an indignant letter to Stalin, survived a superior's attempt to have him dismissed in the purges, and in the summer of 1939 was appointed to command the riposte to the Japanese invasion of Soviet-allied Outer Mongolia. His success there was one of the factors that dissuaded Japan from joining Germany's invasion of the Soviet Union two years later, and was the first of a series of victories he would achieve in the coming war. Another future marshal, I.S. Konev, was accused of 'falsifying his social origins' by claiming to be from a poorer peasant family than was actually the case, concealing the fact that before the revolution one of his uncles had been a policeman, and using army funds to support the families of officers arrested in the purges, but he too somehow avoided being purged himself. Yet another, K.K. Rokossovsky, was arrested and imprisoned in August 1937, but released and restored to rank in March 1940. In 1945 these three, by then all marshals, commanded the three Fronts that ended the war in Europe by taking Berlin.

All three had been NCOs in the First World War, and had the humble class origins (Zhukov and Konev were the sons of peasants, Rokossovsky of a railway engine-driver) deemed appropriate for command in the 'Workers' and Peasants' Red Army'. The fourth member of what became Stalin's 'top team', A.M. Vasilevsky, conspicuously lacked such class 'qualifications'. His parents were an Orthodox Church cantor and a priest's daughter, and in the First World War he was an officer (a staff-captain) in the Tsar's army. With such dubious antecedents, it took the Communist Party ten years (1928–38) to accept his application for membership, but he escaped the purges because the then Chief of General Staff, Marshal Shaposhnikov, sensed his outstanding potential for staff work, and groomed him to become his successor. In May 1942, when ill-health compelled Shaposhnikov to resign, Vasilevsky, by then Head of Operations, succeeded him; apart from two short intervals he held the post till 1949, and then became War Minister.

Stalin acted quickly to try to remedy the numerous shortcomings in training and equipment exposed by the 'Winter War'. He replaced Voroshilov with Timoshenko, who had succeeded in bringing that war to a costly but face-savingly successful conclusion, and Shaposhnikov as Chief of General Staff first with Meretskov and later with Zhukov. Timoshenko tried to refuse, citing lack of knowledge, experience and 'statesmanly wisdom', but Stalin insisted that 'what is needed above all in the army now is firmness, and you have it. In the first instance see to troop discipline and training . . .'.[56] According to Mikoyan, Timoshenko 'had probably never read a book . . . but compared to Voroshilov he was heaven and earth, both militarily and politically'.[57]

This was a not unreasonable verdict. After almost 15 years in charge of Defence, Voroshilov bequeathed to Timoshenko a military machine with no operational plan for a future war, no precise data on the state of the frontier defences, inadequate study of the lessons the German campaigns could teach on how forces operated in modern war, no firm views on the use of tanks, aircraft and airborne forces, inadequate preparedness for war in the western areas where fighting would occur, and serious defects in the mobilisation system and the various arms of service.

Timoshenko took office on 8 May 1940, and about a week later received from Shaposhnikov a General Staff deployment plan. This identified the most likely adversary as Germany, with Italy, Finland, Romania and Hungary as participant allies, and possibly also Japan. They were expected to deploy between 200 and 230 divisions, with over 10,000 tanks and up to 15,000 aircraft. The potential attackers from the west were correctly identified, though their numbers, especially of weapons, were seriously overestimated. The actual invading force totalled about 193 divisions, 153 of them German, with fewer than 4,000 tanks and self-propelled guns and fewer than 4,000 combat aircraft, only about half of them German; the satellite divisions had few tanks and even fewer modern aircraft.[58]

The deployment plan did not attempt to specify when the postulated invasion was likely to take place, but Timoshenko wasted no time in beginning the reforms that the debacles in the Finnish campaign had shown to be necessary. Before the end of May he issued an order on 'Combat and political training of troops for the summer period of 1940', which gave unit and formation commanders only ten days to submit plans for troop training, war games and practice firings, and decreed that they be based on training timetables averaging ten hours a day for infantry, nine for tank crews and artillery, and including fighting by night as well as by day. By June he had decided on five priorities: 1. plans for strategic deployment and mobilisation for war; 2. reorganisation of structures and supply at all levels; 3. monitoring of the programme for re-equipping the armed forces; 4. reform of combat and political training; and 5. personnel matters.

However, the month of June 1940 also saw him preoccupied with a short-term issue, the seizure of Bessarabia. This had been part of the Russian Empire since the early eighteenth century, but the majority of its inhabitants were Romanians, and in 1918, while Russia was embroiled in civil war, Romania had annexed it. The Soviet Union had never accepted the annexation, and in one of the secret clauses of the Molotov–Ribbentrop Pact Germany acknowledged Bessarabia as part of the Soviet sphere of influence. However, Stalin's late addition of Bukovina, on the grounds of its mainly Ukrainian population, raised difficulties, as the Russian Empire had never possessed it, and the Molotov–Ribbentrop Pact did not cover it. Germany therefore declined to put pressure on Romania to cede it, but a compromise was reached by Stalin's reducing his demands to apply only to Northern Bukovina. The timing of the Soviet invasion, coincident with France's surrender, suggests, like the earlier seizures of Eastern Poland, the Baltic States and parts of Finland, that it was not simply opportunistic expansionism, but an element in Stalin's strategic plan to acquire a buffer zone between Germany and the Soviet heartland.

Timoshenko had been born in Bessarabia (in 1897, when it was Russian-controlled), and his brother and sister still lived there; his visit, a few days after Soviet troops under Zhukov reoccupied it at the end of June, lasted long enough for Moscow to enquire anxiously as to his where-abouts,[59] because his presence was required for discussions about the future of mechanised forces.

The Red Army had initially been ahead of the Germans in developing these, with two mechanised corps, combining tanks with infantry in lorries and artillery drawn by tractors (later including self-propelled guns) formed in 1932, and two more by 1934. However, the main pressure for developing such forces came from Tukhachevsky. His relations with Voroshilov had been strained ever since the Civil War, and he had rather played into Voroshilov's hands by submitting a report in January 1930 that called for a peacetime establishment of 310 divisions and 225 machine-gun battalions, with 50,000 tanks and 40,000 aircraft. These were manifestly far beyond the resources of a country just beginning to industrialise (and several times the numbers of tanks and aircraft that sufficed to actually win the war), so Stalin dismissed him as Chief of General Staff and demoted him to command of Leningrad Military District.[60] His eclipse was only temporary, but the increased power it gave to those, such as Voroshilov,[61] Budenny and Kulik, whose thinking was dominated by their Civil War experience, where machines had been few and horses many, meant that the early lead in mechanisation was surrendered to the Germans. In November 1939 the Main Military Council abolished the Mechanised Corps, and suggested replacing them with much smaller Independent Tank Brigades intended mainly for infantry support. Timoshenko argued strongly against this, and Stalin was sufficiently impressed by the German panzer arm's successes in the campaigns against Poland and France to support him, and to order the formation of 'several Corps with 1,000–1,200 tanks'.[62] But by August 1940, when Timoshenko signed the order to create the first of eight new mechanised corps, each comprising two tank and one lorried infantry divisions, the panzers already had 11 months of experience in the highly successful conduct of actual warfare. Even ten months later, on the day of invasion, one of the new corps, Rokossovsky's 9th, had no vehicles for its infantry and only 30 per cent of its war establishment of tanks; those it did have were worn out and unfit for prolonged use. As he put it, the corps 'was incapable of fighting as a mechanised formation'.[63]

Another problem in creating the mechanised corps was that of providing suitable tanks. Those developed, and produced in large numbers during the 1930s, were of 13 different types, and four-fifths (8,391 of 10,508) of the tanks serviceable with the western border military districts on the day of invasion[64] were undergunned and inadequately armoured light tanks, no match for the German medium Mk III and Mk IV. However, study of the experiences of those German tanks in the campaigns of 1939 and 1940 had provided Soviet designers with some pointers towards the optimal combination of armour, suspension, gun and engine-power, and two superior Soviet designs, the KV-1 heavy and T-34 medium, had begun production by the time Timoshenko took office. However, only about 500 KVs and 900 T-34s had been delivered by June 1941, and production of T-34s was temporarily at a standstill because trials of pre-production prototypes and early production models in 1940 had revealed a number of design and production faults. These had prompted Timoshenko to write in November 1940 to Voroshilov, then Chairman of the governmental Defence Committee, suggesting changes to the turret, transmission and suspension. Production was temporarily suspended while a modified version, the T-34M, was developed, with the first deliveries scheduled for early 1942, but the onset of war, and the disruption caused by the need to evacuate the manufacturing base and its labour force to the Urals, Siberia or Central Asia, made it necessary to restart production with the original design. Some of the modifications sought by Timoshenko were gradually introduced, and the tank proved superior to any German counterpart until the new 'Tiger' and 'Panther' and upgunned Mk IV appeared in early 1943. It was not until March 1944 that the final version, the T-34–85, with a more powerful gun, roomier turret, thicker armour and improved transmission, began to reach units and resume earning accolades as the best medium tank of the war.

A further complication was that the main early constraint to production of KVs and T-34s proved to be the provision of diesel engines, and the main reason why the Soviet tank industry continued producing the outclassed T-60 and T-70 light tanks for almost two more years was because they could use truck engines.

Timoshenko set up a special group to study the German campaigns, and took particular note of a book entitled *New Forms of Conflict* by Brigadier G.S. Isserson, head of a faculty in the General Staff Academy, which was based on his studies of the Spanish Civil War and the German campaigns against Poland, France, Yugoslavia and Greece. Isserson emphasised in particular that these had all begun with a ground invasion, supported by air attacks, by forces already fully mobilised and deployed secretly in advance, without the customary features of previous wars such as a formal declaration of war, or the fighting of battles at the frontiers by covering units while the main forces were being mobilised and concentrated. However, several factors prevented a general adoption of Isserson's ideas; some suspected his loyalty, given his past association with 'modernisers' such as Tukhachevsky, many of whom had been shot; he himself had been arrested and imprisoned in 1937,[65] though, like Rokossovsky, he was released in 1940; but perhaps the most insidious obstacle to this new thinking was the boastful doctrine denigrating the value of defensive warfare. This originated in a statement by Frunze, in a 1921 article, that 'only he will win who finds in himself the resolve to attack, the side that only defends itself is inevitably doomed to defeat'.[66] Over time this developed into a dogmatic doctrine, introduced by Tukhachevsky and long proclaimed by Voroshilov, of 'beating the enemy on his own territory and for little blood', which held that any invader of Soviet territory would be met at once by devastating counter-attacks, and driven back to be decisively defeated on his home ground, with the implication that Soviet troops need not train to fight defensive battles, because they would be attacking from the very first day of any invasion.

Another factor disclosed only in post-Soviet times was an overestimation of Soviet strength relative to German that was extraordinary in view of the recent experience of the war against Finland. For example, on 28 December 1940 Army General Pavlov, commanding Western Special Military District, affirmed that a Soviet tank corps could destroy one to two German panzer or four to five infantry divisions, and on 13 January 1941, at a conference of senior officers in the Kremlin, Chief of General Staff Meretskov said 'our division is significantly stronger than a division of the German-Fascist army, and in an encounter battle will undoubtedly beat a German division. In defence one of our divisions will repel a blow by two or three enemy divisions. In an offensive one and a half divisions will overcome the defence of an enemy division . . .'.[67] Seven months later Pavlov would be shot as a scapegoat for the total collapse of his Western Front; Meretskov would survive a period in the hands of NKVD torturers to become a successful Front commander, by never conducting any offensive where he outnumbered the enemy by only three to two . . .

Apart from this boastful dogma, the General Staff's excessive estimate, mentioned above, that an invading force would number 200–230 divisions, must have encouraged the belief that invasion would not come soon; it was twice as many as had sufficed for Germany to conquer the Low Countries and France in six weeks of 1940, and it was not unreasonable to expect that a subsequent doubling of the number of the Wehrmacht's divisions, and at least a quadrupling of its numbers of tanks and aircraft, would take considerable time and visible industrial effort that Soviet Intelligence would inevitably detect before it achieved its goals. Few believed that Germany would risk invading while greatly inferior in numbers of tanks, guns and aircraft.

However, that is what actually happened. Post-war Soviet accounts tried to conceal the facts, but figures from a post-Soviet Russian source[68] indicate that on 1 June 1941 the Wehrmacht had a total inventory of 6,292 tanks and self-propelled guns, and the Red Army 25,479, over four times as many. Of those totals, 5,821 German (92.5 per cent) were serviceable, compared with 19,810 Soviet (77.8 per cent). So even granted that almost one Soviet tank in four was unserviceable, versus only one in thirteen German, the Germans were still outnumbered by over three to one. In 'main battle' (heavy and medium) tanks, the Germans had 2,419 medium and no heavy tanks, whereas the Soviets had 6,640 mediums and 563 heavies, so here also the Germans were outnumbered by about three to one. The best Soviet tanks, the KV heavy and T-34 medium, outclassed the best German tank, the Mk IV, in armour and firepower; the T-34 also outclassed it in speed and manoeuvrability. Granted only 504 KVs and 892 T-34s had been delivered by 1 June, but the Wehrmacht had only 613 Mk IVs on that day, plus 1,806 of the less capable Mk IIIs. The material odds were certainly not in Germany's favour; success would depend entirely on their superior skills in using their inferior assets. That could be expected, given their recent experience of successful campaigning, compared with the Red Army's uninspiring performance against Finland, but the extent of German superiority, especially in the first months, would come as an extreme shock to the Soviet leaders and most of their generals.

The figures comparing the three invading German army groups with the four Special Military Districts (Baltic, Western, Kiev and Odessa) defending the Soviet western borders show the Soviet forces to have had much more firepower per man than the invaders. The four defending Fronts are claimed to have totalled 2,579,444 personnel, the Germans 3,751,900, a ratio of 1:1.45 in the Germans' favour. But in weaponry the picture is entirely reversed, as Table 4 shows.[69]

Table 4. Comparative strengths of the invading and defending forces, June 1941

	Tanks	*Guns/Mortars*	*Combat Aircraft*
German	3,979	39,517	4,371
Soviet	13,375	50,199	8,639
German:Soviet	1 to 3.36	1 to 1.27	1 to 1.98

So in material terms the Red Army in 1941 was far more mechanised than the Wehrmacht. In round figures the Germans and their allies on the day of invasion had three soldiers for every two Soviet soldiers facing them, but only one tank versus three, one aircraft versus two, and four guns or mortars versus five. Stalin was certainly taken by surprise tactically and had damaged military morale by his purges, but he can scarcely be accused of failing to prepare strategically. Arms production programmes he had initiated a decade earlier had ensured that the defenders on the western borders had substantially more weapons of all kinds than the invaders. It could perhaps be expected that the Germans, with the experience gained from their previous successful campaigns, would make better use of what they had, but neither Stalin nor his generals could expect that the performance of their own forces in the first weeks of the invasion would be so appallingly bad.

The Germans also had the advantage of conducting the offensive warfare they were accustomed to, while the Red Army was forced to fight defensive battles, for which it had neither prepared nor been trained. In its instructions and manuals, the utility and necessity of training for defensive fighting continued to be denigrated to the very last. For example, on 20 June, just two days before the invasion, the Main Military

Council adopted a directive 'On the tasks of political propaganda of the Red Army for the immediate future', which contained the passage: 'Experience of military operations has shown that against numerically superior motorised forces a defensive strategy delivered no success and ended in defeat. Consequently it is necessary to use its own offensive strategy against Germany.'[70] It was true, as stated, that the Wehrmacht could only be beaten by adopting its ways of waging war, but to do so required training in tactics combining and coordinating operations by tanks, infantry, artillery and aircraft. Reaching German levels of skill in such tactics would take almost the first two years of the war, and for much of that time the Red Army had to develop and use the previously denigrated defensive strategy and learn the previously untaught defensive tactics.

Up to the day of invasion, 22 June 1941, Germany and the Soviet Union seemed to the outside world more like allies than enemies. On the 13th the Soviet news agency TASS broadcast an official statement, reproduced in the press the next day, describing foreign press reports of imminent war between the Soviet Union and Germany as 'propaganda' by forces hostile to both countries, and 'rumours' of German intent to attack the Soviet Union as 'without foundation'. The rationale behind this statement has never been explained; it was most likely, as Goebbels interpreted it in his diary entry for 15 June, that 'Stalin . . . wants to remove from himself all possible grounds for accusations of unleashing a war', and/or that it was a *ballon d'essai*, released in the hope of eliciting a similar statement from the German side. In fact no such statement emerged: Hitler was too busy that day giving the invading force's commanders their final instructions. Also on that day Timoshenko and Zhukov asked Stalin for permission to put the frontier Military Districts on alert. He refused, and nor did he react to Admiral Kuznetsov's report that German merchant ships[71] were leaving Soviet ports without completing loading or unloading, and would all have gone by 21 June. As the German forces were taking up their starting positions in the last peacetime hours, trainloads of Soviet oil, grain and raw materials destined for Germany were still arriving at the frontier stations. Even when Timoshenko and Zhukov came to Stalin on the evening of 21 June and told him the border guards had reported being told by a German defector that the invasion would begin on the next morning, his first reaction was 'Isn't it that German generals have planted this defector to provoke a conflict?' Only when Timoshenko firmly contradicted him did he authorise putting the frontier Military Districts on full alert, and order his secretary, Poskrebyshev, to summon the other members of the Politburo. Furthermore, when Zhukov gave him the order he had already drafted he rejected it as 'premature', saying 'maybe the question can still be resolved in a peaceful way', and 'we need to give a brief directive, to note that the attack may begin with provocative actions by German units'. When Zhukov gave him a revised text, he read it and made some minor amendments, but did not sign it, instead ordering Timoshenko to do so.[72] Even several hours later, after reports came in of German bombing raids on cities, army positions, naval bases and airfields in the Baltic states, Belorussia and Ukraine, he still grasped at the straw that the attack might be a 'provocation' by some German generals. While waiting for Molotov to return from the German embassy he said, according to Zhukov, 'Hitler surely doesn't know about this', and accepted the reality only when Molotov arrived with the official declaration of war.[73]

In his 'de-Stalinisation' speech at the 20th Party Congress in 1956, Khrushchev claimed that Stalin had been so demoralised that he did nothing for several days. That this was entirely untrue was pointed out (though only after Khrushchev himself had been deposed, in 1964) by several of the political and military leaders, and their denials were subsequently confirmed by publication of the appointment books kept by Poskrebyshev.[74] However, he does seem to have contemplated surrender at one point. According to a post-Soviet account, on 28 June – the day on which Minsk fell – Stalin, Molotov and Beria met the Bulgarian Ambassador Stamenov, and discussed a peace offer under which the Soviet Union would surrender the recently annexed Baltic States and Moldavia, and 'parts of some other republics'.[75]

That this was Stalin's personal low-point of the entire war is also suggested by the events of the next two days. On 29 June he took his four principal subordinates – Molotov, Malenkov, Mikoyan and Beria – to the Ministry of Defence, and there fiercely criticised Chief of General Staff Zhukov (who, according to Mikoyan, burst into tears, left the room and had to be persuaded by Molotov to come back) for his inability to establish communication with the Western Front and find out what had happened to it. As Mikoyan described it later, 'Stalin was depressed and gloomy' when they left the building, and said 'Lenin left us a great heritage, we – his heirs – have stuffed it all up.' Mikoyan continued: 'We were staggered by this expression of Stalin's – had we really lost everything irrecoverably? . . . Stalin went home to the "nearby" dacha at Kuntsevo and had all communication with him cut off.'[76]

The most likely explanation of this withdrawal is depression caused by the apparent collapse of the armies, and particularly by the fall of Minsk, capital of Belorussia, on the same day as the alleged meeting with Stamenov. Minsk was one-third of the way from the frontier to Moscow, and it had taken only a week for the Germans not merely to reach it but to encircle and capture it. If they could maintain that pace, and Soviet forces continued to perform so badly, the panzers could be in Moscow in another two weeks.

Stamenov insisted that the Soviet Union would win, and it seems that at that point Beria instructed Sudoplatov to maintain contact with him and try to persuade him to pass on a peace offer. Sudoplatov's account gave the origin as two German proposals floated in mid-July.[77] He may, after so many years, be slightly wrong in his dates, but a more likely explanation is that he was brought in only after Soviet decryption of Bulgarian embassy messages showed Stamenov's belief in a Soviet victory to be so strong that he was not even passing the Soviet proposals on to Sofia, and that he was given a false account of the proposal's origins because he had 'no need to know' the truth.

That the invasion temporarily threw the Soviet leadership as a whole into a collective state of shock is suggested by its disorganised state during the first week. Not until the ninth day of war, and the second of Stalin's self-seclusion, was any action taken to form a supreme directing body for the war effort; and when it was taken, the moving spirit was not Stalin or Molotov, but Beria. On 30 June he suggested to Molotov that a State Defence Committee should be formed, and all functions of the government, Supreme Soviet and Communist Party Central Committee be transferred to it. Stalin should head it, and its members should be Molotov, Malenkov, Voroshilov and Beria. They resolved to go to Kuntsevo and put it to Stalin. Mikoyan's account continued:

> Seeing Beria with us, the guard opened the gates at once, and we went to the 'boss's' house. We found him sitting in an armchair in the small dining room. On seeing us he literally turned to stone. His head sank down into his shoulders, and his eyes were wide with obvious fear. (He had, of course, decided that we had come to arrest him because we had come without his having sent for us.) He looked at us enquiringly, and forced out a muffled 'Why have you come?' ... Molotov spoke first and, in the name of us all, said power must be concentrated, so that everything for putting the country on its feet could be rapidly decided. He spoke of the proposal to create a State Defence Committee. Stalin changed literally before our eyes.

His former fear was as if it had never been; he straightened his shoulders. But still he looked surprised, and after a short pause said 'Agreed. But who will be its chairman?' 'You, comrade Stalin,' said Molotov. 'Good. But what's the proposed composition of this organ?' Beria replied, 'Like this. You, comrade Stalin, as Head, then Molotov, Voroshilov, and me.' Stalin remarked, 'We must include Mikoyan and Voznesensky.'

There was some discussion about this, resolved by Mikoyan's suggestion that they should be appointed as 'representatives', not members, of the Committee. However, in February 1942 both were made full members.

Responsibilities were allocated there and then. Molotov would monitor tank production, Malenkov aircraft and aviation matters, Voznesensky armaments and ammunition, Mikoyan supplies to the front of food, fuel and materials other than weapons. Voroshilov would oversee the process of forming new armed forces units, Beria maintenance of order and discipline, including preventing desertion.

Most of the members also had ministerial responsibilities – Molotov for foreign affairs, Mikoyan for foreign trade, Beria for the secret police, espionage and counter-espionage – while Voznesensky was head of the economic planning authority, Gosplan, Voroshilov chaired the Defence Committee of the Council of Ministers, and all five ranked as deputy prime ministers under Stalin. As the war went on Stalin placed additional burdens on them. Mikoyan successively served on committees for removing food supplies from the frontier areas (1941), for evacuation of factories and their workers (1942), later (with Malenkov and Voznesensky) for economic restoration of areas recovered from German occupation, and from 1942 was in charge of distributing Lend-Lease supplies. In that year Beria's functions were extended to include control of ballistic missile and atomic bomb development, Voroshilov's to overseeing the increasingly important partisan guerrilla movement behind the German lines. However, the multiple responsibilities of his subordinates were dwarfed by those Stalin concentrated in his own hands. He was simultaneously head (general secretary) of the Communist Party, prime minister, defence minister, supreme commander-in-chief of the armed forces, and chairman of both Stavka (General Headquarters) and the State Defence Committee.

With minor changes of membership, the State Defence Committee remained in existence until the war ended, and proved highly efficacious in enabling Stalin to direct every aspect of the war effort. Even before its formation was announced publicly, on 1 July,[78] it had begun to take major decisions. On 30 June it confirmed the economic mobilisation plan for July–September, and on 16 August the plan for October–December and for 1942 for Trans-Volga, Urals, West Siberia, Kazakhstan and Central Asia. Less than ten weeks after the day of invasion, the Soviet leadership was preparing for a long war, and implicitly accepting further loss of territory in the European USSR. Evacuation from the west and south-west of plants producing aero-engines and aircraft, tanks and armour-plating was already under way, and programmes for increasing agricultural production in the eastern areas were being drafted. The Trans-Siberian Railway had been double-tracked in the 1930s; now subsidiary single-track railways connecting Siberia with the Urals and Volga regions began to be double-tracked, for ease in handling the anticipated increased traffic in westbound coal, oil and minerals, and (later) tanks, guns and ammunition and Lend-Lease shipments. Most of the rails for these projects were found by dismantling the uncompleted Baikal–Amur main line, a grandiose Five-Year Plan undertaking, parallel to the Trans-Siberian but a long way north of it.

The already low Soviet standard of living would inevitably plunge even lower, as industry, construction and capital investment were shifted to the defence sector. The working hours were increased and numbers of rest days reduced, and the burden on the peasants, still a majority of the population at that time, weighed especially heavily. Compulsory deliveries from collective farms to the state were increased, while most of the able-bodied men were conscripted into the army, leaving what was still a mainly unmechanised agriculture, despite official propaganda that featured tractors and combines, to a labour force of women, old people and adolescents. Furthermore, a 'scorched earth' policy was proclaimed on 29 June. Where the Red Army had to retreat the population was called upon to 'remove all railway rolling stock, leave the enemy not one locomotive, not one wagon, not a kilo of bread nor a litre of fuel . . . collective farmers must drive cattle away, and hand grain over to custody of organs of the state, for it to be taken out to the rear areas'. Any valuable property or food stocks that could not be removed were to be destroyed. These measures condemned the 73 million inhabitants who remained in the occupied areas to hardship and hunger, but at that time the regime regarded any who stayed behind either as potential collaborators with the invaders, or as not useful enough to the war effort to be worth evacuating. In due course this attitude would come to be somewhat modified by a realisation of the inhabitants' utility as sources of information about the enemy and as a support base for the increasingly important partisan movement behind enemy lines, but that came only much later.

There were no precedents or plans for an evacuation on the proposed scale. Priority was given to machinery, materials and skilled employees of defence-industry plants, and trains conveying them had priority over everything except those carrying troops and military supplies. Evacuation centres at loading and destination points began to be set up on 5 July; these provided basic food and medical care, but conditions on the journey were often primitive. A Party official at Chelyabinsk, in the Urals, described the first trains to arrive there:

> People travelled in open wagons or sometimes just on flat trucks. It was good if there was a tarpaulin with which they could cover themselves against the rain . . . but sometimes there wasn't even that. There were lathes and materials, and a few things belonging to the evacuees . . . In the most favourable situation there were two or three covered trucks for women with children. Instead of 36 people, up to 80–100 were crammed into them.[79]

Experience with the evacuations suggested that most Russians would tolerate hardships in the national interest, but incidents during the first weeks of fighting suggested that non-Russian minorities would be rather less inclined to do so. From the outset Stalin envisaged a protracted war, and accepted that initially much territory and manufacturing capacity would be lost; Hitler, on the other hand, banked on winning before the first winter, and at least until mid-October that appeared possible.

Chapter Two

'Industrialise or go under'

Before considering the events of 1942–43 that finally swung the strategic balance decisively in the Soviets' favour, it is worth taking a look at how the mid-1942 situation came about. Some of its origins long pre-dated the invasion, and it had several aspects, not least in the personalities of Hitler and Stalin, but also in the internal situations each faced and the complexities of international relations during the late 1930s.

It was a firm tenet of Soviet leadership thinking that a coalition of the capitalist world's major states would ultimately seek to evade their inevitable demise by making war on the Soviet Union. Early expectations of widespread revolutions had proved false, but the doctrine of 'socialism in one country' expressed a siege mentality, of a state subsisting in a hostile world while preparing for an unavoidable armed conflict at some time in the future. No timetable was postulated for this trial of arms, except for a general statement by Stalin in 1931 that the Soviet Union had ten years to industrialise or 'go under'.

To examine Stalin's industrialisation in detail is beyond the scope of this study, but the main points are highlighted in Table 5. A tenfold increase in heavy industry, versus only slightly more than fourfold in light industry and a mere one-third increase in agriculture, points to a clear priority of defence over consumption. That industrial labour productivity more than trebled mainly reflected the superiority of the

Table 5: Some basic indicators of Soviet economic development, 1928–40[80]

In each case the 1928 level = 100
In 1940:
  Industry: heavy, 1,000, light, 420
  Capital investment: 670
  Numbers of industrial and non-manual workers: 300
  Agricultural output: 130
  Labour Productivity: Industry, 310, railways, 280, construction, 250, agriculture, 170

newly built plants over the old ones, but the table shows that agricultural productivity actually declined severely: in 1940 there were 70 per cent more farm workers than in 1928, but they produced only 30 per cent more food.

A factor which perhaps should have somewhat modified the very low German, British and American opinions of the Red Army was its convincing defeats of Japanese encroachments at Lake Khasan in the Soviet Far East in 1938 and at Khalkhin Gol in Outer Mongolia in May–September 1939. Here, however, remoteness, the small scale and short duration of the 1938 fighting, and the coincidence of the climax in Mongolia with the German invasion of Poland and the British and French declarations of war, combined to divert the outside world's attention from them. Later events in South-East Asia and Oceania would tend to suggest that Western discounting of these Soviet victories also owed much to a gross underestimation of the capabilities of Japan's armed forces. Be that as it may, the low opinions were further fortified by the copiously reported contrasts between the Red Army's ineptitude in the 1939/40 'Winter War' with Finland and the Wehrmacht's successes in the series of short sharp campaigns that between September 1939 and mid-1941 gave Hitler, at a very small cost in German lives, control of most of main-land Europe and expanded the war to North Africa, where Rommel's Afrika Korps for two years created problems for the British 8th Army out of all proportion to its small size.

There was also a political reason, which Stalin did not mention to Timoshenko and Zhukov, for rejecting their advocacy in mid-May of a pre-emptive attack. In the eyes of the outside world Germany and the Soviet Union were allies, under the Molotov–Ribbentrop Pact, right up to the day of invasion. Soviet historians regularly described the German attack as 'treacherous' ('*verolomnoie*', literally 'faithbreaking'), inadvertently illustrating how seriously the Soviet leadership took the pact. The signatories had both invaded several countries, and that the two dictators were in effect seen as co-conspirators was evident from one of the stranger episodes of the 'Phoney War' period, the decision of the Chamberlain and Daladier governments on 19 December 1939 to send an Anglo-French expeditionary force to invade Norway and go on to help Finland in the Winter War against the Soviet invaders. Its main purpose was at the very least to seize the railway to Narvik, along which German iron ore supplies from mines in northern Sweden travelled in winter, when the Gulf of Bothnia was frozen, and probably to seize the mines themselves – but if the pledge to aid Finland with military force meant anything, it meant that Britain and France, already at war with Germany, contemplated going to war with the Soviet Union as well. There was strong public support for Finland in both countries, and in both the Soviet 'image' was already poor beforehand, because of its deal with Germany, its collusion in the invasion of Poland, and the conduct of the local Communist parties which, in obedience to Moscow's line, were depicting the war as 'imperialist', blaming the British and French governments for starting it, and attempting to stir up unrest in their war industries. The French allocated 57,000 troops to the proposed expedition, and the British Cabinet ordered the Chiefs of Staff 'to plan for landing a force at Narvik for the sake of Finland'.[81]

One post-Soviet source cites the memoirs of a French diplomat for evidence of how German agents exploited the episode by circulating 'beyond the English Channel' rumours of a possible peace with Britain and France that 'would be concluded at the expense of Russia, against which the Wehrmacht would act immediately after conclusion of an armistice. England would receive Turkestan. The frontier between Iran and Turkey would be advanced to the Caspian Sea. Italy would receive a share of oil, and Germany would annexe Ukraine.'[82]

It does not say how much credence these rumours received in Moscow, but even the lesser threat of Anglo-French military aid to Finland had to be taken seriously, because it indicated that the Allies saw no difference between the two dictatorships and even contemplated fighting both simultaneously, or even worse, making peace with Germany and joining it in a 'crusade' against the Soviet Union. Another post-Soviet account deals in greater detail with the episode, citing documents published after the war, such as reports to Moscow from the Soviet ambassadors in London and Paris, messages to their respective foreign ministries by British, French and United States embassies, and accounts of meetings of the British and French governments and their military advisers. It is clear from these that both governments seriously contemplated conflict with the Soviet Union as a by-product of their plans. For example, at a War Cabinet meeting on 12 December 1939 Churchill (then First Lord of the Admiralty) strongly supported the French proposals to land forces in Scandinavia. He acknowledged that participation by British forces would inevitably involve them in 'broad-ranging military actions with Russia', but hoped these 'would not extend beyond local limits'.[83]

The Soviet government knew enough from its own ambassadors'

reports to be aware of the potential unwanted consequences of its war with Finland, and resolved to avoid them by finding a quick end to the war. The task was entrusted to Marshal Timoshenko, who succeeded, though at high cost, in breaking through the fortified 'Mannerheim Line', whereupon Finland sought an armistice. Probably to the benefit of the Allies and posterity alike, it was concluded on 12 March 1940, before the Anglo-French expedition could get under way.

Soviet congratulations offered to Germany for some of its subsequent victories, and speed in withdrawing recognition from the governments-in-exile of invaded states, did nothing to improve Anglo-Soviet relations in the period before the invasion. If Stalin had accepted Timoshenko's and Zhukov's May 1941 recommendation of a pre-emptive attack, the world, including all the Soviet Union's potential allies, would probably have seen it as a mere falling-out between gangsters. It was politically essential for the outside world to see the Soviet Union as a victim of unprovoked German aggression.

In Stalin's lifetime the real reasons for the retreats of 1941 and 1942 were never discussed publicly, because they were always presented as a deliberate drawing-on of the Germans in order to annihilate them. After his death it was admitted that they had been forced retreats, and he was blamed for ignoring the evidence that invasion was inevitable and imminent. It is indisputable that he committed very damaging errors, but some of the criticisms seem overdone. The 'Red Orchestra' spy ring in Germany had forecast several previous invasion dates, all of which had proved wrong. It was therefore not unreasonable that he rejected the allegedly correct forecast, as the source, Richard Sorge, a journalist in Tokyo and friend of the German ambassador, was himself suspect. During the purge of Soviet Intelligence he had more than once been 'invited' to return to Moscow, but had always claimed to be too busy to do so. The 'Centre' therefore saw him as possibly a German- or Japanese-controlled double-agent, and treated his reports with suspicion. Besides, if the networks in Germany kept making wrong predictions, why should anyone believe that someone in Tokyo had got it right – especially as Sorge, too, had previously wrongly predicted the invasion date as 1 June?[84]

In the nine months preceding the invasion Stalin received at least fifty warnings of it, and may well have received more.[85] Some were imprecise ('beginning of 1941', 'spring 1941', 'end of April or start of May', 'by beginning or end of May', 'by end of May', 'any time after 16 June', 'in second half of June', 'after victory over England or conclusion of an honourable peace with it'). Others gave precise dates (15 April, 14, 20 May, 8, 15, 20 June, 'between 20 and 25 June'), but none gave the right one. It was also claimed, after the war, that Dekanozov, the Soviet ambassador in Berlin, had provided the correct date in a message sent on 18 June, prompting Beria on 21 June to ask Stalin to recall and punish him 'for bombarding me with disinformation about an alleged attack on the USSR that Hitler is preparing'.[86] This looks unlikely. Dekanozov, a Georgian, as were Beria and Stalin, was not a career diplomat, but a senior NKVD official, widely regarded as Beria's man in the Foreign Ministry. He was one of the group of Beria's six closest associates, all tried, like Beria, on trumped-up charges in 1953, and was shot just 90 minutes after him. Besides, in the alleged memorandum Beria addressed Stalin by name and patronymic, as 'Iosif Vissarionovich'. This is a normal, respectful, Russian way of addressing a superior, but all Stalin's close associates knew that he disliked it intensely.[87] A genuine note from Beria would have addressed him in the way he preferred, as 'Comrade Stalin' (precisely as Beria and Molotov did in Mikoyan's account of the creation of the State Defence Committee, mentioned in Chapter One), or perhaps, though less likely, by his Georgian nickname of 'Koba'. Besides, post-Soviet research in the archives has shown that in the months preceding the invasion Beria had received regular reports from NKVD frontier guards of German activities just across the border, and considered many of them important enough to be brought to the attention of Stalin and Molotov, despite knowing full well that their content ran counter to Stalin's strongly held opinion.

Dekanozov's message of 18 June was genuine, and so was its source (codename 'Breitenbach', a Gestapo official), but Beria's alleged response of 21 June was most likely a forgery, inserted to discredit him ahead of his trial in 1953 on manufactured charges, for which no real evidence was ever produced, of counter-revolutionary conspiracy 'to seize power, and liquidate the Soviet worker-peasant system with the aim of restoring capitalism and domination by the bourgeoisie'.[88] A note that appeared to show him attempting, implicitly on the German behalf, to mislead Stalin right up to the last moment before the invasion would provide convenient support for the charges.

The British warnings must also have been less categorical than is sometimes claimed. Churchill did not personally become convinced till the end of March 1941 that an invasion of the Soviet Union was inevitable, while the Chiefs of Staff, Foreign Office and Joint Intelligence

Committee did not come to endorse this view until the first two weeks of June; as late as 12 June the War Cabinet was unsure whether Germany would simply invade or issue demands to which the Soviet Union might yield. Deciphering of German messages had inclined Bletchley to more definite views that the invasion was inevitable and imminent, but certainty arrived there only with messages deciphered on 14 June, and even they did not provide the actual date.[89] So Stalin was by no means alone in his uncertainty.

In his books *Icebreaker* and *M-day* Victor Suvorov has claimed that the German invasion on 22 June 1941 narrowly pre-empted a Soviet attack scheduled for 6 July, which was intended to enable the Soviet Union to dominate not only Germany but all the countries it had recently conquered. The evidence he cited in support included the massing of Soviet troops in the frontier areas and of aircraft on airfields close to the frontiers, from where they would reach targets faster and need less fuel, so could carry bigger bombloads. He quoted the passage already mentioned from Stalin's speech of 5 May 1941, and some extracts from Soviet military memoirs that he interpreted as indicating an intention to attack, and also noted the assembly of particularly large Soviet forces in Ukraine along the frontier with Romania, which he claimed were intended to seize Germany's main source of oil at Ploesti.

It is certain, as Stalin later told Churchill, that he saw war with Germany as ultimately inevitable, but had hoped to postpone it for at least six more months. Stalin did not say whether in that event he would have attacked first, or simply been in a better position to repel invasion. There are, however, several reasons to reject Suvorov's contentions. First, the pre-war doctrine of 'beating the enemy on his own territory' was always presented as describing the presumed fate of any invader; the Red Army was supposed to drive him out at once.[90] This, of course, could serve as a cover for aggression; an aggressor's claim to be responding to a prior attack by the victim is common enough – to justify their recent invasions, Hitler had used a faked Polish attack on the Gleiwitz radio station, Stalin a faked Finnish artillery bombardment. In the later stages of the impending war, Stalin would come to prefer chasing German forces out of Soviet territory to encircling and destroying them on it, on the grounds that to do so liberated occupied territory more quickly, so that it could be sown with food crops and the enemy deprived of time for destroying industries, and that the hostile forces could then be encircled and smashed on their home ground.[91] But in 1941 the 'doctrine' was untested and no

more than a boast. It did, however, appeal to the general military preference for offence over defence, because to plan to fight a defensive battle
means at least temporarily surrendering the initiative to the enemy, and
may also have reflected the victory of one purged military intellectual over
another, specifically of the offensive-based doctrines promoted by
Tukhachevsky over the more defence-oriented ideas of General A.A.
Svechin.[92] Both the German and the Soviet armies trained predominantly
for offensives, and their recent experiences had been almost entirely in
conducting them, but in 1941 both would suffer serious defeats – the
Soviets during the first five months, the Germans in December, largely
because they had not trained to fight defensive battles.

Secondly, inconsistent with preparations to invade are the lengths to
which Stalin went to avoid 'provoking' the Germans, particularly his ban
on firing on Luftwaffe reconnaissance aircraft. These flew over regularly,
often deep into Soviet territory, but Stalin's ban continued to be applied
even after one of them force-landed and was found to have been
photographing the frontier areas, including military camps and airfields.[93]
Stalin never explained why he imposed this restraint. He may have hoped
to postpone or even prevent the invasion by impressing the Germans with
the numbers and equipment of the forces that would oppose it; but whatever his reasons, if he was about to attack Germany, he would hardly have
given it total freedom to photograph the final few weeks of preparation.

Third was his hostile reaction to Timoshenko's and Zhukov's advocacy
in mid–May of a pre-emptive attack. If a full-scale Soviet invasion of
German-occupied Europe was intended for early July, planning must
already have been far advanced by mid–May, Timoshenko and Zhukov
would be directing it, and would be in overall charge of the invasion.
Stalin's warning that 'heads would roll' if anything was done to provoke
the Germans is inconsistent with that scenario. It is, however, consistent
with his having received Hitler's alleged letter of 14 May, just delivered
by air, containing assurances of peaceful intent that he wanted to believe
and hinting at possible 'provocations' by generals who did not share these
views – a straw that Stalin would clutch at even after the invasion had
begun.

Fourth, the concentration of forces in the area bordering Romania was,
as mentioned above, the result of Stalin's erroneous assumption that an
invasion's objectives would be primarily economic, so that the main
thrust would be south of the Pripyat marshes, and that was where the
strongest Soviet forces should be deployed.

Fifth is Rokossovsky's detailed account of the condition of 9th Mechanised Corps, which he commanded on 22 June 1941. It was deployed at the border, and if Suvorov's account is correct, would be invading German-occupied Poland in two weeks' time. Yet on the day of invasion it had only 30 per cent of its tanks, most of them obsolete and so worn out that Rokossovsky had had to restrict crew-training hours, and it had no vehicles for its infantry.[94]

Finally a general point about the extent of Stalin's ambitions is his attitude to the Second Front. He told Milovan Djilas in 1944 that nations imposed their social systems wherever their armies penetrated, and that, of course, is precisely what happened after 1945. That Stalin constantly pressured Roosevelt and Churchill for a Second Front up to late 1942 could be explained by his perceived need to relieve the strains on the Red Army. However, the series of Soviet victories beginning in November 1942 with Stalingrad and culminating in the recapture of Kiev in November 1943, accompanied by the Anglo-American expulsion of Axis forces from Africa and the invasion of Italy, made it clear that the strategic balance had swung decisively against Germany and its defeat was only a matter of time. Provided the Western Allies continued to bomb and blockade Germany, and maintained Lend-Lease supplies to the Red Army, it could probably win the land war without the Second Front; after all, by 6 June 1944, when that Front was launched, Soviet forces had been advancing almost continuously for ten months and three weeks. If there had been no Second Front the most likely outcome would have been the imposition of Soviet-style Communism on the whole of German-occupied Europe, a possibility that certainly worried Churchill.[95] Had Stalin's objectives been as expansive as Suvorov claimed, it could be expected that after mid-1943 he would have abandoned or at least much reduced his pressure for the Second Front.

However, Churchill's account of the 'Big Three' conference at Tehran in November–December 1943[96] makes it clear that nothing like that happened. Stalin pushed as hard as ever, asked many searching questions and undertook to mount a Soviet offensive in support of the Second Front, to prevent the Germans moving troops from east to west. He kept his word: Operation 'Bagration', launched in Belorussia on 23 June, two and a half weeks after D-day, by four Fronts with 2.4 million troops was one of the largest and most successful Soviet offensives of the entire war. While still in progress it was joined on 13 July by a second offensive, Lvov–Sandomir, by the 1st Ukrainian Front, and a third, on 20 August, by the 2nd and 3rd Ukrainian Fronts in Moldova and Romania. Between them they involved 4.7 million Soviet troops. 'Bagration' alone destroyed 17 German divisions, reduced another 50 to less than half strength and forced the transfer of 46 divisions, most from elsewhere on the Eastern Front but some from the west.[97] All three offensives were terminated on 29 August; by then the success of the Second Front was assured, and so, by Stalin's own reasoning, but contrary to Suvorov's depiction, was Western Europe's future within the Anglo-American sphere of influence. No archival evidence has been found to indicate that Stalin intended to invade Germany in 1942, but he certainly cannot have been intending to do so in July 1941, and Molotov claimed that he had said before then that the Soviet Union could not meet Germany on equal terms until 1943.

Returning to the summer of 1941, there were several differences among the German war planners about the details of the intended invasion, but the military consensus was that destroying the Red Army must take precedence over pursuit of economic objectives, hence the deployment of two army groups north and only one south of the Pripyat marshes.[98] The Soviet deployment, with an opposite bias, reflected Stalin's misreading of Hitler's objectives.[99]

Soviet-era accounts of the war tended to exaggerate German numbers and understate Soviet ones, particularly in the early period. As mentioned in the previous chapter, only in post-Soviet times were such facts disclosed as that the Red Army at the outbreak of war had far more tanks, guns and aircraft than the three invading army groups. However, the aircraft were mostly inferior to the Luftwaffe's, their crews lacked the training and experience of their German counterparts, and most of the tanks were obsolete or inadequate; although they included at least 1,400 (some reports say as many as 1,861) of the new KV-1 heavy and T-34 medium tanks, which were superior to anything the Germans then had, more than half the entire inventory consisted of (10,508) light tanks, with neither armament nor armour adequate for taking on the German Mk III or Mk IV mediums.[100] Besides, inadequate training, especially of driver-mechanics, shortages of fuel and spare parts, lack of radios (even as late as mid-1943 only tank company commanders and above had transmitters; the rest had a receiver or nothing) and German superiority in coordinating operations of tanks, mechanised and marching infantry, tactical air and artillery support more than nullified the Soviet advantage in numbers. The Wehrmacht's qualitative edge was gradually eroded as Soviet commanders and troops gained experience, but the Red Army had been at war for fully two years before it scored a major victory in the summer, with no help from Generals Winter and Mud.

An example of the Soviet problems in the early days of the war was a report of 8 July from South-West Front, which noted that in a mere two weeks the 41st Tank Division had already lost 22 of its 31 KVs. But only 5 of them were lost to enemy action: the other 17 included 5 sent for repair and not recovered, and 12 destroyed by their own crews. The losses were explained primarily by weaknesses in the crews' technical training, poor knowledge of the tank and lack of spare parts, but in some cases crews had blown up tanks that had stopped because of a simple engine malfunction that they did not know how to rectify. As late as February 1942 Zhukov found it necessary to issue an order criticising his Western Front tank units for 'great and unjustified losses', incurred because

> tanks are thrown into battle without preliminary and thorough reconnaissance, coordination on the spot with infantry, artillery and aircraft . . . time is not devoted to preparation . . . regrouping is conducted in daylight under enemy air and artillery strikes. Commanders of tank units put their brigades into battle without appropriate technical preparation, reconnaissance, preparing evacuation resources, and try to resolve combat assignments by tanks alone, without infantry . . . when they receive a task the tankers resolve it without the necessary skill, in a straight line and most often by a frontal attack.

He noted that nine tank brigades, which between them had received 739 tanks, had only 153 serviceable on 15 February. Of the remaining 586, 264 were under repair; the other 322, many of them repairable, were still on the battlefield, because no attempt had been made to retrieve them.[101]

The precise extent of Soviet manpower losses in the first three weeks of the invasion was also fully disclosed only in 1993. An official publication[102] included the following figures for North-West and West Fronts for the 18 days between 22 June and 9 July, and for South-West Front to 6 July. The publication in question has been severely criticised in Russia as understating Soviet losses, but the figures are the most comprehensive available, and even if understated they indicate a catastrophic start to the Red Army's war. In the Soviet terminology 'irrevocable' losses were killed, captured or missing, 'sanitary' wounded, injured or sick. The figures for South-West Front include the losses, but not the initial strength, of 18th Army of South Front. It can be seen from the table that the three principal Fronts defending the western border in the Baltic provinces, Belorussia and Ukraine lost 30 per cent of their manpower killed, captured or missing in less than three weeks. Worst affected was Western Front, facing Army Group Centre; by 9 July it had 'irrevocably' lost over half (54.6 per cent) of its troops, at an average loss rate of about two divisions a day, equivalent to 36 of its 58 divisions.

Table 6. Soviet manpower losses in the first three weeks of invasion

Front	Initial strength	Losses	
		'Irrevocable'	'Sanitary'
North-West	440,000	73,924	13,284
West	625,000	341,012	76,717
South-West*	864,600	165,452	65,755
Total	1,929,600	580,388	155,756

An especially ominous sign was that 'sanitary' losses of the three Fronts were only 8.1 per cent of their initial strength, whereas 'irrevocable' losses were 30 per cent. In most military campaigns the wounded outnumber the dead by at least 2 to 1, so 'irrevocable' exceeding 'sanitary' losses by almost 4 to 1 suggests that both deaths and woundings were vastly outnumbered by surrenders, desertions or defections. The initial strength of all three Fronts included conscripts from the recently annexed territories (mostly Lithuanians, Latvians, Estonians and Finns in North-West Front, Poles from West Belorussia and West Ukraine in the other two, and in South-West Front also Romanians). Their brief experience of Soviet rule had given many cause to hate it and few any motivation to fight for it, and, following the famines, deportations and killings that had accompanied forced collectivisation of agriculture in the 1930s, the same was true of many Soviet Ukrainians; nor was it a negligible factor among other Soviet ethnicities, Russians included, and especially Russian or Ukrainian Cossacks, particularly while the Germans appeared to be winning. In fact desertion and defection levels would remain significant until the third quarter of 1943, when the outcomes at Kursk, in North Africa and in Italy finally convinced most potential deserters or defectors that Germany was no longer to be seen as the winning side.

Some idea of the scale of desertion and defection in the first weeks, and of the brutal methods used to counter them, can be gained from reports to his superiors by Brigade Commissar Mikhaylov, head of the Political Propaganda Directorate of South-West Front. On 26 June 1941, 'In 41st

Rifle Division from 22 to 25 June officers shot 10 conscripts for cowardice and desertion.' On 3 July

> in units of 6th Rifle Corps up to 5,000 deserters have been detained and sent back to the front. 100 deserters have been shot . . . unit commanders have shot 101 for desertion . . . In 99th Rifle Division 80 conscripts from Western provinces of Ukraine i.e. recently annexed Polish or Romanian territory refused to fire during a battle. All were shot in front of the ranks . . . during battle a company commander of 895th Regiment . . . withdrew the company from the front without permission . . . the division commander, Major-General Smekhotvorov, shot him on the spot.

On 6 July, 'From 22 June to 1 July . . . 26th Army lost 391 killed, 953 wounded, 772 missing, and up to 4,000 (mostly from Western provinces of Ukraine) dispersed i.e. deserted or defected.'[103]. So in the latter case twelve went missing or 'dispersed' for every one killed. Hardly a good start.

A summary report of the activities of NKVD 'blocking' detachments, stationed behind the troops in the line, noted that from 22 June to 10 October 1941 they had detained 657,364 soldiers who had fled from their units. They had arrested 25,878 (3.9 per cent) of them, formed the rest into units, and sent them back to the front line. Those arrested included 1,505 spies, 308 saboteurs, 2,621 defectors, 2,643 cowards/panickers, 3,987 rumour-mongers, 1,671 men with self-inflicted wounds, and 4,371 (unspecified) 'others'. Of those arrested, 10,201 (39.4 per cent) had been shot. Assuming those shot included all the alleged spies, saboteurs, defectors, cowards and self-wounders, totalling 8,748, so must also have been 1,453 of the 8,358 rumour-mongers or 'others' – so even careless talk carried a one in six chance of receiving a bullet.[104] Even as late as November 1942 defection was still a problem. One account for that month from a sector where the adversaries were on opposite banks of a frozen river mentioned the use of artillery to break up the ice to deter defectors from crossing to the German side, and when that proved ineffective NKVD blocking detachments had to be stationed in front of the troops as well as behind them.[105]

The 657,364 attempted deserters detained over the first 111 days of war average 5,922 a day. To those must be added the numbers of dead, missing or captured, and non-combat losses (deaths in accidents, by execution or suicides). Figures for these cover the whole of 1941, and for the main Fronts were as follows:[106]

Table 7. Soviet Army 'Irrevocable' losses, 1941

Front	Killed	Missing or captured	Non-combat losses
North–West	31,511	142,190	8,563
West	106,997	798,465	50,831
South–West	60,016	607,860	49,957
South	32,362	188,306	17,909
Total	230,886	1,736,821	127,260
Daily average	1,196	8,999	659

So, on average over each of the first 193 days of war, for every two who died in battle, one died a non-combat death, seven surrendered or 'went missing', and in the first 111 days, as the previous table showed, another six tried to 'go missing' but were caught. The non-combat deaths repay further scrutiny, because they show a very high level in 1941, and seeking the most likely explanation for this requires comparison with the following two years. Over Fronts that existed for more than one year the figures for non-combat deaths were as follows: daily averages are for 193 days in 1941 and 365 in the other two years.[107]

Table 8. Soviet Army non-combat deaths, 1941–43

Front	1941	1942	1943
North–West	8,563	8,970	2,504
West	50,831	25,095	5,541
South–West	49,957	5,533	–
South	17,909	10,862	–
Bryansk	3,044	7,088	726
Leningrad	8,284	6,371	4,431
Karelian	632	1,491	406
Kalinin	7,973	13,984	2,488
Volkhov	–	8,935	1,590
Transcaucasus	–	8,235	905
Stalingrad/Don	–	12,948	835
Totals	147,193	109,512	19,426
Daily average	763	300	53

It is very unlikely that the dramatic fall in 1943 was due to a reduction in accidental deaths; they would be more likely to increase, because of the larger size and increased mechanisation of the army, with horse-drawn carts replaced by much faster American trucks and jeeps, mostly with inexperienced drivers. The most likely explanation is that many of the non-combat deaths were executions for cowardice or attempted desertion/defection. As already noted, these were widespread in the early period, and several post-Soviet accounts noted that both were still serious problems at the end of 1942.[108] The German defeats on the Eastern Front and in Africa seriously damaged the image of the Germans as 'winners', so henceforth there were fewer attempts to desert. But even as late as July 1943 fear of desertion or defection was acute enough for Stavka officials to order all Estonian, Latvian or Lithuanian soldiers, and all of any ethnic origin who had been in German captivity, to be removed from every unit about to fight the battle of Kursk, and sent to the rear.

Rokossovsky described in his memoirs numerous instances of panic flight he witnessed in the early days,[109] including the arrival at his command post of a general who had tried to stop fleeing infantrymen, and escaped being shot by them only by jumping from a moving lorry and hiding in a field of tall rye. All these passages were edited out of Soviet-era editions.

As the above figures indicate, it took only three weeks of war to show up serious morale and organisational problems that required prompt and drastic action. On 15 July Stavka issued a Directive to all commanders of Directions, Fronts, Military Districts and Armies. It made several points. First, the existing mechanised corps were too cumbersome, immobile, unwieldy, sluggish and unmanoeuvrable. At the first opportunity they must be disbanded and reorganised as independent tank divisions; their motorised infantry would become ordinary infantry divisions, and the vehicles thus freed used to create army transport battalions, for transferring troops between sectors and bringing up ammunition. Secondly, large armies with intermediate corps headquarters were hard to organise for, and direct in, battle, 'especially bearing in mind the youth and limited experience of our staffs and commanders'. They must be replaced by armies of at most five or six divisions, directly subordinate to army commanders, with corps level abolished. Thirdly, for combating enemy tanks, infantry divisions must wherever feasible be provided with at least a company of medium or light tanks, and if possible also a platoon of three KV heavy tanks. Fourthly, for raiding into the German rear, existing (horse) cavalry corps and divisions must be reformed into light divisions of 3,000 men each, and new ones created. Fifthly, air force corps, multi-regiment divisions and sixty-aircraft regiments were very ponderous, clumsy and vulnerable to air attack, and their size impeded their control by necessitating dispersal between several airfields. Air corps must be replaced by smaller air divisions, of only two regiments, each with 30 aircraft.[110]

The Directive specified that all these changes must be introduced 'gradually and without detriment to current operations', but that such radical reorganisation was prescribed after a mere three weeks of war pointed clearly to the damage caused by the purges and rapid post-1939 expansion, as the reference to the 'youth and limited experience of staffs and commanders' implicitly acknowledged. At this stage the Stavka judgement clearly was that few Soviet officers could handle anything larger than a division; a mechanised corps, of only three divisions, was deemed too 'unwieldy', the new light cavalry divisions, of only 3,000 men, were really only reinforced regiments, and the standard 'rifle' (infantry) division would eventually be reduced from almost 15,000 to about 9,000 men. As time passed Soviet skill in handling large numbers would come to surpass even that of the Germans, but in 1941 the only quick-fix solution was to make formations smaller.

Another radical element of reorganisation was introduced simultaneously, for immediate, not gradual, implementation. This was the re-creation of the Institute of Political Commissars by the Supreme Soviet Presidium on 16 July, followed the next day by a Stavka order for its implementation.[111] Political Officers had been introduced in 1917 by the Provisional government, to provide a check on the reliability of officers commissioned under the recently abdicated Tsar Nicholas II, and Lenin's government extensively used dedicated Communist 'commissars' for the same purpose in the civil war that followed its seizure of power in November of that year. In principle, and usually in practice, a professional commanding officer's order was valid only if countersigned by the commissar. In August 1934 the principle of *edinonachalie* (unified command) was introduced, giving the professional officer precedence, with the political officer defined as his 'deputy' for political matters such as propaganda and troop indoctrination. In June 1937 the political commissars were restored to equal status with commanders, and military councils (comprising the commanding officer, chief political officer, chief of staff and sometimes a local Communist Party representative) were reintroduced at the level of army or fleet and military district, clearly in order to tighten Party control of the military during the purge which had begun with the trial and execution in that month of Marshal Tukhachevsky and six other high-ranking officers. Presumably as a gesture of Stalin's and the Party's renewed trust in the purged officer class, unity of command had been restored in August 1940, the political officers losing the title of 'commissar' and again becoming 'deputy commanders for political matters'. However, the disastrous start of the war, particularly the large-scale surrenders, revived Stalin's suspicions about the professional military's loyalty, so on 16 July the Institute of Military Commissars was re-established. The Stavka order issued on 17 July changed the titles of the political sections of divisions and above from Directorate or Department of Political Propaganda to Political Directorate/Department. It did not specifically state that the political officers had equal status with commanders, but implicitly did so by removing their 'deputy' status, and renaming them 'military commissars' of regiments and above, or 'political leaders' (*Politruki*) of lower-level units. At the highest levels, of Front or Direction, the order made no real difference, because there the 'Member of the Military Council' was always a senior Communist Party official, usually close to, and with ready access to, Stalin, irrespective of his formal status relative to command-line officers. But below that level the change indicated to the professionals that the Party's eye was again on them. Even when officially only 'deputies', the political officers had been widely seen by commanders as Party spies (the first step to dismissal or arrest in the purges was often a calling to account by a unit's Party branch, initiated by a political officer), and that most of them lacked military training commensurate with their status earned them resentment, including among the rank and file. Learning of Hitler's notorious 'commissar order', that political officers were to be shot on capture, many removed their rank badges, only to have their own men point them out to the Germans. The regime, however, saw their position as convinced Communist Party members making them more reliable than the military professionals. The newly appointed Head of the Main Political Directorate, Lev Mekhlis, paraded his distrust of officers to the extent of having some arbitrarily shot and threatening many others with the same fate. Only in October 1942 was the institution again abolished. The political officers were again demoted to 'deputy' status, and at the same time Tsarist-epoch gold braid and shoulder-boards with rank badges were restored, both gestures reflecting the renewal of the Party's (i.e. Stalin's) confidence in the military.

Panic, desertion and defection were enough of a problem in the early weeks of war for Stalin to issue Order no. 270 on 16 August 1941. Its preamble included statements such as 'in the ranks of the Red Army, that is steadfastly and self-sacrificingly defending its Soviet motherland from the vile invaders, there are unstable, mean-spirited, cowardly elements. And these cowardly elements are not only among private soldiers, but also among command personnel . . .'. The Order stipulated that 'Commanders and political officers who in battle tear off their rank badges and desert to the rear or surrender to the enemy are to be considered malicious deserters, and their families arrested', and ordered 'all higher-level commanders and commissars to shoot such officer deserters on the spot'. Families of private soldiers who surrendered were to be 'deprived of state allowances and assistance'. Division commanders and commissars were ordered to remove battalion or regiment commanders who went into hiding during battle, demote them to privates, 'or if necessary shoot them on the spot', and replace them with 'bold and brave' NCOs or privates who had distinguished themselves in combat. The Order was 'to be read out in all companies, cavalry troops, batteries, squadrons, commands and staffs' but not made public:[112] in fact it was not published until 1988.

Having unveiled the 'stick', Stalin took three more months to produce a 'carrot' for officers in the shape of Order no. 929 of 20 November. This reflected the catastrophic effects of five months of disastrous fighting on an army short of experienced officers. It reduced the time of front-line service before consideration for promotion to two months for lieutenants, three for senior lieutenants and captains, four for majors and five for lieutenant-colonels, and halved those terms for officers wounded in battle or decorated for bravery. A 'carrot' for the lower ranks was a daily issue of 100 grams of vodka, presented to the troops as 'a manifestation of the Party and Government's special care for Red Army men'.[113] Later 'carrots' instituted substantial cash payments for tank or gun crews and infantry anti-tank riflemen who knocked out an enemy tank or self-propelled gun; adding these cash incentives undoubtedly increased the exaggerations normal in combat reports, when several crews fire at the same target and all in good faith claim its destruction. When the archives were opened numerous combat reports were found to have claimed the destruction of far more German tanks than actually existed; whether and to what extent acceptance of the exaggerated figures created undue optimism in Stavka and the General Staff, thereby prompting some unsuccessful Soviet offensives, has yet to be researched.

As noted above, Stalin's mistaken assumption about German aims had resulted in higher numbers of Soviet forces facing lower numbers of Germans south of the Pripyat marshes compared to north of them. According to a post-Soviet assessment, the South-West Front had almost as many men (1.4 versus 1.5 million) as Army Group South, and far more weaponry – 1.7 times as many guns and mortars (26,580 to 16,008), 2.6 times as many combat aircraft (4,696 versus 1,829) and no less than seven times as many tanks (8,069 versus 1,144).[114] Consequently its retreat was initially much slower and less chaotic than that on the two northern sectors, but once past the eastern end of the marshes this dangerously exposed its northern flank. Zhukov, realising the risk of encirclement, advised Stalin on 29 July to pull the Front back to east of the Dnepr river. However, this would have meant abandoning Kiev, which Stalin refused to authorise, whereupon Zhukov resigned, or was dismissed, as Chief of General Staff. He asked for a field command, so Stalin put him in charge of the Reserve Front, which, despite its name, was in the front line, and authorised him to carry out his proposal for an offensive against the 'Yelnya salient', which Stalin had previously denigrated as 'nonsense', but which Zhukov considered necessary because of the salient's dangerous potential as a launching-point for an eventual attack on Moscow.

This operation, which began on 30 August and ended on 8 September, was insignificant in the short term; it was brief, conducted by only a single Army (24th), did not achieve any encirclement, and the ground gained had soon to be abandoned in the general retreat during October that marked the last phase of the Battle of Smolensk and first phase of the Battle of Moscow. However, it was of considerable long-term significance, because the Germans had to abandon the salient. For the first time in the entire war a large German ground force, including the elite Waffen SS Das Reich Division, had been not just stopped in its tracks, but forced to retreat. This success contrasted with the previous Soviet disasters and the failure of the offensive launched on 1 September by the Western Front, and marked the beginning of Zhukov's rise to become Stalin's chief military troubleshooter.

A number of post-Soviet authors have criticised Zhukov as militarily only semi-literate, pointing to his lack of training at senior level such as a Staff College. However, he did on a number of occasions show far more than average skill in interpreting enemy intentions and deciding how to frustrate them. He had already exhibited this quality at the end of July, when he advocated withdrawing to east of the Dnepr, but his advice had not been taken. In mid-August, while preparing for the Yelnya operation, he noticed a decline in activity against his Front and the two others deployed to cover the routes leading to Moscow, and concluded that this meant the Germans intended to use their mobile forces (Guderian's 2nd Panzer Group) instead for a southward drive to encircle the South-West Front, defending Kiev. On 19 August he sent a message to that effect to Stalin, and recommended deploying a strong force in the Bryansk area, to attack Guderian's east flank when he appeared. This time Stalin accepted his advice, and instructed Yeremenko, commander of the just-established (14 August) Bryansk Front accordingly. Yeremenko promised to dispose of 'that rascal Guderian', who, as Zhukov had forecast, duly appeared a few days later. However, despite being sent additional artillery and air support and several infantry divisions, Yeremenko failed to stop the 2nd Panzer Group, and on 16 September it linked up with Kleist's 1st Panzer Group to complete the encirclement of most of the South-West Front.

Despite Yeremenko's failure, Zhukov's correct reading of German intentions, as early as 19 August, obviously reinforced by his success at Yelnya, raised his status in Stalin's eyes. Only after the war did it become known that the leading German generals (Commander-in-Chief Brauchitsch, Chief of General Staff (OKH) Halder, the Commanders-in-Chief of Army Groups Centre (Bock) and South (Rundstedt), and the Panzer Group commanders Hoth and Guderian) had unanimously argued against the southward diversion and for a continuation of the direct drive on Moscow. Guderian had objected so strongly to his orders, on the grounds that it would be difficult to go south, fight an encirclement battle and get back north in time for an attempt to seize Moscow before winter, that on 24 August he had a meeting with Hitler, which Halder, who shared his reservations, initiated specifically so that he could present his objections. In his account of the meeting Guderian claimed to have done so but been overruled, and to have been surprised by the angry scene with Halder that followed.[115] Halder, however, noted in his diary that Hitler had not overruled Guderian, but had convinced him.[116] The point remains that Zhukov predicted what Guderian would do five days before Guderian himself ceased arguing that he should not do it. If that was a lucky guess, it would not be the only one in Zhukov's subsequent career. He was not always right, but he was wrong less often and less harmfully than others; Stalin's recognition of his ability to predict enemy plans elevated him above his coevals, and he had charge of nearly all the most important assignments for the rest of the war.

The first such assignment followed immediately after his success at Yelnya. On the evening of 9 September Stalin summoned Zhukov to Moscow, congratulated him on it, then told him 'a very serious, I'd almost say hopeless, situation has arisen at Leningrad', which on the previous day had lost its last land connection to the rest of the country, with the German capture of Shlisselburg initiating a 905-day siege, and had suffered its first massive air and artillery bombardments. Zhukov replied, 'If it's that difficult there, I'm ready to go and command Leningrad Front.' Stalin asked when he could go, and authorised him to take over command from Voroshilov immediately on arrival. He then asked him what he thought of the situation in Ukraine; Zhukov again urged withdrawal across the Dnepr, but the dictator undertook only to discuss the matter with the local commanders,[117] and when he did so, on 11 September, he again forbade retreat from Kiev or the destruction of any bridge over the Dnepr without his consent; then when Budenny, commanding the entire southern 'Direction', also urged withdrawal, he sacked him and replaced him with Timoshenko. He too favoured a retreat, as did Kirponos, but was prepared to authorise it only orally, and Kirponos refused to act without written orders. Preservation of an entire Front took second place to post-purge fear of incurring Stalin's displeasure.

Another significant event at this time was the beginning of Zhukov's close association with Vasilevsky, then Deputy Chief of General Staff and Head of its Operations Directorate, destined to succeed Shaposhnikov as Chief in mid-1942 and become second only to Zhukov in Stalin's estimation. Before leaving for Leningrad Zhukov sought Vasilevsky's opinion about the fighting in Ukraine, and Vasilevsky said he too thought withdrawal across the Dnepr was seriously overdue.[118] That they were right was proved within a week. The encirclement completed by Guderian and Kleist closed the ring on three of the South-West Front's armies and parts of two others. The Germans claimed to have taken 665,000 prisoners; only in 1993 did post-Soviet disclosures show that their claims had not been wildly exaggerated. The South-West Front, with 864,600 troops initially committed to action, lost 165,452 (19 per cent) of them 'irrevocably' (i.e., killed, captured or missing) in the first two weeks of war, then in the next 88 days, from 7 July to the final surrender on 26 September, lost another 531,471. An ominous sign was that its 'sanitary' losses in the same period were only 54,127; in round figures, ten Soviet soldiers died, surrendered, deserted or defected for every one wounded or sick – an even worse result than in the two Fronts to its north.[119]

The depth of Stalin's pessimism about Leningrad (since 1991 again St Petersburg) was shown by another secret order, suppressed until well after the war. This order, issued on 6 September and classified 'Top Secret. Of Special Importance', was for Baltic Fleet sailors 'in the event of withdrawal from Leningrad' to prepare all port installations for destruction, and to sink ships, including all warships, in places where they would prevent the Germans using the waterways or berths. The authority for the Order was a message signed by Admiral Kuznetsov (under protest), Marshal Shaposhnikov and Stalin.[120] When Zhukov arrived in Leningrad on 10 September he immediately countermanded it, and by a combination of decisive actions, dismissals, shootings and blood-curdling threats (for example his order of 17 September that anyone who left his post without a written order was to be shot at once)[121] brought stability to the wavering defence. He was lucky in one respect; five days before he arrived, Hitler had notified Army Group North that he intended to send all bar one panzer corps of its mobile forces (Hoepner's 4th Panzer Group, of five panzer and two motorised infantry divisions) to Army Group Centre to take part in Operation 'Typhoon', the attempt to take Moscow. However, the defenders did not know that at the time, because Army Group North's remaining forces mounted numerous attacks as part of the process of diverting Soviet attention from the preparations for 'Typhoon'. Only at the end of September, when reconnaissance found the Germans digging bunkers, installing stoves in them and planting mines in front of their positions, could it be firmly concluded that they were going into winter quarters and settling in for a siege. The front line here, except along the south shore of Lake Ladoga, where in January 1943 the Leningrad and Volkhov Fronts, in Operation 'Iskra' ('Spark'), restored a slim but vital rail and pipeline connection from the 'mainland', would remain little changed until the siege was lifted in January 1944.

Germany's victories in Ukraine and the Baltic States had a price – postponement of the attack on Moscow to allow time for Army Group Centre to receive Hoth's 3rd Panzer Group from Army Group North, and to retrieve Guderian's 2nd Panzer Group from Ukraine – placing the start of the offensive perilously close to the rain and mud of autumn and the snow and ice of winter. Nevertheless it had great successes to report very soon after it was launched on 30 September; by 7 October the 3rd and 4th Panzer Groups had encircled most units of seven Soviet Armies (3rd, 13th, 19th, 20th, 24th, 32nd and 50th) of the Kalinin, Bryansk and Reserve Fronts. Some elements managed to break out eastward, but according to Field-Marshal von Bock's diary some 558,000 men had been captured by 15 October, and another 115,000 by the 19th.[122] However, the autumn rains had begun on 9 October and from the 13th became heavy, turning the terrain into a sea of mud in which vehicles could only move if towed by tractors, every gun needed ten horses to pull it, and standard German Army carts had to be jettisoned because they were too low-slung and replaced by whatever local carts could be commandeered from nearby collective farms. Supplies of all kinds arrived late or not at all, and the troops went hungry except for what food they could loot from villages or farms; they were cold, for lack of winter uniforms and shelter, and lousy and dirty, because the Red Army destroyed as many buildings as it could before retreating.

The most authoritative post-Soviet account does not quite confirm the totals in Bock's diary, but admits that 514,338 'irrevocable' losses[123] were incurred between 30 September and 5 November, 382,000 of them in the first 12 days, at an average daily loss rate of 31,833. A full-strength Soviet infantry division in June 1941 numbered 14,483 men,[124] so even taking the lower Soviet figures the losses averaged over two full-strength divisions-worth a day for 12 successive days. In fact, not 24 but 45 divisions were destroyed, as most had fallen well below full strength during the long retreat from the frontiers, and by mid-August Stavka had decided to reduce their war establishment to 11,000.

'Typhoon' started well for the Germans. In two weeks they had smashed three Soviet army groups (the West, Bryansk and Reserve Fronts), and killed or captured well over half a million troops. At this stage the Wehrmacht was suffering more hardship from mud, inadequate supply and medical services (casualties from sickness and frostbite outnumbered those from enemy action), frost, snow and sheer exhaustion than from anything the Red Army was doing.

However, that was about to change. Stalin telephoned Zhukov with orders to come back to Moscow at once, and when he arrived, on 7 October, told him the situation was very serious – 'I can't get comprehensive reports from West Front Konev and Reserve Front Budenny about the true state of affairs, and we can't take any decisions because we don't know where or in what strength the enemy is attacking, nor what condition our own troops are in' – and told him to go to Western Front Headquarters, find out the situation 'and ring me from there at any time'.

Zhukov went first to the General Staff, where Shaposhnikov told him what was known, and handed him a Stavka Directive ordering both Front commanders to tell him what they knew, and to implement 'obligatorily' any orders he might give about employing and directing their troops. Western Front HQ had been his own during August, so finding it was no problem, but the information he received there added little to what Shaposhnikov had told him. At the start of 'Typhoon' the Western, Reserve and Bryansk Fronts had between them 1.25 million troops, 990 tanks, 7,600 guns and mortars, and 677 aircraft. According to Zhukov the reinforced Army Group Centre was reckoned to have 40 per cent more men, 70 per cent more tanks, 80 per cent more artillery and twice as many aircraft.[125] Some of these figures are undoubtedly exaggerated; Army Group Centre, for example, started the battle with 70 divisions (14 panzer, 8 motorised infantry and 48 infantry); even if they were all at full strength they would total at most 1.2 million, not 40 per cent more but slightly less than the initial strength of the three Soviet Fronts, and their air support, Luftflotte 2, had about 1,000 aircraft, not the 1,350 or so implied by Zhukov's statement. Nevertheless, even those ratios should still have favoured the defenders, were it not that the Germans had so regularly defeated vastly superior numbers; Soviet practice considered successful offensives needed a superiority of 3 to 1, and even on the exaggerated Soviet figures the Germans had nothing like that. In his memoirs, written many years later, Zhukov severely criticised the three Front commanders:

> Despite the enemy superiority in manpower and equipment, our forces could have avoided encirclement. To do so it was necessary to determine in good time and more correctly the direction of the main enemy thrusts, and concentrate the bulk of troops and resources against them, at the expense of inactive sectors. This was not done, and our fronts' defence did not withstand the concentrated enemy blows. Yawning gaps formed, and there was nothing to close them with, because the commands had no reserves left . . .

When he originally wrote it, his criticism was even more severe: in post-Soviet editions the above passage is preceded by one that reads 'On the basis of Intelligence data, Stavka forewarned the Front commanders, by a special directive on 27 September, of the possibility of an offensive on the Moscow axis by major enemy forces within the next few days. Consequently surprise by the offensive, in the sense there was at the start of the war, was lacking', and it is followed by 'By the end of the day on 7 October, all roads to Moscow essentially were open.'[126] Both passages were removed from Soviet editions; if Zhukov, who was never noted for sparing others' feelings, felt so strongly about Konev's, Yeremenko's and Budenny's errors when writing his memoirs over 20 years later, it is easy to guess what he said to and about them at the time, and this helps to account for the post-war criticisms of him by Konev and Yeremenko, both of whom survived several subsequent dismissals and reappointments to achieve eventual success as Front commanders, and clearly resented his earlier castigations of them.

At 2.30 a.m. on 8 October Zhukov telephoned Stalin and reported the situation: 'The main danger now is the weak coverage on the Mozhaisk line. Because of that enemy armoured forces could appear suddenly at Moscow. Forces must be brought up to the Mozhaisk defence line from wherever possible.' Stalin asked, 'Where now are Western Front's 16th, 19th and 20th Armies and Boldin's group? Where are Reserve Front's 24th and 32nd Armies?' Zhukov replied, 'They're encircled west and south-west of Vyazma.' He then set off to look for the headquarters of Budenny's Reserve Front, defending the south-western approaches to Moscow.

Nobody could tell him where it was, but eventually some signals troops he found laying telephone lines told him where it had moved to, just two hours earlier. The situation there was even worse than at Western Front – 'I learned very little specific about the situation of Reserve Front's forces or about the enemy' – and nobody even knew where Budenny was. Zhukov set off to look for him, and found him in the apparently deserted town of Maloyaroslavets. He said he had had no contact with Konev for over two days, had been with the 43rd Army on the previous day, and as his own headquarters had moved in his absence, he did not even know where it was. When asked who was guarding the road from Yukhnov, believed to be in enemy hands, Budenny replied that on his way from there all he had seen were three policemen. Zhukov told him where his headquarters were, and instructed him to go there, report the situation to Stalin, and tell him that he, Zhukov, would go on to the Yukhnov area, then to Kaluga. However, on his way to Yukhnov he was stopped by soldiers who told him the enemy were in front; in fact they turned out to be troops from the headquarters of a tank brigade of Stavka Reserve which, in the prevailing confusion, had been in position nearby for two days, but had been given no orders whatsoever. Zhukov later found out that an improvised unit of 400 frontier guards, formed by a major on his own initiative, had blown up the bridge over the River Ugra and, assisted by a detachment of officer cadets from training schools in Podolsk, held the Germans up for five days. Most of them had been killed, but the time they gained was valuable because hasty improvisation was now the order of the day; for the time being the lines at Maloyaroslavets would be manned by officer cadets from two other training schools in Podolsk.

While in the Kaluga area Zhukov received another message from Stalin, ordering him to be at the Western Front headquarters on 10 October, but when he arrived at the Reserve Front headquarters on the evening of the 8th the Chief of Staff told him that Stavka had dismissed

Budenny and appointed him, Zhukov, to command the Front. He rang
the General Staff to ask which of these apparently conflicting orders he
should obey, and Shaposhnikov told him that the State Defence
Committee was considering merging Reserve Front with Western Front
and giving him command of both. When he arrived at Western Front
headquarters on the 10th, Stalin telephoned and confirmed him in the
dual command. Then came another passage deleted from Soviet-era
editions of the memoirs:

> Stalin asked 'What shall we do with Konev?' For the enemy's
> smashing of Western Front, which Konev commanded, the
> Supremo intended to have him court-martialled. And only my
> intervention saved him from a heavy fate. I must say that until the
> Kursk battle Konev commanded forces badly, and the State
> Defence Committee more than once [actually six times] removed
> him from command of a Front.[127]

Many Soviet generals, Zhukov, Yeremenko and Konev among them,
appeared to regard politeness as 'bourgeois', and proved their 'proletar-
ian' credentials by offering rudeness and sometimes even physical
violence to subordinates. Rokossovsky, commanding 16th Army, was a
noted exception, and his relationship with Zhukov was complicated by
another factor. In the mid-1930s Rokossovsky commanded the 7th
Cavalry Division, and Zhukov was his subordinate, commanding one of
its regiments. But in August 1937 Rokossovsky was arrested and imprisoned, accused of spying for Poland (apparently for no other reason than
that his father was Polish). But by March 1940, when he was released and
restored to the rank of major-general, Zhukov had defeated the Japanese
in Mongolia and risen meteorically to army general, three ranks above his
former superior. In the battle of Moscow Rokossovsky was an army
commander under Zhukov, and he seems to have had some difficulty
accepting the role reversal. At one point he proposed to withdraw to east
of the Istra reservoir, to shorten his line and secure a more easily defended
position. This made sense for his army, but would have exposed the flank
of the neighbouring 5th Army, forcing it also to withdraw, so Zhukov
vetoed it. Rokossovsky then went over his head to Chief of General Staff
Shaposhnikov, who gave his approval, whereupon Zhukov sent an angry
message, 'I command the Front's forces . . .' and later turned up at
Rokossovsky's headquarters, along with Govorov, commanding 5th
Army:

'What, are the Germans chasing you again? You've more forces than you need, but you can't use them. You can't command! Here's Govorov, he's got more of the enemy than you have in front of you, and he's holding him and not letting him through. I've brought him here to teach you how to fight.'

Although Rokossovsky knew, and knew that Zhukov also knew, that Govorov was only facing ordinary infantry, whereas he had to contend with the tanks and motorised infantry of the panzer divisions, he solemnly thanked Zhukov for giving him and his assistants a chance to learn, and Zhukov left the room to telephone for the latest information. Suddenly he came charging back in, slammed the door and bellowed at Govorov, 'What are you doing? Who've you come to teach? Rokossovsky?! He's repelling assaults by all the German panzer divisions and beating them. And some lousy motorised division arrives against you and chases you dozens of kilometres. Get out of here, go to your place! And if you don't restore the situation . . .', etc, etc. A fresh German motorised division had indeed arrived, and driven 5th Army back some 15 kilometres, while Zhukov had irresponsibly deprived it of its commander by taking him to 'teach' Rokossovsky how to fight.[128]

Despite his reservations about Konev, Zhukov recommended putting him in charge of the forces on the Front's northern sector, the Kalinin (now Tver) axis, guarding the approach to Moscow from the north-west along the main road from Leningrad; Stalin agreed, and when the Stavka order was issued, putting Zhukov in charge from 6 p.m. on 11 October, it included the appointment of Konev as his deputy. As Zhukov had requested, substantial forces now began to arrive at the Mozhaisk defence line from Stavka Reserve and from other Fronts, including 14 infantry divisions, 16 tank brigades and over 40 regiments of artillery, and the battered 5th, 16th, 43rd and 49th Armies began to be made back up to strength.

Strong forces had initially been kept in Siberia and the Far East, in case Japan also attacked, but during September and October information from a variety of sources, including the deciphering of Japanese diplomatic and military messages,[129] made it clear that at least currently it had no such intention.[130] That made it possible to bring several divisions from the east to Moscow, but they would take some time to arrive. In the meantime Zhukov deployed the available forces to defend the four principal lines of approach to the capital, and mobilised engineering troops and civilians to create defence in depth by digging trenches and anti-tank ditches. Over

250,000 Muscovites, mostly women and teenagers, spent October and November on these works, while men were organised into 14 divisions of *'opol'cheniie'*, a militia similar to the Local Defence Volunteers ('Home Guard') hastily formed in the UK in 1940, but, unlike them, they were destined to be thrown into battle almost at once, poorly equipped and practically untrained; inevitably they suffered very heavy casualties but they helped to buy time.

On 15 October the State Defence Committee ruled that on the next day ministries and other government bodies, embassies, General Staff directorates and military academies must be evacuated from Moscow, mostly to Kuybyshev (now Samara). Stalin was also supposed to leave that day, but decided not to go. However, when news of the evacuation spread there was widespread panic, quelled only by the proclamation on 20 October of a 'state of siege' (effectively the imposition of martial law) in Moscow and adjacent areas, and by arrests (and some shootings) of 'panic-mongers' and looters.

Meanwhile the Western Front continued to lose ground. On 17 October its northern sector became a new Kalinin Front, with three armies and with Konev as commander, though he remained subordinate to Zhukov; but on that very day the 40th Panzer Corps took Kalinin and on the next the 57th Panzer Corps entered Mozhaisk and Maloyaroslavets, putting German tanks within 96 kilometres (60 miles) of Moscow. Expectation of victory had already led Brauchitsch to issue an order on 14 October that Moscow was not to be occupied, nor any offer to surrender it accepted. Hitler had earlier decreed that Leningrad and Moscow were to be razed to the ground, the population starved out or 'encouraged' to flee, and a huge lake to be dug where Moscow had stood.

The Red Army was also faring badly elsewhere. On 16 October the last shipload of defenders left Odessa, on the 18th the Germans broke through the Soviet defences of the Crimea and on the 19th began a major offensive into that peninsula. On the 25th they took Kharkov, Ukraine's second city (and the USSR's fourth largest), while the Leningrad Front spent nine days (20–28 October) trying and failing to break the blockade. As the rain and mud gave way to snow and ice, the ground hardened and the Germans began to find the going easier, but everything else more difficult. The campaign had been meant to end before winter came, so no account had been taken of the likely effects of cold on troops still in summer uniforms, or on vehicles, many of them up to their axles in mud, which now froze them in, or their engines, which could only be kept serviceable by running them continuously, or by having a fire or heater under them when switched off, both options requiring fuel that often was not available. The ability to maintain artillery support was regularly limited by the need to scrape every shell clear of the frozen grease that made it too bulky to load. These and many other problems created by the Russian winter had to be overcome in an environment of increasing Soviet resistance, with new armies being formed and fresh divisions arriving from Siberia and Central Asia. Supply provision still presented problems for both sides; whenever Zhukov and his Chief of Staff, Lieutenant-General Sokolovsky, went to see Stalin, they always took a 3-ton truck with them, in the hope that he would tell them where to pick up some rifles or other small items.

However, Zhukov sensed a weakening in the German attacks as November went on. They continued to make small inroads into the Soviet defences, which in places were then only 20 miles from the city's outskirts, and at one point on the main highway to Leningrad, now marked by a monument, a reconnaissance unit penetrated to only 22 kilometres (about 14 miles) from the Kremlin; but in Zhukov's perception the German effort tangibly lacked the scale and impetus of 'Typhoon's' earlier days. This perception was correct; Halder wrote in his diary on 30 November that losses in killed, missing, wounded and sick from the start of the invasion to 26 November totalled 743,112, including almost 25,000 officers; the three army groups had lost half their infantry and were 340,000 men under strength. These losses were small compared to the enemy's, and were mainly in wounded and sick, most of whom would return to the ranks in due course; but they were also several times the losses that had been incurred in conquering Poland, Western Europe and the Balkans, and the stated aim of 'Barbarossa' – to defeat the Red Army before the winter – was obviously not being achieved.

The last days of November also saw substantial Soviet reinforcements arriving. On the 24th the 10th Army, and on the next day the 26th and 61st Reserve Armies, each of seven infantry and two cavalry divisions, all ordered from assembly areas on the Volga, detrained and were deployed just south-east of Moscow. Zhukov would later write that at that time neither he nor the General Staff planned anything beyond stopping the Germans, but his existing forces had practically brought them to a standstill already, and he obviously knew of the additional armies' arrival, because he telephoned Stalin on 29 November to ask for two of them. That he had something more ambitious in mind than just 'stopping' Army Group Centre emerges from his account of the conversation. He said Stalin asked him, 'Are you sure the enemy has reached a crisis, and isn't in a position to introduce some large new force into the affair?' Zhukov replied that the enemy was 'worn out', but unless his 'dangerous penetrations' were liquidated he could later bring in large fresh forces 'and then our position would become more difficult'. Stalin said he would consult the General Staff, and later that evening telephoned to tell Zhukov he could have not two but all three of the newly arrived armies, and must submit his plan for using them. Compiling it took less than a day, and Stalin approved it at once.

The major threat Zhukov aspired to eliminate was that posed by Army Group Centre's mobile forces (the former panzer groups, now redesignated panzer armies), located on its flanks with the obvious aim of by-passing Moscow from north and south and meeting east of it to achieve an encirclement. So he sent in most of the additional forces against Guderian's 2nd Panzer Army on the south flank, around Tula, and Hoth's 3rd and Hoepner's 4th Panzer Armies on the north side. He expected the counter-attacks to gain about 37 miles in the north and 100 in the south, but when the first assaults showed the Germans to be even weaker than he expected, the attacks more or less spontaneously developed into a general counter-offensive. There was no formal directive instituting one, but now there was a possibility that the Soviet mobile forces could not only push their German counterparts back, but get behind and encircle the foot soldiers who constituted the majority of Army Group Centre. Few tanks and vehicles were available, so the mobile forces sent into the enemy rear were mostly horse cavalry, skiers and parachute troops. Against the over-extended, exhausted and largely worn-out forces of Army Group Centre these improvised, but mostly fresh, mobile forces proved more than adequate to force the enemy into retreat. By the end of December Zhukov considered the first stage of the counter-offensive completed, and hoped to be given additional forces to renew it.[131] However, as will be seen, Stalin believed the Germans completely spent, and had more ambitious ideas.

Hitler's first reaction to Zhukov's counter-offensive was to issue Directive no. 39 on 8 December, face-savingly attributing the entire responsibility for the need 'to abandon immediately all major offensive operations and go over to the defensive' to the winter weather and consequent difficulty in bringing up supplies, rather than to the Red Army's resistance. The statement of the defensive operations' purpose – 'to hold areas of great operational or economic importance to the enemy, enable the forces to rest and recuperate as much as possible . . . and thus to establish conditions suitable to the resumption of large-scale offensive operations in 1942' – implicitly assumed that the Soviet forces were completely exhausted, and could do little or nothing to affect the situation. However, as the Soviet attacks not merely continued but escalated, creating an adverse turn in German fortunes not limited to Army Group Centre, the tensions between Hitler and his generals became exacerbated. Field-Marshal von Rundstedt had already resigned from command of Army Group South at the end of November, after Hitler refused him permission to withdraw from Rostov to a more defensible line along the River Mius, and during December there was a spate of resignations and dismissals, mostly over conflicts between Hitler's order of 16 December forbidding any withdrawals and the professionals' assessments that they were necessary to shorten lines or were forced by enemy action. Leeb was dismissed from command of Army Group North, Bock from Army Group Centre, and Brauchitsch from his position as Commander-in-Chief of the Army, a post that Hitler assumed himself. In January Hoepner (4th Panzer Army) was also dismissed, Strauss (9th Army) retired on health grounds, Rundstedt's replacement, von Reichenau, died of a heart attack (Hitler replaced him by re-employing Bock), and von Kluge, the new commander-in-chief of Army Group Centre, dismissed Guderian for disobeying the 'stand fast' order and making an unauthorised retreat.

On the Soviet side Zhukov intended to follow up the successful December counter-offensive with further attacks aimed at restoring the front line to where it had been before the launching of 'Typhoon'. However, Stalin had more far-reaching aims. At a meeting of Stavka on 5 January 1942 he had Shaposhnikov outline a plan for a general offensive along the entire front from Leningrad to the Black Sea, and then said 'the Germans are currently dispirited because they were beaten in front of Moscow and had prepared badly for winter. Now is the best moment for going over to a general offensive.' Zhukov argued strongly for an offensive confined to the central sector, on the grounds that there the Germans had not yet been able to restore the fighting strength of their units, whereas at Leningrad and in the south they could resist Soviet attacks from strong defensive positions. He was supported by Voznesensky, in charge of economic matters, on the grounds that material resources were insufficient to support a general offensive, but Stalin's mind was made up, and the offensive went ahead. Resources for it were indeed insufficient (Zhukov wrote that his artillery had only enough shells to fire one or two rounds a day),[132] and little more was gained before mid-April, when the mud of the spring thaw imposed a pause on both sides. It had failed to achieve Stalin's over-ambitious objectives, and was undoubtedly a mistaken strategic decision. At the beginning of 1942 no fewer than eleven reserve armies had been formed. If they had all been allocated to Western Direction, then Army Group Centre, with many of its units already worn down to only a third of full strength, could possibly have been wiped out before the spring thaw began. Instead, in his over-confident belief that the Germans were worn out everywhere, Stalin distributed the new armies between four Fronts, so that none had the overwhelming strength necessary for a real killer punch.

Nevertheless, the Soviet recovery was by any standard a remarkable achievement. Up to the end of November 1941 the Red Army had experienced losses in troops and equipment on a scale unprecedented for any other army in history. Even on the 1993 official figures for the losses of 1941, widely criticised as understated, 3.14 million troops – nine out of every ten who saw action in the first 193 days of war – were dead, captured or missing.[133] In addition, nine of every ten tanks, guns, mortars and combat aircraft, and two out of every three rifles, automatics or machine guns with which they began the war had been lost, and the arms industry had been able to replace only 27 per cent of the tanks, 58 per cent of the artillery weapons, 55 per cent of the aircraft, and 66 per cent of the small arms.[134] To have survived such losses was remarkable enough; to have won an important victory in such circumstances was even more noteworthy.

Unfortunately, Zhukov's success in December went to Stalin's (though not Zhukov's) head. He persuaded himself that the Germans were exhausted, ignored the reality that the Red Army had far fewer tanks, guns and aircraft than it had had at the outbreak of war, that even rifles were in short supply, and ammunition seriously deficient, and ordered a general offensive. Detailed figures for the whole of this offensive are not in the public domain, but some idea of them can be gained from the partial figures available. Zhukov's counter-offensive at Moscow (5 December–7 January) incurred irrevocable losses of 139,586. In the follow-up, the Rzhev-Vyazma operation (8 January–20 April), undertaken (reluctantly) by Zhukov and the same two Fronts as part of the general offensive, losses were 272,320, i.e. almost double those of the first offensive, for less territory regained and fewer Germans killed or captured.[135]

So the Germans were beaten but not routed, and the Soviet counter-offensive achieved only a few of its objectives. It was nevertheless of enormous significance as Germany's first strategic–scale defeat on land in the war, marking the failure of the Barbarossa plan; it also ensured that the Soviet regime and its armed forces would survive the winter, and thus made inevitable a prolonged war in which time would not be on Germany's side.

Chapter Three

'Stand Fast!'

With the clear vision conferred by hindsight, the first eleven days of December 1941 can be seen as the time when Germany lost the Second World War. On the 5th, the start of the Soviet counter-offensive at Moscow showed that the Barbarossa plan to eliminate the Red Army before winter had failed. On the 7th the Japanese attack on Pearl Harbor brought the USA into the war, and on the 11th Hitler declared war on the USA (a move that the Tripartite Pact required Germany to make only if the USA attacked Japan); in so doing, Hitler greatly eased President Roosevelt's task of overcoming both the wishes of the outraged US military to give priority to avenging the Japanese assault and isolationist opposition to involvement in any European war, and he directed the country's immense resources to defeating Germany first.

However, except to a few far-sighted statesmen, such as Churchill, it was less clear at the time that Hitler had doomed Germany to inevitable defeat, and neither Hitler nor most of his generals then believed he had. The generals could attribute the setbacks in Russia partly to the Führer's vacillation over priorities during the summer but mainly to the Russian winter, and if the Red Army had handled that season better than the Wehrmacht, the answer must be to overcome it before the next winter. Besides, Army Groups North and South had not suffered greatly from the winter fighting, and Army Group Centre, though severely battered and driven back, had weathered the storm of the Soviet counter-offensive, retaining most of its fighting qualities, and could be made back up to strength by the summer campaigning season.

The spring thaw imposed a lull by turning the terrain, with its few (mostly unsurfaced) roads, into mud. The German army intelligence section *Fremde Heere Ost* (Foreign Armies East) had already conceded by the end of October 1941[136] that its previous assessments had underestimated not only Red Army numbers but the ability of the Soviet economy to arm, clothe, feed and transport its soldiers, and of the political leaders and the military at all levels to improvise solutions to problems. However, Hitler's self-confidence had survived the winter setbacks and even been increased by his belief, endorsed by at least some of his generals, that his 'stand fast' order had prevented Army Group Centre's retreat from becoming a rout. He now returned to the position he had held briefly in the previous summer: that the main offensive should now be in the south, aimed at destroying the Red Army south and west of the Don, capturing major grain-growing areas and the Donbass with its industries and mines, to reach the Volga somewhere in the neighbourhood of Stalingrad, thus cutting off Soviet oil supplies, which mostly came from the Caucasus along that river or railways parallel to it, then advancing into the Caucasus to seize the oilfields for Germany's own use. Stalin's belief that the economic targets would be Hitler's prime objective, though mistaken in the previous year, was now proved right, though he still believed Moscow was the main single target and did not know that it was not on the German agenda for 1942.

The Chief of General Staff of OKH, Halder, expressed a preference for limited attacks by Army Group Centre, and for no major offensive anywhere until the Wehrmacht had fully rebuilt its strength. Hitler brushed his views aside, arguing that the winter counter-offensive had exhausted the Red Army, that the Soviet war effort would collapse without the oil of Transcaucasus, so attacking in that direction would compel the Soviet main forces to engage and be destroyed in defending the oilfields, that a success in that area would inspire Germany's allies and impress Turkey, and that the prospect of Anglo-American landings on the continent in 1943 made it all the more necessary to win the war in the East in 1942.

However, before mounting the offensive two obstacles in the south must be dealt with; the Crimea must be seized, to eliminate any possibility of its use to mount bombing raids against the Romanian oilfields at Ploesti, and to deprive the Soviet Black Sea Fleet of its main base at Sevastopol; and in Ukraine the front line must be straightened by removing the Soviet-held Barvenkovo salient.[137]

Hitler laid out the tasks in Directive no. 41, issued on 5 April 1942. In the Crimea Manstein moved swiftly. He attacked the three armies of the Crimean Front in the Kerch peninsula on 8 May, and by the 15th had effectively wiped them out; remnants of one brigade survived in underground quarry workings until early October, and a few escaped across the Kerch Strait, leaving all their heavy equipment behind, but the rest were killed or captured. For only 7,500 casualties Manstein took 170,000 prisoners, 1,100 guns, 250 tanks, 300 aircraft and 3,800 vehicles.[138]

Sevastopol would not fall until 4 July, but after elimination of the Crimean Front it could expect relief only by sea, and not much of that.

It is not clear why Hitler made elimination of the Barvenkovo salient a necessary preliminary to the general offensive. He had previously rejected suggestions for shortening the lines of Army Groups North and Centre by withdrawing from salients they held around Demyansk and Rzhev respectively, on the grounds that to do so would also shorten the Soviets' line and release more of their troops for offensives. But his decision fortuitously resulted in another German victory, because, unknown to him, the Soviet South-West, Bryansk and South Fronts were about to attack out of the salient, aiming to recapture Kharkov.

In the Soviet planning for the summer campaigning season the General Staff was considerably influenced by the fact that at its nearest point, in the Rzhev-Vyazma salient, the front line was still less than 160 kilometres (100 miles) from Moscow. No attempt to forecast the German summer offensive's likely objectives could entirely exclude the possibility of a renewed effort to take Moscow, and Stalin, who believed it probable, insisted on retaining large forces close by. In 1941 he had first under-estimated the German threat to the city, then overestimated the extent of the Wehrmacht's exhaustion.[139] Now, perhaps overcompensating for his 1941 errors, he overestimated the threat to the capital.

He was undoubtedly encouraged in this by Operation 'Kremlin', a deception campaign conducted by Army Group Centre. This included frequent reconnaissance flights over Moscow and the printing of detailed city maps, intended for Soviet patrols to capture, to give the impression that intensive planning for a new assault against the capital was under way. The loss in 1941 of over 3 million Soviet troops[140] by death, capture, deser-tion or defection, and of about 900,000 reservists and potential conscripts from territory overrun by the Germans before they could be mobilised, had created a shortage of even basically trained troops, so retention of large reserves close to Moscow reduced those further south below an adequate level for the sector where the offensive actually took place.

According to Zhukov, Stalin on several occasions in the spring of 1942 stated his belief that the Germans would mount two strategic offensives, the first against Moscow, the second against the south and Trans-caucasus, but would not launch the second unless and until the first had succeeded,[141] because to do so would over-extend their forces. Stalin was, of course, right about the second offensive, but wrong about the first. As for planning Soviet actions, he conceded that the limited success of the winter's general offensive, relative to its human and material costs, meant that the Red Army had as yet insufficient men and weapons to undertake such large-scale operations. It must for the time being confine itself to 'active strategic defence', by which he meant limited offensives, in several areas, including attempts to retake the Crimea and Kharkov.

Like Halder, both Shaposhnikov and Zhukov favoured staying on the defensive until at least early summer to build up reserves, then mounting a small number of strategic-scale counter-offensives; the main one of these, in Zhukov's view, should be against Army Group Centre in the Rzhev-Vyazma salient, which he had unsuccessfully attempted to eliminate before the spring thaw. There were two reasons for Zhukov's preference: the first was that Army Group Centre was both the largest and the most battered element of the invading forces, and the second was his acceptance of the generally held but erroneous belief that Moscow must still be the Wehrmacht's main target. This belief was asserted yet again in the Stavka assessment that 'in the coming campaign the most important directions for us will be Leningrad, Moscow, Voronezh and Donbass-Rostov, and the main one among them is that of Moscow'.[142] Three of these predictions were correct, but the one that was wrong was that defined as 'the main one' – yet another sign that because of inadequate Intelligence information the Soviet Supreme Command did not know what the Germans planned for the summer campaign of 1942.

This would have detrimental consequences in the coming summer. By early 1942 eleven new Reserve Armies had been created, and Zhukov favoured using them for an offensive to try to finish off Army Group Centre, where many units were known from prisoner interrogations to have been worn down to a third of their war establishment. But despite Stalin's apparent acceptance of the previous winter's lessons, he still wanted a general offensive, and instead of concentrating the eleven new armies on one or two of the Fronts, he retained two in reserve and dispersed the other nine between five Fronts, three to Western, two each to Volkhov and North-West, one each to Bryansk and South-West Fronts.[143] The consequence was not only insufficient strength to achieve a breakthrough anywhere, but acute difficulties in supplying the widely dispersed forces with ammunition, fuel, food and forage for their still mostly horse-drawn transport.

In early March Marshal Timoshenko, Commander-in-Chief of South-West Direction, submitted a plan to initiate a major offensive out of the Barvenkovo salient by Bryansk, South-West and South Fronts. After the General Staff had studied it, Shaposhnikov told the State Defence

Committee at the end of March that he opposed it as too difficult to organise, and because the reserves needed were unavailable. Stalin cut him off:

> It's not for us to sit with arms folded and wait till the Germans strike first. We must ourselves strike a number of pre-emptive blows on a broad front, and test the enemy's preparedness. Zhukov proposes developing an offensive on the western axis and defending on the remaining fronts. I think that's a half-measure.[144]

Timoshenko then defended his proposal, and Zhukov continued to argue against Stalin's insistence on mounting several simultaneous offensives, but it earned him only the dictator's displeasure. Even before he arrived back at his headquarters, Stalin had abolished his post of Commander-in-Chief of Western Direction, thereby removing Kalinin Front from his control and leaving him in command of only Western Front.[145]

The German plan for liquidating the Barvenkovo salient (Operation Fridericus I) comprised simultaneous attacks at its neck, from the south by von Kleist's 1st Panzer and Hoth's 17th Armies, and from the north by Paulus's 6th Army. It was timed to begin on 18 May, but Timoshenko had already moved two armies and parts of two others into the salient, and began his offensive on 12 May, before the German 6th Army was fully in position. The Viennese 44th Division, holding the northern neck, came under heavy pressure, but managed to hold on until Kleist's panzers and Hoth's infantry attacked the salient from the south on 17 May. They advanced 40 kilometres (25 miles) on the first day, on the next captured Barvenkovo and Izyum, and by the 19th had ripped an 80 kilometre (50 mile) hole in the Soviet front. The success of the 'one-armed Fridericus' threatened all Soviet forces in the salient, and their systematic destruction began on 22 May, after VIII Corps of 6th Army, advancing from the north, closed the ring by meeting up with Kleist's panzers.

The Soviet General Staff had been quick to realise the danger, and on both 17 and 18 May Vasilevsky asked Stalin to cancel the offensive, but initially he accepted Timoshenko's assurances that all was well and refused to do so. During the 18th Timoshenko too became apprehensive, and that evening had his 'Member of Military Council' (political overseer) Nikita Khrushchev telephone Stalin to seek permission to abandon the offensive. Stalin refused even to receive his call, instead ordering Malenkov to take it, instructed to 'tell him orders are implemented, not discussed, and hang up'.[146] The next day he finally agreed to abandonment, but it was too late.[147] The Germans destroyed the Soviet 6th and 57th Armies and most of the 9th and 38th Armies, and killed or captured about 240,000 Soviet troops; only some 44,000 managed to fight their way out, mostly with only their personal weapons. In the twelve days from 18 to 29 May Army Group South had smashed 29 Soviet divisions[148] at a cost to itself of only some 29,000 casualties – and this a month before the main offensive even began.

A post-Soviet 'balance sheet' of losses on both sides up to the end of April 1942, when the spring thaw imposed a pause, can be summarised as follows: in manpower the Red Army had lost close to 7 million men – 4,091,000 killed, captured or missing, and 2,784,500 wounded or sick. The total German casualties, at 1,005,600, were less than a sixth of the Soviet figures but amounted to 31 per cent of the invading force, and difficulties in providing replacements were already being encountered. Between 1 November 1941 and 1 April 1942 German 'arrivals' on the Eastern Front were 450,000, but 'departures' were 786,000. An OKH report of 30 March 1942 judged only eight of the 162 Eastern Front divisions as fully capable of action; Army Groups North and Centre were assessed as having only 35 per cent and Army Group South about half of the infantry with which they had begun the invasion. Compared to Soviet losses of over 20,000, German losses of 3,319 tanks and 173 self-propelled guns up to 20 March 1942 were also tiny, but Germany's lack of preparation for a long war was reflected in the fact that up to that date only 732 of the tanks and 17 of the guns had been replaced.

OKH concluded, and Hitler agreed, that only one of the three army groups could be made strong enough to mount the summer offensive, so Army Group South was strengthened at the expense of Army Groups North and Centre. Elements of ten of their panzer and seven of their motorised infantry divisions were transferred south, and in recognition that their winter losses could not be completely replaced, the infantry establishment of all bar six of their 75 divisions was reduced from nine battalions to six, with corresponding reductions in their artillery and support services. By these expedients Army Group South was more than trebled, from 20 to 68 divisions, all bar three of them at or near full strength, though with shortages of officers and NCOs, and with 1,495 tanks.[149]

Hitler's Directive no. 41[150] of 5 April also implicitly acknowledged the reduced strength of Army Groups Centre and North, specifying that 'the armies of the Central sector will stand fast', i.e. make no attempt to take Moscow, while 'those in the north will capture Leningrad' and 'those on the southern flank will break through into the Caucasus. In view of conditions prevailing at the end of winter, availability of troops and resources, and transport problems, these aims can be achieved only one at a time'. The main operation, by Army Group South, involved 'decisively attacking and destroying Russian forces stationed in the Voronezh area to south, west or north of the Don' by 'a series of consecutive, but coordinated and complementary, attacks'. The first of these was intended to capture Voronezh, after which the infantry divisions must establish 'a strong defensive front' while mobile forces continued advancing south-eastwards with their left flank on the Don, in support of the second attack, an eastward thrust from the Kharkov area. The third attack was to combine the continuation of the eastward advance along and across the Don with a northward drive from the Taganrog area, to link up 'in the Stalingrad area' and 'finally establish contact with the armoured forces advancing on Stalingrad'.

It is not clear how forces advancing along the Don were to link up near Stalingrad (now Volgograd), which is on the Volga, about 45 miles east of the Don, or 'finally establish contact with armoured forces advancing on Stalingrad', not previously mentioned but by implication *not* those conducting the third attack. Nor did the Directive specify whether or not the 'mobile forces advancing on Stalingrad' were meant to capture it, and although the 'General Plan' section of the Directive specified that the purpose of 'destroying the enemy before the Don' was 'to secure the Caucasian oilfields and the passes through the Caucasus mountains', this was not further mentioned. That clearly meant that the offensive, as originally planned, envisaged the drives to Stalingrad and the oilfields as consecutive, precisely as Hitler had said in the preamble to the Directive, but he would change his mind soon after the offensive began.

Like Directive no. 41, the operational plan drawn up by Field-Marshal von Bock's staff saw the seizure of Voronezh as necessary only to secure flank and rear protection for the main drive along the Don, and to disrupt Soviet north–south rail communications behind the front line. Stalin in fact had advance information to this effect before the offensive began, from documents outlining its first phase, *Fall Blau* ('Case Blue'), found in an aircraft shot down over Soviet positions on 19 June. Timoshenko sent them at once to Moscow, but Stalin was so convinced that the capture of Voronezh would be followed by a northward drive against Moscow that he dismissed them as a disinformative plant, and when on the next day Timoshenko, who believed them genuine, asked for reinforcements to meet the expected attack, he replied, 'if they sold divisions in the market

I'd buy you five or six, but unfortunately they don't'.[151] Then he ordered five armies, including three from Stavka Reserve, to be sent to defend Voronezh, and a day later, on 21 June he abolished Timoshenko's post of Commander-in-Chief South-West Direction.

Bock in his turn did not realise that the increase in the forces facing him at Voronezh was due to the mistaken belief that he meant to follow its capture with a northward push towards Moscow. He interpreted it instead as meant to threaten the flank and rear of Army Group South's drive along the Don, and under that misconception he retained so many of his mobile forces (24th Panzer Corps of the 4th Panzer Army) at Voronezh that Timoshenko's troops were able to trudge away eastwards, pursued only by German infantry, also mostly on foot.

In mid-July Hitler transferred his headquarters from Rastenburg in East Prussia to Vinnitsa in Ukraine, and began increasingly to interfere in the direction of the campaign. He dismissed Bock again, this time permanently (and would later blame the catastrophic outcome of the campaign entirely on his actions at Voronezh), and at the same time divided Army Group South into two, Army Groups A, to drive for the Caucasus oilfields, and B, to make for the Volga. Field-Marshal List became Commander-in-Chief of Army Group A on 9 July, and Field-Marshal von Weichs replaced Bock at Army Group B. This division was previously intended, but as conducted it marked a major change in Hitler's thinking, because the two objectives, planned as consecutive, were now to be pursued simultaneously.

The reasoning behind this decision is unclear. It could not be based on any victory comparable to those of 1941, nor even to Manstein's more recent ones in the Crimea and at Barvenkovo; in the summer offensive's first two weeks only 30,000 prisoners had been taken and there had been no major hauls of abandoned equipment. It seems that in July his entire headquarters experienced a period of premature euphoria, generated both by the haste of the Soviet retreat, with its abandonment of the major Donbass industrial and mining area, and by the combined effect of recent successes elsewhere. In May there had been Manstein's Crimea and Barvenkovo victories, in Africa Rommel had beaten the British at El Agheila and invaded Egypt, while the Japanese had compelled the last American forces in the Philippines, at Corregidor, to surrender, and had driven the British out of Burma. On 21 June Tobruk had surrendered, and on 4 July Manstein's forces had captured the Soviet Black Sea Fleet's main base at Sevastopol. There may also have been an element of wishful-thinking belief in Japanese propaganda claims that the lost battles of the Coral Sea in May and Midway in June had been victories, but even without them there was plenty to be euphoric about, and the mood seems to have seized even the congenitally sceptical Halder. When Hitler said to him on 20 July 'the Russian is finished', he could reply only 'I must admit it looks like it', even though the circumstances suggested not a rout but a fairly orderly Soviet withdrawal.

However, the retreat along the Don, though not comparable to the often chaotic headlong flights of 1941, was no exception to the generalisation that long retreats are bad for morale. General Vassiliy Chuikov, soon to become famous in command of the 62nd Army's determined defence of Stalingrad, was not the only Soviet officer to write that July of standing with a drawn pistol gathering stragglers into improvised forces at the Don bend. The public did not know that if Stalin had accepted Vasilevsky's advice to cancel the Barvenkovo offensive, or had sent Timoshenko the reinforcements he requested, matters might have turned out very differently. All the people knew was that vast areas of the south, with industries built up recently and through great sacrifices, were being abandoned, and unflattering comparisons were being drawn with both the staunchness of the defenders of Leningrad and Moscow and the competence of the generals who commanded them. In the months ahead the defenders of Stalingrad would more than match those, but nobody, including themselves, yet knew that.

However, by mid-July Stalin, Stavka and the General Staff had finally accepted that this time Moscow was not the target, and began sending units from the strategic reserve to the south. Stalin's displeasure with Timoshenko had not abated, although having made him a scapegoat for the disaster at Barvenkovo and contemplated trying him for treason, he apparently accepted Zhukov's defence of him.[152] The demotion of Timoshenko on 21 June had left him in command of a single Front, the South-West, renamed the Stalingrad Front on 12 July,[153] but Stalin removed him on 23 July, replacing him with Lieutenant-General V.N. Gordov, promoted from command of the 21st Army. Stalin's anger with Timoshenko gradually evaporated, and in October he gave him command of the relatively less active North-West Front. He retained it until March 1943, then until the end of 1944 served as a Stavka Representative, overseeing several important operations but, like Voroshilov and Budenny, no longer commanding forces in the field. That role was now entirely in the hands of younger generals.

*   *   *

The extent of the German advances in the offensive's first month prompted Stalin to issue Order no. 227 on 28 July. It became notorious as the 'Not a Step Back' order, but was perhaps equally notable for the starkness with which it argued why there must be no more retreats:

> The population of our country, which relates to the Red Army with love and respect, is beginning to become disillusioned with it, is losing faith in the Red Army, and many of them curse the Red Army for giving up our people to the yoke of German oppressors while itself escaping to the east. . . . Every commander, Red Army man and political worker must understand that our resources are not unlimited. The territory of the Soviet state is not a desert, but people . . . our fathers, mothers, wives, brothers, children. The territory the enemy has seized and is trying to seize is grain and other foodstuffs for the army and the rear, metal and fuel for industry, mills and factories supplying the army with weapons and ammunition, railways. After the loss of Ukraine, Belorussia and the Baltics, the Donbass and other provinces we have much less territory, hence many fewer people, much less grain, metal, mills and factories. We have lost over seventy million of population, over 800 million *puds* [about 13 million tonnes] of grain a year, and over ten million tonnes of metal a year. We now have no superiority over the Germans in human reserves or in grain stocks. To retreat further means to destroy ourselves, and, along with that, to destroy our Motherland.[154]

The Order was read out to all troops, but not published until 1988. In much of the post-Soviet debate it is treated as yet another instance of Stalin's cruelty, but most survivors of the war who expressed an opinion about it said they thought it was justified by the situation; in some respects it resembled Joffre's order to his troops before the equally desperate and decisive Battle of the Marne in 1914. In addition to exhortations to shoot deserters or panic-mongers on the spot (which Order no. 270 of August 1941 already authorised commanders to do), Order no. 227 prescribed the creation of penal companies and battalions for lesser offenders. These were given the most dangerous assignments, and anyone wounded, or surviving for three months in action, was to be restored to rank and position; anecdotal evidence suggests that few of them were that fortunate.

The Stalingrad Front's line now stretched for 700 kilometres (almost 440 miles), so to make it more manageable it was divided on 5 August,

Gordov retaining its northern half, the other becoming a new South-East Front under Colonel-General A.I. Yeremenko. Each had four armies (a Soviet army was roughly equivalent to a German Korps) and one air army, but their divisions were much below strength – on 22 July, for example, against a revised war establishment of just under 11,000, 19 of the Stalingrad Front's 38 divisions had fewer than 3,000 men, and none of the others had more than 8,000.[155] On 12 August Stalin sent Chief of General Staff Vasilevsky to coordinate the work of the two Fronts, and placed both under Yeremenko's operational control. But on 23 August three divisions of the 14th Panzer Corps reached the Volga in Stalingrad's northern outskirts, splitting the defences and cutting the 62nd Army off from the rest of Stalingrad Front, while bombers of Luftflotte IV made over 2,000 sorties, creating enormous destruction and panic in the city.

The next phase of the German plan called for the 14th Panzer Corps to thrust south to the city centre, while the 51st Corps was to drive due east from its bridgehead at Kalach to cut the 62nd and 64th Armies off from each other, and the IV Panzer Army was to come in from the south to complete the annihilation of the defenders. So seriously did Yeremenko take the threat, including the risk of the Germans getting across the Volga, that when engineer officers came to him on 23 August, to report completion of a pontoon bridge for bringing in supplies, he congratulated them and ordered them to destroy the bridge immediately.[156] However, when the 14th Panzer Corps attacked south next day, Yeremenko's hastily organised defenders, including the remnants of shattered units and companies of semi-trained factory workers, proved effective enough to stop them in the morning and drive them back 2 kilometres in the afternoon. On the 25th tanks and infantry of the 6th Army attempted to break into the city centre from the west, but were halted at the outskirts. Yeremenko then sought to cut off and destroy the 14th Panzer Corps units in the city's north near the tractor factory, but several counter-attacks that he mounted on the 25th and 26th were beaten off. Only after the war did he find that they had worried the 14th Panzer Corps commander, General von Wietersheim, so much that he ordered a retreat, but was overruled by Army Group B's commander, von Weichs.

On 27 August Stalin appointed Zhukov Deputy Supreme Commander, ordered him to go to Stalingrad as soon as possible, and told him three additional armies were being sent there. Zhukov first spent a day in the General Staff familiarising himself with the situation, then flew to Stalingrad on the 29th.[157] Apart from two brief visits to Moscow, on 12–14 and 26–28 September, he stayed there till 3 October.[158]

The first Soviet attempt to relieve the situation at Stalingrad was by a southward push from north of the city by three armies newly arrived from reserve. Stalin ordered the first of these, 1st Guards, to attack southwards from Loznoye on 2 September, to drive the Germans away from the Volga, link up with the 62nd Army, and provide cover for the deployment of the other two armies (24th and 66th), which were also to be put into action immediately, 'otherwise we will lose Stalingrad'.[159] However, Zhukov found on arrival that the forces could not be concentrated and supplied in time to attack before 6 September. He reported accordingly to Stalin, and so did Vasilevsky, who returned to Moscow on 1 September. However, on 2 September, influenced by pessimistic reports from Yeremenko about the exhausted condition of his units in the city, Stalin ordered all three armies to attack not later than the 5th. They complied, but five days of inadequately prepared and supplied attacks brought large losses for little gain; however, they tied up substantial German forces that otherwise might have been sent against Yeremenko, and may thus have saved the city's defenders from being overrun. The attritional damage they inflicted can be illustrated by the figures of tank strengths of two of the divisions involved in repelling the Soviet September offensive. In early July the 60th Motorised Infantry Division had 57 tanks and the 16th Panzer Division 100. On 18 November they had 21 and 31 respectively.[160]

On 12 September Zhukov flew back to Moscow and reported to Stalin, who asked him what additional forces the Stalingrad Front needed in order to liquidate the German 'corridor' and join up with the South-East Front. Zhukov replied, 'as a minimum one more full-strength army, a tank corps, three tank brigades, and not less than 400 howitzers . . . and for the period of the operation not less than one air army'. Vasilevsky endorsed Zhukov's view, and Stalin reached for the map that showed the locations of Stavka Reserves. While he was studying it, Zhukov and Vasilevsky moved away, and began talking in low voices of the need to find 'some other solution'. The acuteness of Stalin's hearing surprised them; he asked 'What other solution?' and continued, 'Go to the General Staff and do some good thinking about what must be undertaken in the Stalingrad area. What forces, and from where, can be redeployed to reinforce the Stalingrad grouping, and at the same time think about the Caucasus front too. We'll meet here again at nine o'clock tomorrow evening.'[161]

That day, 12 September, was notable for two other events. Colonel-General Friedrich Paulus, commanding 6th Army, met Hitler at Vinnitsa to discuss plans for taking Stalingrad. This was not militarily necessary – the passage of oil tankers could be blocked by artillery from positions on the Volga's west bank north and south of the city, and by aircraft from several nearby airfields – but the capture of 'Stalintown' had become an obsession with Hitler because of the political symbolism of its name. On the same day General Vassiliy Chuikov was appointed to command 62nd Army, defending the ruins of the city. It was in dire straits; Chuikov wrote in his memoirs that its three armoured brigades had only one serviceable tank between them, its infantry divisions were worn down to about a battalion each, and the only units even near full strength were two infantry brigades and a division of NKVD (Interior Ministry) troops, with no tanks, field or anti-tank guns, and with a commander initially not disposed to take orders from an army officer. Chuikov even had difficulty finding his headquarters, and when he eventually located it, he found his Chief of Staff, Major-General Krylov, berating the army's tank commander for the unauthorised movement of his headquarters to the Volga bank, behind that of the army on the Mamayev Kurgan, the dominant hill in the city centre. Chuikov gave him until 4 a.m. to move his headquarters forwards, and warned him that any repetition would be treated as treason and desertion (for which he would be shot). The tank commander complied, but a few days later he and his counterparts commanding the engineers and artillery pleaded illness and removed themselves to the east bank. Chuikov did not say what action he took against them.

Chuikov was immediately faced with another crisis. He spent 13 September planning a counter-offensive, to start on the next day, and designed to drive the Germans back out of artillery range of the central landing stage on the Volga, the main point for reinforcements and supplies arriving and wounded departing. However, this was forestalled by a German offensive that began at 6.30 a.m. on the 14th; directed at central Stalingrad from north and south, it involved two panzer and four infantry divisions, one of them motorised, and included an artillery bombardment of the Mamayev Kurgan so intensive as to render Chuikov's command post there untenable. He went to the east bank and crossed back to a purpose-built command centre known as the Tsaritsa bunker, which was not only much safer than the dugouts on the Mamayev Kurgan, but also had far superior communications. Unfortunately he could occupy it for only three days because the Germans advanced into the Tsaritsa river valley to within machine-gun range of the bunker, and he had to move to improvised dugouts on the Volga bank, below some oil tanks that were assumed to be empty, but were later found to be full when German aircraft succeeded in setting them on fire. The defence of Stalingrad need not be detailed here but a few points are worth noting.

Morale in the 62nd Army had been badly affected by the prolonged retreats, and was temporarily worsened even further by Chuikov's decision to evacuate his heavy artillery to the east bank. This was militarily entirely justifiable, since they would still be well within range for firing on targets in the city with spotters there to direct their fire, and it would be far easier for them to work the guns and receive ammunition. However, the sight of them departing convinced some of the troops that the city was about to be abandoned. Discipline began to break down as troops started to refuse to obey orders and officers abandoned their men, and plans to bring the 13th Guards Division across during the hours of darkness had to be given up as by then there might be nowhere to land them. Instead elements of the division began to cross in the late afternoon of 13 September under improvised smokescreens that did little to conceal them from the prowling aircraft of Luftflotte IV. Over half the troops did not survive the crossing, but those who did went straight into action with extreme determination, recaptured the Mill, one of the main buildings overlooking the crossing, and drove the Germans back, enabling the rest of the division to cross during the night. On the 16th one of its regiments recaptured the Mamayev Kurgan, and that boosted the defenders' morale.

There had never been a battle of such scale and duration in a large city, so there were few precedents for either side to draw on. Chuikov, with some advice from Rodimtsev, who had experienced street fighting in the Spanish Civil War, reorganised the 62nd Army into combat groups combining infantrymen, machine gunners and sappers, with each group capable of defending or seizing a building. Chuikov ascribed this idea's origin to noticing during the fighting at the Don bend that German success depended heavily on excellent coordination between three elements – aircraft, tanks and infantry – not, as he asserted, of especially high quality individually. He observed that the tanks did not advance until the aircraft had pounded the Soviet positions, and the infantry did not go forwards until the tanks had reached their objectives. He also felt the German infantry disliked fighting at close quarters, noting that they often opened fire with their automatic weapons when well out of range. Whether or not this last observation was justified, he concluded that the best way to break the chain would be to keep his troops so close to the

Germans that they could not use their aircraft, field artillery or tank guns for fear of hitting their own men. The infantry would then have to engage in the close combat he believed them to dislike, against Soviet soldiers who had not been demoralised beforehand by air or tank attacks or artillery bombardment.

What Chuikov had observed was, of course, the standard German procedure that had served them so well in all their campaigns, and knowledge of it should not only have emerged from Soviet study of those campaigns but have been prescribed for Soviet generalship, because the Red Army's inability to match the Germans' skill in coordinating different arms of service was among the main reasons for its early disasters. Although the Soviet air forces were regarded as part of the army, whereas the Luftwaffe was independent, Soviet skill in air support of ground operations did not begin to match German levels until mid-1943. Chuikov's statement that he derived his understanding of German methods only by personal observation suggests that even well into the second year of war dissemination to Soviet field commanders of knowledge about the enemy's *modus operandi* was still inadequate. That deficiency was partly remedied by Stalin's Order no. 325, which discussed the reasons for past failures and specified the roles for tanks and mechanised infantry. It was to be read by all officers down to company commanders but it was not issued till 16 October, and would be inapplicable in the special conditions obtaining at Stalingrad, where the opposing sides were often in adjacent buildings or even adjacent rooms. However, it showed that German methods were being studied, and it would become increasingly relevant as Soviet mechanised forces increased in numbers and size up to tank armies.

Chuikov propagated his doctrine under the slogan 'Every German must feel he is living under the muzzle of a Russian gun'. The corollary, that every Russian would then be living under the muzzle of a German gun, did not need to be stated; the troops were so aware of the fact that much would depend on sustaining morale, and here sticks and carrots, especially in relation to senior officers, had to be combined.

The German army on the whole observed the convention that a general should share the fate of his troops, but until then the Red Army had taken the pragmatic view that even beaten generals were better than none at all, and regularly made special efforts to rescue them even while abandoning their troops. Chuikov took steps to sustain morale by visiting front-line positions regularly, talking to the troops there, ensuring that his chief subordinates did the same, maintaining his command post in the city rather than on the east bank (except for a brief period on 14–15 October, when all his communications had been destroyed and the Germans were only 300 metres away)[162] and having those who put their own safety ahead of their duties removed – in some cases undoubtedly shot. Using a combination of barbed wire, trenches linking the larger and stronger buildings, and the gunfire of the heavy artillery deployed on the east bank, directed by spotters located on upper storeys or roofs, the 62nd Army built an integrated defence system that was – just – strong enough to keep the Germans busy in the city from mid-September to mid-November. The 'carrots' included rewards, medals and publicity for acts of daring and self-sacrifice, the 'sticks' the threat of being shot or dispatched to a penal unit. The 62nd Army could reasonably be described as exhibiting 'mass heroism', but between them the four armies (from south to north the 51st, 57th, 64th and 62nd) of the Stalingrad Front involved in the defensive battle shot 13,500 of their own men for cowardice or desertion,[163] and dispatched unknown numbers of lesser offenders to penal units or prison.

In Moscow Zhukov and Vasilevsky spent 13 September reviewing the possible options, starting from the premise that interrogation of prisoners indicated the Germans were overstretched, their strongest armies, 6th and 4th Panzer, so worn down by the fighting in Stalingrad that they would be unable to take it, but pinned down there because Hitler's orders forbade them to withdraw. The reinforcements they needed to achieve their set tasks in the North Caucasus and Don–Volga areas were not available, and manpower shortages were such that they had had to entrust defence of the long west–east flank along the Don to satellite forces from Hungary, Italy and Romania. These were less well equipped and less experienced than the Germans, and were reckoned incapable of fighting even a strong defensive battle; most importantly, many of the soldiers and at least some of the officers had no wish to die in distant foreign fields for an ally who often displayed disrespect or even contempt for them.

The Soviet side, in contrast, was building up a strategic reserve of full-strength armies, including tank formations, well equipped with the newest weaponry, and the process would be completed during September–October. Zhukov and Vasilevsky therefore proposed continuing to wear down the Germans by active defence of the city, while preparing a counter-offensive that would change the strategic situation radically to Soviet advantage. Stalin was still busy at 9 p.m., but received them at 10, and they outlined to him a plan for a major three-stage counter-offensive: first to encircle the Germans in the Stalingrad area by a southward push against the Romanian 3rd Army west of the Don and a northward drive to meet it, secondly to create a stable 'external front' against relief attempts, and thirdly to destroy the encircled forces. Stalin responded that currently there were insufficient forces for such a large operation, but Zhukov assured him they would be available by the end of October. Then Stalin asked whether it would not be better just to try a pincer movement east of the Don, to which Zhukov replied that this could too easily be parried by panzer divisions from the Stalingrad area; by attacking west of the river the offensive would have a major water obstacle protecting its left flank. Stalin reacted cautiously, saying 'There's need to think some more about the plan and count up the resources. But for now the most important task is to hold Stalingrad . . .'. At that point his secretary, Poskrebyshev, entered to report that Yeremenko was on the telephone. Stalin took the call, and on his return told Vasilevsky to order Rodimtsev's 13th Guards Division from the Stavka Reserve to cross into Stalingrad at once, and to see what else could be sent over, as Yeremenko expected a new German onslaught the next day. Turning to Zhukov, he told him to phone orders to Golovanov (commanding the Long Range Bomber Force) to throw in his bombers, and to Gordov to attack north of the city in the morning to pin the enemy down.

Having dealt with the immediate situation, Stalin turned his attention back to the proposed counter-offensive, ordering Zhukov to fly to Stalingrad at once to study the situation in the areas (Kletskaya and Serafimovich) from which its northern pincer would start, and Vasilevsky to go in a few days' time to make a similar study of the South-East Front's left wing, where the southern pincer would originate. 'We'll continue the conversation about the plan later. For the time being, no one except us three must know what we discussed here.'[164] This last point was observed so punctiliously that the presence of Zhukov and Vasilevsky in Stalin's office on 12 and 13 September was not even recorded in Poskrebyshev's appointments book.

Within an hour Zhukov was on his way to Stalingrad. He stayed there for two weeks, until Stalin summoned him and Vasilevsky back to Moscow on 26 September for more detailed discussions of the planned offensive. On 28 September the Stalingrad Front was renamed the Don Front, and Gordov was replaced by Rokossovsky; the South-Eastern Front was renamed the Stalingrad Front, with Yeremenko retaining command; and a new army group, the South-Western Front, under Lieutenant-General N.F. Vatutin, was established west of the Don Front. After further discussion Zhukov and Vasilevsky signed the map-plan for the proposed offensive, and Stalin endorsed it. Then he ordered Vasilevsky to ask the three Front commanders what they thought they should do, but without yet telling them what was planned, and told Zhukov to go back to instruct the Don Front's command on the need to give the Stalingrad Front all possible help. On 29 September Zhukov ordered the Don Front to maintain constant activity so as to prevent the enemy transferring units away to storm Stalingrad, to which Rokossovsky objected that he had too few troops and resources to achieve 'anything serious'. Zhukov knew that was true, but could not yet tell Rokossovsky why German attention must be kept fixed on the city, or why nothing 'serious' enough to prompt them to withdraw must be attempted, so he merely answered that without active aid the Stalingrad Front would be unable to hold the ruins. He then returned to Moscow to do more work on the plan.

By the end of September almost all of the 62nd Army's original complement had been killed, captured or wounded, and six infantry divisions and a tank brigade had been ferried across the Volga to replace them. On the German side Hitler's demands that Army Group B take Stalingrad had prompted von Weichs during September to remove some of his stronger units from the Don Front's sector into the city, replacing them by units 'burnt out' by fighting there and by Romanian 3rd Army elements, which were less well equipped and certainly less motivated than even their 'burnt-out' German counterparts. To Soviet advantage it would be these that bore the first brunt of the imminent counter-offensive.

Although the Soviets did not know it, events within the German High Command were also working in their favour. On 9 September Hitler, dissatisfied with Army Group A's slow progress into the Caucasus, dismissed Field-Marshal List and took command of it himself. On the 24th he sacked Halder as Chief of General Staff of OKH and replaced him with Zeitzler, who had none of the status and respect that the field commanders had accorded his predecessor. He also quarrelled with Keitel and Jodl, the heads of OKW, and rumours spread that both were to be dismissed. In the event neither was, but rumours that Paulus would replace Jodl after taking Stalingrad may have been among the factors that prompted Paulus, whose previous career had been almost entirely as a staff officer, to make renewed efforts during October; whether or not this was so, he was in any case bound by an Army Group B order of 6 October, which emphasised that Hitler had defined the complete capture of Stalingrad as its most important task, and that therefore all available forces should be used to fulfil it. During October repeated German attacks were mounted, giving Paulus control over nine-tenths of the city area, and reducing the 62nd Army's tenure to two strips along the Volga bank, neither more than a few hundred metres wide and both under constant artillery fire. Casualties on both sides were heavy, but Paulus's were harder to replace. The final German attack, on 11 November, reached the river at a point south of the Barricades factory, splitting the 62nd Army into three sectors but unable to dislodge any of them.

Zhukov, Vasilevsky and Colonel-Generals N.N. Voronov, Head of Red Army Artillery, and A.A. Novikov, Head of Air Forces, arrived at the South-West Front on 30 October and spent a week there briefing and preparing the commanders down to division level for the counter-offensive. On 6 November they moved on to the Don Front, and on the 9th to the Stalingrad Front, returning to Moscow on the evening of the 12th and reporting to Stalin the next morning. They told him that delays in the arrival of troops, food, ammunition, fuel and anti-freeze at the Stalingrad Front, and in arranging air support for the Stalingrad and South-West Fronts, would necessitate postponing the offensive by a few days. Stalin raised no objections and ordered them both to fly back to Stalingrad to check once more that the forces and commanders were adequately prepared. On the 14th Zhukov was with Vatutin and Vasilevsky with Yeremenko, and on the 15th they received a message from Stalin authorising Zhukov to set the start date. After consulting Vasilevsky, he set it as 19 November for the South-West and Don Fronts and the 20th for the Stalingrad Front, then on the 17th he was summoned back to Stavka to finalise preparations for the offensive (Operation 'Mars') against Army Group Centre by the Kalinin and Western Fronts, which he was to direct.[165]

Before considering the counter-offensive and its consequences, it is worth considering how the concealment that made it an almost complete surprise was achieved. The preparations required enormous movements of troops, equipment, ammunition, winter clothing, fuel, food and forage for the draught-horses; for example, in the first 20 days of November 111,000 troops, 14,000 motor vehicles, 7,000 tonnes of ammunition, 427 tanks and 556 guns were ferried across the Volga to meet just the requirements of the Stalingrad Front.[166] All movement was at night, units observed radio silence and their operators stayed as long as possible at their old locations, transmitting routine messages to convince German radio-intercept and direction-finding stations that everything was normal. Trains took most of the troops to the nearest railhead as late as possible, coping with the inevitable congestion by ignoring the normal signalling system, and having flagmen dispatch the trains at 12-minute intervals.[167]

However, complete concealment of such large-scale deployments was impossible. For example, Romanian units facing the 21st Army's bridgehead west of the Don detected the 5th Tank Army's movement into the bridgehead, and reported to 6th Army headquarters that they could hear tank motors running there at night. Since the bridgehead was to be the launch-point for 5th Tank Army's southward drive to Kalach, the 21st Army had been ordered to enlarge it and did so by mounting a surprise attack on 21 October. Neither Paulus, nor his staff nor anyone at OKH seems to have wondered why the Soviets wanted to enlarge the bridgehead, nor connected their actions with the Romanian reports. The 3rd Army was merely ordered to restore the situation, and duly counterattacked on the 23rd but without success.

Naturally the Soviet General Staff could not simply rely on the Germans failing to detect signs of imminent action at Stalingrad; steps must also be taken to mislead them by drawing their attention elsewhere. The most important, and most credible, of these diversions would be the mounting of an apparent third attempt to eliminate Army Group Centre's potential threat to Moscow by expelling it from the Rzhev–Vyazma salient. The actions taken in this direction have spawned two controversies in post-Soviet times; first, whether the offensive against that salient in November–December 1942 (Operation 'Mars') was a diversion, to prevent Army Group Centre sending troops south to Stalingrad (Operation 'Uranus'), as Zhukov's and other Soviet-period accounts maintained, or whether, as David Glantz has claimed, it was meant to be the main assault of the winter campaign, or alternatively, as Aleksey Isayev contended, it was linked with and implicitly equal to 'Uranus', then, as both argue, was subsequently ignored or played down only because it was a disastrous failure.[168]

Both claims rest largely on data showing the numbers of troops, tanks, guns and aircraft allocated to the Fronts (Kalinin and Western) engaged in 'Mars' as much exceeding those allocated to 'Uranus', on the paucity of mentions of 'Mars' in Soviet-era accounts, most of which ignore it completely, on the unfavourable descriptions of it in participants' recollections, and, not least, on Zhukov's extraordinary economy with the truth in the brief account in his memoirs of the date and circumstances of its origin.

Taking that last item first, Zhukov presented 'Mars' as almost a last-minute afterthought. He wrote that on the evening of 13 November 1942 he and Vasilevsky met Stalin, who confirmed their plan for the counter-offensive to be launched at Stalingrad in the next few days, and that they both then drew his attention to the likelihood that

> as soon as a serious situation developed at Stalingrad and in the North Caucasus, the German high command will be forced to re-deploy some of its forces from other areas, especially from the Vyazma area, to help the southern group. To prevent that happening, an offensive operation must be urgently prepared and conducted in the area north of Vyazma, in the first instance to smash the Germans in the area of the Rzhev salient. For this operation we proposed drawing on troops of Kalinin and Western Fronts.
>
> 'That would be good,' said Stalin. 'But which of you will under-take this affair?' Alexander Mikhailovich and I had agreed on our proposals about this beforehand, so I said, 'The Stalingrad operation is already prepared in all respects. Vasilevsky can take coordination of actions of the forces in the Stalingrad area on himself, and I can take preparation of the offensive by Kalinin and Western Fronts on myself.'[169]

Zhukov went on to cite an order to the Kalinin and Western Fronts, issued on 8 December over his and Stalin's signatures, leaving the reader to assume, though without actually saying so, that it was the first order relating to 'Mars', whereas archival evidence shows conclusively that 'Mars' was originally intended to start in mid-October, i.e. to precede the counter-offensive in the south, so planning for it must have begun in September, at the same time as that for 'Uranus' and 'Saturn'. The primary evidence is a Western Front Directive dated 1 October, containing very detailed instructions to the commanders of the 20th and 31st Armies 'for destruction of the enemy Sychevka-Rzhev grouping', ordering them to 'submit plans for Operation "Mars" by 5 October', and be ready to attack by the 12th.[170] This completely demolishes Zhukov's presentation of it as first proposed only on 13 November, and there is further confirmation in Stavka Directive no. 170651, issued at 3.50 a.m. on 13 October, which ordered the transfer of five divisions from three other Fronts to the 43rd Army of the Kalinin Front, stating specifically that this was 'for the forthcoming Operation Mars'.[171]

Zhukov's economy with the truth and the ignoring of 'Mars' in most descriptions of the Stalingrad campaign certainly indicate that something went wrong. It is clear that more was expected of 'Mars' than it delivered, and Drs Glantz and Isayev have performed a service to scholarship in drawing attention to this. However, the difference in context between 'Mars' and 'Uranus/Saturn', and five very important pieces of evidence of which neither of those authors was apparently aware, tend to contradict Glantz's argument that 'Mars' was more important than 'Uranus', and Isayev's contention that it was equally important, and point to its being, at least in Stalin's mind, a 'diversion', and acknowledged by Zhukov as such, as support for 'Uranus', though he may covertly have hoped to make it an equal partner to that offensive.

Taking first the difference in context, absolutely vital to success at Stalingrad was the basic assumption that the non-German forces guarding the German flanks – for 'Uranus' the Romanian 3rd and 4th Armies, for 'Little Saturn' the Italian 8th and Hungarian 2nd Armies – were all much weaker than the German elements of Army Group B. They were specifically targeted for that reason, and the assumption was proven correct from the very first day of 'Uranus'. No such assumption could be made in respect of 'Mars', as Army Groups Centre and North had no vulnerable non-German forces for it to exploit; the Rzhev-Vyazma salient was manned by 30 experienced German divisions, which had been in position for well over a year and had already withstood two previous major offensives, in January–April and July–August, both conducted by Zhukov. The smaller Demyansk salient, a little further north, had been held by Army Group North for even longer, and contained 12 divisions. Thanks to air supply it had survived being cut off for several weeks in February–April 1942, and since then had withstood repeated attempts by the North-West Front to eliminate it. In both salients the Germans had made good use of their time to prepare strong defensive positions, whereas in contrast the 20 German divisions of the 4th Panzer and 6th Armies that would be encircled in the Stalingrad area, and the Romanian 3rd and 4th Armies immediately protecting their rear, had been in position only since mid-August or, in the Romanian case, September, and had had no time or opportunity – nor was there a perceived need – to establish solid defensive lines before they faced an unexpected Soviet onslaught of a magnitude they had simply not thought possible. Hindsight is not needed for this judgement; Stalin, Zhukov, Vasilevsky and the General Staff planners of both 'Mars' and 'Uranus/Saturn' knew all these facts beforehand, and it strains credibility to assume that they would have given priority to the immeasurably harder and far less promising of the two tasks they faced.

It is also relevant that Stalin thought the original concept of 'Uranus/Saturn' itself very ambitious. 'Uranus' was to involve encircling most of Army Group B, and 'Saturn' to cut off Army Group A in the Caucasus. Granted the means of achieving these results would be initially at the expense of Germany's allies, it would then be necessary to take on two of the four German army groups; in the event that plan did prove too ambitious, and Army Group A was allowed to escape for the time being. If, in addition, 'Mars' was really meant to be the most important operation of the 1942/3 winter, then Stalin, his two chief military troubleshooters and the General Staff were aspiring to destroy three of the four army groups, including the strongest, Centre, in two overlapping and almost simultaneous operations. Stalin certainly displayed at times a tendency to underestimate the Germans and set over-ambitious tasks; he did so in early 1942 and would do so again in early 1943. However, both those episodes followed successful Soviet counter-offensives; in contrast, when planning for 'Uranus/Saturn/Mars' began in September, he had little cause for euphoria. All offensives attempted during the previous six months had failed, two of them (Barvenkovo and Crimea) disastrously, whereas the Germans had advanced to the Volga and Caucasus in less than two months, and were still being held only with difficulty. When on 12–13 September Zhukov and Vasilevsky put their proposal for the Stalingrad counter-offensive to him, his initial reaction was to suggest that it should be scaled down somewhat. That he could move within a few days not only to approving an operation he at first thought might be over-ambitious, but also to adding an even larger preceding and/or simultaneous offensive against Army Group Centre seems unlikely; the limited evidence about his state of mind in that period provides no support for such a conclusion.

Another extremely important difference in the context is that Army Groups North and Centre had (and did in fact soon exercise, in February–March 1943) the option of controlled withdrawal from the two salients, a recourse not available to the forces at Stalingrad, first because Hitler had categorically forbidden it, and secondly because the Soviet encirclement was quickly made too strong to be broken through. This is discussed below.

Of the five important pieces of additional evidence, the first and most significant is the memoirs of former NKVD General Pavel Sudoplatov, published in English in 1994 and in Russian in 1996.[172] Sudoplatov provided detailed evidence that 'Agent Max', cited by Dr Glantz as giving the Germans advance warning of 'Mars' in a message of 4 November

1942, was a Soviet-controlled double agent, and, having been his controller from July 1941 through most of the war, gave a comprehensive account of him and his activities. 'Max' was Alexander Demyanov, and he and his wife were both long-standing NKVD agents (in his case since 1929), with pre-revolutionary aristocratic and current artistic connections that made it easy for them to establish contacts during the 1930s with foreign journalists and diplomats in Moscow, including in the German embassy. Just before the war the Abwehr recruited Demyanov, as the NKVD intended it should, and in July 1941 Sudoplatov's superior, Beria, agreed to his being used in operations 'Monastyr' (Monastery) and 'Prestol' (Throne), both fake anti-Soviet underground organisations created by the NKVD to attract and uncover collaborationist or espionage networks. After receiving training, Demyanov was ordered to 'defect' in December 1941, and did so by skiing across to the German lines outside Moscow at night, posing as an emissary of 'Prestol'. The Germans initially distrusted him, but eventually accepted and trained him, then in February 1942 parachuted him back into Soviet territory, tasked to re-establish himself in Moscow, use his connections to penetrate Red Army staffs, and also organise sabotage on the railways. A 'safe house' was established at his apartment, through active participation by his wife and her father, a German-educated noted medical specialist. Couriers sent there by the Abwehr were mostly 'turned', but some were arrested and jailed for credibility's sake. The 'legend' constructed for Max was that he was a disgruntled ex-Tsarist officer, currently a signals officer on the General Staff, who had sources of information among other equally disgruntled ex-Tsarist officers serving under Marshal Shaposhnikov (himself a former Tsarist officer, as was Vasilevsky, who succeeded him in mid-1942). He also created a mythical group conducting sabotage on the railways, and to enhance his credibility Sudoplatov had some items about official concern at such sabotage planted in Soviet newspapers that the Germans could acquire in neutral Stockholm or Lisbon.

Sudoplatov wrote that 'disinformation transmitted by "Heine-Max" was composed in the Operations Directorate of our General Staff, with one of its leaders, General Shtemenko, taking part, then vetted in the General Staff Intelligence Directorate and handed over to the NKVD, to ensure it was received in convincing circumstances'. He specifically mentions the 4 November message, in order to emphasise that

> disinformation sometimes had strategic significance. Thus on 4 November 1942 'Heine-Max' reported that the Red Army would

strike a blow at the Germans not at Stalingrad but in the North
Caucasus and at Rzhev. The Germans expected the blow at Rzhev
and repulsed it. But the encirclement of Paulus's grouping at
Stalingrad was a complete surprise for them. Not suspecting this
'radio game' Zhukov paid a high price – in the offensive at Rzhev
thousands and thousands of our soldiers died under his command.
In his memoirs he admits that this offensive operation's outcome
was unsatisfactory. But he never realised that the Germans had been
forewarned of our offensive on the Rzhev axis, and that was why
they threw such a quantity of forces into it.[173]

How seriously Gehlen took Max's reports, and how thoroughly he was
misled, can be seen from his report of 6 November 1942, which was based
on Max's message of the 4th. It referred to a fictitious 'War Council'
meeting chaired by Stalin on 4 November[174] that decided to 'carry out all
planned offensive undertakings, if possible before 15 November, insofar
as the weather permits. Mainly from Grozny; in the Don area at
Voronezh; at Rzhev; south of Lake Ilmen, and Leningrad . . .'.

All these offensives duly took place, though mostly not until January
1943. But 'Uranus', to be launched on 19 November, was not mentioned,
and Gehlen's report of 6 November stated unequivocally that 'the point
of main effort of the coming operations looms with increasing distinct-
ness in the area of Army Group Centre', while 'the enemy's attack
preparations in the south are not so far advanced that one need reckon
with a major operation here in the near future simultaneously with the
expected offensive against Army Group Centre'.[175] In a further report on
12 November Gehlen slightly qualified that assertion by mentioning a
possible offensive in the south, but assessed it as only a flank attack
intended to induce a German withdrawal from the Stalingrad area. In his
post-war memoirs he inflated that qualification into an advance warning
of 'Uranus', claiming that it began 'precisely where we had predicted',
but he clearly had no idea of its intended scale, nor that its purpose was
not to force the Germans to withdraw, but to encircle and destroy them,
nor of the existence of its southern pincer; nor, even writing 25 years after
the war, had he realised that Max was Soviet-controlled. On the contrary,
he wrote that 'events over the next months showed that this report of 4
November must have been genuine'.[176] In fact the references in Max's
message to Rzhev and 'south of Lake Ilmen' were specifically intended to
focus German attention on the two salients (that centred on Demyansk
was indeed just south of Lake Ilmen), and thereby distract it from the

preparations in the south. Incidentally Shtemenko, whom Sudoplatov mentions as vetting Max's messages, was one of the most senior officers in the Operations Directorate; in fact he became head of it in May 1943. However, not even he could authorise a leak on this scale; the idea may not have originated with Stalin, but could not have been implemented without his endorsement.

The second important source is the memoirs, published in 1973, of Colonel-General K.N. Galitskiy, who in November 1942 was in command of the Kalinin Front's 3rd Shock Army, tasked with taking the rail and road centres of Velikiye Luki and Novosokolniki, on a sector of the front line between the two salients, in an operation to be conducted simultaneously with 'Mars'. On 19 November Zhukov arrived at his headquarters, and Galitskiy outlined his plan for taking both centres in an operation lasting 10 to 12 days. To everyone's surprise, Zhukov flatly rejected it, saying,

> an army's combat operations are organically linked to the operations of the Front's forces and those of our armed forces as a whole. One plan, even if profoundly thought out, is in no position to change the situation suddenly and radically. Therefore the main thing in an army's operations is its role and significance on the operational and strategic scales. All these blows, interacting among themselves, are securing the counter-offensive by Soviet forces at Stalingrad that has begun today; they are tying down the enemy's reserves. That is also 3rd Shock Army's basic role in the forthcoming fighting on the Velikiye Luki axis.

He went on: 'To draw enemy forces onto itself is 3rd Shock Army's main task. Whether or not you take Novosokolniki, we shall nevertheless consider the task fulfilled if you draw the enemy's forces on to yourself and he is unable to take them away from your sector for transfer to the south . . . That is 3rd Shock Army's main task.'[177]

The context of Zhukov's point was well enough known to Galitskiy not to need elaborating, but it is important to note. The 3rd Shock Army's sector lay between the two salients, which were manned by 42 seasoned German divisions. The capture of Velikiye Luki and Novosokolniki would deprive the Germans of an important lateral rail connection between Army Groups North and Centre, and would also lodge Soviet forces between the two salients, well placed for attacking either or both. Zhukov had only to look at a map of the front line to see that abandoning the salients would greatly shorten it, and thereby free up substantial German forces for deployment elsewhere; aware from prisoner interrogations, and from the entrusting of the long front along the Don to Romanian, Italian and Hungarian formations, that the Germans had serious manpower shortages, it would be reasonable for him to conclude that once Velikiye Luki fell, they might abandon one or both salients, and would send some or all of the 'freed' divisions to the south. If Galitskiy's original plan worked, it would be completed by 4–6 December, and that might lead the Germans to cut their losses early. They would then have a number of divisions available for dispatch to the south soon enough to create problems for Operation 'Uranus', which had begun on the very day of Zhukov's visit; so in effect he ordered Galitskiy to 'win more slowly'.

Unfortunately Zhukov's memoirs contain no discussion of his plans for 'Mars', other than the misleading statement about its origins mentioned above, and no precedent has so far been found in Soviet archives for his departure, mentioned by Galitskiy, from Stavka's (and his own) normal requirement to have offensives conducted as strongly and quickly as possible. However, proof that Zhukov had yet again correctly foreseen a German course of action would soon be forthcoming. Galitskiy reduced the size and intensity of his attacks. Velikiye Luki held out until 17 January, and the operation was concluded on the 21st. Zhukov's reasoning was then proved totally correct; Zeitzler, Chief of Staff at OKH since September, had already unsuccessfully sought Hitler's consent to abandon the Demyansk salient in early December, but as soon as Velikiye Luki and Novosokolniki fell, he renewed and increased pressure for abandonment of both salients, receiving Hitler's permission for Rzhev-Vyazma on 25 January and for Demyansk on the 31st. The formal order for both withdrawals was issued on 6 February, four days after the final surrender at Stalingrad, and they were completed by 28 February (Demyansk) and 14 March (Rzhev-Vyazma). The consequent shortening of Army Group North's line freed at least six divisions, some of which were immediately employed against Operation 'Polar Star', an attempt to follow up the January success of Operation 'Iskra' (Spark) in restoring Leningrad's land connection to the 'mainland' by encircling a large part of Army Group North. 'Polar Star' used forces of three Fronts (from south to north North-West, Leningrad and Volkhov), Zhukov was again in charge, and perhaps it qualifies better than 'Mars' for the title of his 'greatest defeat'. The weather was partly responsible; the spring thaw came early, and Zhukov, reporting to Stalin early in March, noted:

in the last 15 days, because of rain and thaws, the roads are becoming impassable. The marshes where the troops now have to function are beginning to show themselves, to flood and be completely covered with water. The forecast predicts warm weather from 15.3.43. I very much fear that we will be sitting with our groupings in the marshes here and in terrain hard to traverse, without achieving our aims under 'Polar Star'.

He concluded by advising Stalin simply to set more modest limits of advance, and prepare the starting area for a spring offensive; Stalin accepted his advice, and 'Polar Star' was terminated on 17 March.

However, even granted the unfavourable weather conditions, the main reason for the operation's failure was the North-West Front's inability to break through the German defences; four successive attempts along the line of the River Lovat, on 28 February, 4, 6 and 11 March, were beaten off by German divisions that had just been withdrawn from the Demyansk salient and had taken up their positions along the river only on the day before the first Soviet attack. The Front's commander, Marshal Timoshenko, ordered his troops onto the defensive on 18 March, and the front line in that sector remained practically unchanged for nine more months, until the siege of Leningrad was fully lifted in January 1944.[178]

Zhukov's reasoning in respect of Galitskiy's operation applied even more strongly to 'Mars' proper; if the Germans assessed the early stages of it as too strong for successful resistance, it would be open to them to avoid a potential disaster by withdrawing from the 540-kilometre (340-mile) front in the salient to a line about 175 kilometres (110 miles) long across its neck, which could be defended by eight divisions, leaving up to 22 others free for use elsewhere, including in the south. That Zhukov was sensitive to the dangers of too-early success is shown not merely by his comments to Galitskiy but by the fact that only one-third of the Kalinin and Western Fronts' forces were committed to 'Mars', whereas in the south at least half the available forces were committed initially, then further reinforced by two later-arriving armies (2nd Guards and 5th Shock) from Stavka Reserve. Intriguingly, the 43rd Army, to which the mid-October Stavka Directive cited above ordered five divisions sent specifically for use in 'Mars', did not in fact take part in it. That also tends to support Galitskiy's account of Zhukov's rejection of his original plan for a quick victory; the Germans must be pressed so generally that they could not disengage, but not so hard that they abandoned the salients.

Like Max's message of 4 November, when interpreted in the light of Sudoplatov's disclosures, Zhukov's instructions to Galitskiy contradict the contention that 'Mars' was more important than 'Uranus'. However, Zhukov's references to 'interaction' between blows could perhaps be taken to imply linkage between 'Mars' and 'Uranus' as equally important partners, as Isayev argued; but that interpretation too is contradicted by his explaining his decision exclusively in terms of the contribution the 3rd Shock Army's efforts would make to 'Uranus', and not even mentioning 'Mars', which he himself would launch just six days later.

There is also a question whether stated aims are always to be taken literally. To ensure that the troops fought hard enough to convince the enemy, they would not be told that they were engaged in a 'diversion'. Nor was such information withheld only from Soviet junior ranks. Two such instances, one from 'Mars', the other from Kursk, can serve to illustrate this. The first is in the memoirs of Marshal of Armoured Forces Babadzhanyan, who participated in 'Mars' as a colonel commanding the 3rd Mechanised Brigade of 3rd Mechanised Corps under General M.E. Katukov. At the end of October the corps began to redeploy from Kalinin (now Tver) to positions about 200 miles away, between Rzhev and Velikiye Luki. The move coincided with the autumn rains, the roads became almost impassable, vehicles, when not bogged down, moved at a maximum 10kph, and the corps arrived at its destination in sore need of time to overhaul and repair its equipment. 'However, they hurried us – not much time had been allocated to prepare for an offensive.' Babadzhanyan was taken to the commander of the 22nd Army, Lieutenant-General Yushkevich, whose infantry his brigade was to support, and briefed that 'we are conducting an extremely serious operation – the enemy's Rzhev salient must be liquidated. The defence must be broken through whatever happens.' Babadzhanyan went on: 'Only considerably later did we learn why they rushed us so, not letting us recover our wits after such a difficult march; in the south, at Stalingrad, our forces had gone over to the counter-offensive, and there must be no letting enemy forces be redeployed to the Stalingrad area. There was only one way to pin down enemy forces here – attack.'[179] Here too action in 'Mars' is defended as a contribution to the success of 'Uranus', but only as something Babadzhanyan learned after the event; Yushkevich's briefing of him defined the operation in far more apocalyptic terms.

The implication is that even a brigade commander had no 'need to know' what the true objective was, and this interpretation finds support in the third piece of evidence, the memoirs of his corps commander in 'Mars', the future Marshal of Armoured Forces M.E. Katukov, promoted after 'Mars' to command the 1st Tank Army, which fought at Kursk in July 1943. Katukov wrote that in ordering a counter-attack during the defensive battle there, Vatutin told him 'advance a kilometre then another, and that's alright. The main thing is to tie up German forces.' Katukov continued:

But in setting the task to Corps Commanders, Generals Kravchenko and Burkov, we didn't confine their attacks to just those 2 kilometres. On the contrary, we pointed them towards a deeper penetration of the fascist defence. We did this deliberately, taking account of purely psychological factors. If you tell people they are being sent into battle with very limited aims, just to attract the enemy's attention to themselves, they won't act as energetically as when it's up to them to breach the enemy defence with the intention of smashing right through its entire depth.[180]

Here even the two corps commanders who would have to carry out the assignment were deemed to have no 'need to know' its true objective, and, like Babadzhanyan, were told that it was more far-reaching than was actually the case.

The fourth item of evidence is in the memoirs of Army General A.I. Gribkov, who as a captain on the General Staff took part in 'Mars'. The corps he was attached to (Solomatin's) fought for several days in encirclement, and after the remnants of it had managed to break through to the Soviet lines on 15 December, he and the corps commander were immediately taken to Zhukov, who conceded that the corps had suffered heavy losses, but said it had 'fulfilled its task. The Germans did not venture to remove the tank divisions from your front and send them to Stalingrad.'[181] Here Zhukov may have been making the best of a bad job, but the view he expressed then is consistent both with what he had told Galitskiy before 'Mars' began, and, of course, with what actually happened.

The fifth item relates again to the differing contexts of 'Mars' and 'Uranus'. It occurs in the preface Isayev provided to the Russian translation of Dr Glantz's book, published in 2007. While not taking issue with the main theme of the book, he cites criticisms of 'Mars' in the memoirs of General A.I. Radzievsky, who served in it as Chief of Staff of the 2nd Guards Cavalry Corps, and who wrote:

The concept of 'Mars' consisted of fragmenting the defence in the Rzhev salient area by eight blows of Western and four blows of Kalinin Front, destroying the forces defending it, then emerging into the Smolensk area. Simultaneously Kalinin Front undertook an offensive at Velikiye Luki and Novosokolniki with the forces of 3rd Shock Army. Because overall thirteen shock groupings were created, most of them . . . were small, three–four divisions with a mechanised or tank corps. The multiplicity of blows, more than half of which were for pinning-down, led to dispersion of firepower. Although the artillery density of some groupings reached 70–85 or even 100 guns and mortars per kilometre on the breakthrough-sector, half of them were mortars, which could fire only on the forward positions.

Isayev went on to support Radzievsky's criticism, noting that the strongest blow at Stalingrad was dealt by a group of mobile forces comprising two tank corps and a cavalry corps, supported by 632 field guns, 297 anti-tank guns and 1,609 mortars, whereas the assault force of the 20th Army in 'Mars' comprised only one tank and one cavalry corps, supported by 525 field guns, 175 anti-tank guns and 1,546 mortars.[182] The two points made here are, first there were many blows but none was very strong, and secondly that despite the availability of larger forces the strongest attack mounted in 'Mars' was not nearly as strong as its counter-part at Stalingrad. Both Radzievsky and Isayev implicitly assume that this resulted from bad planning; apparently neither asked himself why Zhukov and Vasilevsky, who conceived both operations, and who directed their detailed planning, and Stalin, whose approval they received for both, devised such different plans for two operations to be conducted within the same time frame. They opted for 'Uranus' to open with three very heavy blows and to seek very quick results. For the first phase five tank corps (1st, 4th and 26th from the north, 4th and 13th from the south) were employed to achieve the encirclement, while elements of six armies (from north to south the 21st, 65th, 24th, 66th, 62nd and 64th) maintained pressure along the existing front line to prevent the Germans dis-engaging. Encirclement was achieved in four days and extended westwards for another seven, so that by 30 November the new German front line was at minimum about 65 and at maximum 110 kilometres (42–70 miles) from the trapped forces. These major results were achieved in a mere twelve days, but when Galitskiy put forward a plan to achieve a much more modest result in a similar time-period, Zhukov flatly rejected it, and told Galitskiy his main task was not to capture the objective but to pin down enemy forces so that they could not be sent south.

As Radzievsky noted, 'Mars' opened with thirteen blows smaller than any in 'Uranus', and Isayev confirmed this. However, neither they nor Glantz considered why the same three men who masterminded and controlled both operations planned them so differently. In Isayev's foreword to Glantz's book he compared 'Mars' with Brusilov's offensive of 1916, which achieved initial success by ignoring convention and attacking everywhere, then stated that 'what worked in a limited way against the Austrians in 1916 was completely ineffective against the German Army of 1942; the difference was that the German reserves at Rzhev were motorised or received vehicular transport for transfers from one sector of the front to another . . .'[183] Isayev then argued that 'Zhukov strongly overestimated the possibilities of the Kalinin and Western fronts' forces in proposing to carry out after 'Mars' a large-scale encirclement of Army Group Centre.' Two points arise here. First, there is no evidence that any such follow-up to 'Mars' ever existed. Secondly, overestimating one's own forces involves underestimating those of the enemy. Zhukov, preparing his third offensive against the Rzhev salient in eleven months, would hardly be likely to underestimate an enemy against whom both his previous offensives had achieved only limited and costly success. Is it not more likely, especially given what he told Galitskiy, that the conduct of 'Mars' as thirteen limited-strength operations was precisely calculated to keep the Germans too busy everywhere to disengage and thereby free forces for the south, but not so overwhelmed anywhere as to compel them to consider abandoning the salient – as noted above, they eventually did so, but too late to affect the situation at Stalingrad. That Soviet casualties in 'Mars' were so heavy was mainly due to the deliberate advance warning conveyed via Agent Max, about which Zhukov was not told. Sudoplatov did not say who authorised such an important leak, but in military matters the only higher authority than Zhukov was Stalin himself. Isayev mentions Max not at all, Glantz only briefly, and neither appears to have seen Sudoplatov's disclosures about Max's double-agent role and the purpose served by his 4 November message.

Isayev's comparison of 'Mars' with Brusilov's offensive of 1916 seems strained. There is nothing to suggest that Soviet planning was influenced by it, and if any lesson was drawn from it, it would surely be that too-early success can lead to disaster. Brusilov's initial successes, achieved in June–August 1916, tempted Romania into declaring war on 27 August and seizing Transylvania from Austria-Hungary. That brought about an instant German riposte, which saw Romania defeated and almost totally occupied by the end of the year, and Russia's strategic position far worse after than before Brusilov's successes.

However, Isayev does give some attention to what might have happened if 'Mars' had not taken place. He noted that Manstein's relief attempt was spearheaded by three panzer divisions, the full-strength 6th, transferred from France, and the much under-strength 17th and 23rd. If not 'tied up' by 'Mars', three more panzer divisions, the 12th, 19th and 20th, could have been added, and with six panzer divisions instead of three, the relief force might have got through. He also noted that post-ponement of Operation 'Citadel' from May to July (usually ascribed mainly to Hitler's desire to have as many as possible of the new Tiger and Panther tanks) was also due to the time Model needed to restore the combat strength of divisions that had fought in 'Mars', and that not all of them could be restored by then. For example, the 1st Panzer Division did not return to the line until the autumn of 1943, the 20th Panzer Division had a combat strength of only 2,837 men on 4 July, the 6th Infantry Division only 3,121 on 2 July,[184] both less than half the acceptable minimum for divisions about to fight a major battle.

A few other points in the argument about 'Mars' versus 'Uranus' merit attention. One is that during the 69 days between Zhukov's and Vasilevsky's first formulation of the Stalingrad counter-offensive plan on 12 September and its launching on 19 November, Zhukov spent 43 days in the Stalingrad area, versus only 18 days in Moscow (12–13 September, 3–6, 12–20, 26 and 29–30 October), eight (21–25 and 27–29 October) at the Kalinin Front,[185] one of the two allocated to 'Mars', and none at all specifically at the other, the Western Front. As noted above, its HQ was close enough to visit from Moscow, but even if he spent half his Moscow days there, the total of 17 'Mars'-associated versus 52 'Uranus'-associated days still points to 'Uranus' as the more important of the two.

Because losses in 'Mars' were heavy and the stated objectives not achieved, most Soviet-era accounts, like Zhukov's own, said little or nothing about it, and the study *Grif Sekretnosti Snyat* ('*Secret Stamp Removed*', hereafter *GSS*), an otherwise comprehensive listing of most major Soviet operations, defensive or offensive, with numbers of troops engaged and details of the losses incurred, did not even mention it. Generals who took part in 'Mars', such as Getman and Solomatin, truth-fully described their difficulties and failures in their memoirs, but, as Dr Glantz rightly pointed out, Soviet-era censorship prevented the full story being told. However, Sudoplatov's disclosure that the Germans were warned of 'Mars' in advance surely means the 'full story' would have been withheld even if the operation had been a complete success, for fear of incidentally disclosing the fact that the many thousands killed in it had been deliberately sacrificed to ensure the success of 'Uranus'. Zhukov's counterfactual references probably reflected his chagrin at its relative failure, contrasted with the successes achieved by his lower-profile colleague Vasilevsky and his former superior Rokossovsky at Stalingrad. However, none of this justifies contending either that 'Mars' was the winter's main operation, or that it was of equal status with 'Uranus', or that this was subsequently concealed merely because 'Uranus' succeeded and 'Mars' did not.[186]

The argument also rests on some other factors susceptible to explanations different from those offered. It is true that the 1.89 million troops, 3,375 tanks and huge numbers of guns and aircraft of the Kalinin and Western Fronts were much more than the 1.14 million men and 1,463 tanks available to the three Fronts (Don, Stalingrad and South-West) conducting 'Uranus', but it would surely be surprising if it were not so. Behind the Kalinin and Western Fronts was Moscow, the most important target in the country, and in front of them was Army Group Centre, the most powerful of the invading forces. The totals cited also included the manpower and weapons of the Moscow Defence Zone, which took no part in 'Mars', and suffered only 376 combat deaths in the whole of 1942.[187]

Though the German offensive plan for 1942 did not even mention Moscow, the Soviet General Staff's assessment of tasks for that summer (presumably influenced by the German deception campaign) defined four axes as under threat, and defence of the Moscow axis as the most important task. So if Zhukov believed the key to victory must be the destruction of Army Group Centre, he was not alone. Deception campaigns by both sides also played their part. In 1942 the Germans for long prevented Soviet reserves from being sent south by conducting Operation 'Kremlin', suggesting Moscow was their real target, and the Soviets, through Max, leaked information on 'Mars', including the fact that Zhukov would be in command. The German defeats at his hands at Leningrad and Moscow, the narrow margin by which they had survived his second offensive at Rzhev, in July–August 1942, and Stalin's appointment of him as Deputy Supreme Commander in August would all naturally induce them to view, as the Soviet planners meant them to, any operation he headed as more important than one conducted by the far less prominent Vasilevsky.

It would also seem axiomatic that when a disinformation campaign mentions four out of five planned offensives, the one it does not mention must be the most important. There are also three problems with Glantz's table that allocates 56 infantry divisions to 'Mars' and the hypothetical follow-up operation, 'Jupiter', versus 52 to 'Uranus/Saturn'. The first problem is that since 'Saturn' (modified as 'Little Saturn') took place but 'Jupiter' did not (there is no positive evidence that it even existed, as Dr Glantz admitted),[188] the 19 divisions and 5 tank corps claimed as allocated to it should be deducted, leaving the total involved in 'Mars' at 37 divisions and 6 tank corps – not much more than the 30 German divisions manning the Rzhev salient. The second problem is that although the 66th and 2nd Guards Armies are mentioned as supporting 'Uranus', they are not included in the totals of forces allocated to it. Each had six divisions, and the 66th Army was in action from the very first day of 'Uranus', while the 2nd Guards was sent from reserve in early December and dispatched to the Myshkova river to repel Manstein's attempt to relieve Stalingrad. It is hard to see why twelve divisions that saw a great deal of action in 'Uranus/Saturn' are excluded from the totals for it, while nineteen divisions that saw no action at all are included in those for 'Mars/Jupiter'. The third problem is that *Grif Sekretnosti Snyat*[189] lists the Stalingrad offensive operation as involving not 52 divisions but 74, far more than the 56 allegedly allocated to 'Mars and Jupiter', and double the 37 listed as specifically allotted to 'Mars'.

Dr Glantz also assessed Soviet casualties in 'Mars' as about 335,000 (100,000 killed, captured or missing, 235,000 wounded). However, to his credit he also included figures given by General Krivosheyev, the chief editor of *Grif Sekretnosti Snyat*, in a letter to a western publisher, of 215,674 casualties (70,374 dead/missing, 145,300 wounded). Even these lower figures confirm that 'Mars' was extremely costly; of the 43 major Soviet operations tabulated in *Grif Sekretnosti Snyat*, only eight had higher daily average losses than 'Mars', and its average of 8,295 compares badly with the 6,392 a day of the highly successful offensives at Stalingrad. However, operations there lasted 76 days, three times as long as 'Mars', so actual losses, 485,777 (154,885 dead/missing, 330,892 wounded) were over double those of 'Mars'. The figures also indirectly confirm Isayev's contention that the sacrifices in 'Mars' did contribute to the success of 'Uranus' and 'Little Saturn'. If Hitler had yielded to Zeitzler's urging at the beginning of December instead of the end of January, a large proportion of the 22 divisions freed by abandoning the Rzhev salient could have been sent south, some to reinforce Manstein's relief attempt, others to 'corset' the Italians and Hungarians against 'Little Saturn'.

Army General Mahmut Gareyev, in 1942 a junior officer in 'Mars', wrote that throughout the operation he and his colleagues cursed the Supreme Command for the disparity between the objectives set and the resources provided. Many unit diaries and reports cited in studies of 'Mars' confirm this complaint by mentioning shortages or complete lack of ammunition, food, fuel and forage. Also the postulation of the existence of Operation 'Jupiter' is based solely on reports of a major build-up of forces in the Soviet 5th and 33rd Army sectors during October–November. If 'Mars' was really the main offensive, it would seem logical for Zhukov to have committed some or all of those forces when it was seen to be faltering, as he had done at Leningrad and Moscow in the previous year. There are only two possible explanations for his abstention: either that he wanted to use them but Stalin overruled him, or that he never intended to use them. Neither is consistent with the argument that 'Mars' was the main or equal-main operation and 'Jupiter' meant to follow it, and that he never intended to use them seems more likely from a passage in his memoirs. He wrote that when the Western Front's attacks failed to achieve their objectives, Stalin sent him to Konev's headquarters, and there he concluded 'to repeat the operation was pointless. The enemy had guessed our intention and was able to bring substantial forces into the area from other sectors.'[190] That supports Sudoplatov's statement that Zhukov was never told of the deliberate leaks that had been made through Max.

'Mars' was terminated on 20 December, either because it was a costly failure, or because it was no longer needed, or a combination of both. All three cases are tenable, but on balance the last seems most justifiable. Manstein's attempt to have Hoth break through to Stalingrad, begun on 12 December, was stalled for three days at Verkhne-Kumsky, and when it reached the Myshkova river, the 2nd Guards Army was already taking up blocking positions on the north bank. Further west Operation 'Little Saturn', launched on 16 December, had ripped through the Italian 8th Army in two days. By the 19th Soviet forces had captured the main bases and supply dumps at Kantemirovka, and were about to take the airfields at Tatsinskaya and Morozovskaya, the western termini of the air supply route to Stalingrad. By then Soviet Intelligence must have worked out, from the observed frequency of flights and known maximum payloads of the aircraft, that the airlift was proving totally inadequate to meet even the minimal requirements of 22 divisions and that the need to use airfields further west would reduce its capacity even more. 'Mars' could be called off because by 20 December it was proving both costly and unnecessary. That equates to partial, but by no means total, failure.

A further point concerns objectives. Certainly German losses in 'Mars' were far fewer than the Soviets', but Germany was much less able to replace them. Galitskiy's capture of Velikiye Luki and Novosokolniki in late January created a new threat to the Demyansk and Rzhev salients that Army Groups North and Centre obviously lacked the resources to elim-inate. As noted above, during February–March 1943 they abandoned both salients, thereby shortening the front line by at least 250 miles.[191] This reduced Stavka's and Stalin's concern about threats to Moscow and Leningrad, and also shortened the Soviet front line by the same amount, enabling some divisions to be moved to reinforce weak sectors and others to be withdrawn to recuperate, replace battle losses and train for the summer offensive. The Red Army may even have benefited as much from the move as the Germans did. Incidentally, when in the previous year the two army group commanders-in-chief had sought permission to abandon both salients, Hitler had refused on the grounds that the withdrawals would also shorten the Soviets' front line and release reserves.[192] So if 'Mars' was a diversion, it was a success, though an expensive one; if in-tended as more, it was a partial failure, but the balance of evidence does not support the view that it was meant to be either equal to or more im-portant than 'Uranus'. Marginal to the argument, but perhaps a pointer to Stalin's assessment of success and failure, is that on 18 January 1943 he promoted Zhukov to (5-star) marshal, and Vasilevsky to (4-star) army general. Then in March, after the Germans completed their withdrawal from the salients, he had the rank of marshal conferred on himself. This was purely symbolic; he already had all the power he needed, as head of the Party and government and Supreme Commander-in-Chief of the armed forces, but the timing was significant, marking the final removal of the most direct potential threat to Moscow, though not of residual fear for its safety, which, as will be seen, even affected planning for Kursk, and identifying himself with the success achieved by the hitherto distrusted military professionals.

There remains, of course, a possibility that Zhukov covertly hoped to make 'Mars' more than a diversion, and that his cavalier and misleading treatment of it in his memoirs reflects his chagrin at its outcome. His personality may have governed his actions more than his orders did, and here some incidents that illustrate his usual approach may be relevant.

In Leningrad in September 1941 he ordered an engineer officer to have one hundred dummy tanks made overnight by the Marinskiy Theatre workshops, and threatened him with court-martial if they were not ready by next morning.[193] Then on 28 September he had all units notified that the families of any soldiers or sailors who surrendered would be shot, and so would the offenders on their return from captivity. This outdid even Stalin's notorious Order no. 270 of 16 August, which threatened the families only with 'loss of state benefits and assistance'.[194]

Former front-line soldier V.P. Astaf'yev commented: 'When Konev led us we advanced more slowly, but were all right for food, boots, clothing, some awards, a little human existence. But Zhukov replaced Konev – and in mud, bad weather, no boots, into the attack, forward, forward . . .'.[195] General P.I. Batov, commanding the 65th Army in June 1944, wrote that in all his service he 'never experienced such a humiliation' as the dressing-down Zhukov gave him because he had not yet taken the Belorussian town of Baranovichi. Zhukov's ire was apparently motivated solely by his wish to have a victory to report to Stalin before Vasilevsky took the Lithuanian capital, Vilnius; when Batov woke Zhukov early the next morning to report Baranovichi taken, Zhukov's only reaction was 'no news from Vilnius? Then let me sleep some more.'[196] In the final operation to take Berlin, in 1945, Stalin exploited the rivalry between Zhukov and Konev by drawing the demarcation line between their Fronts (1st Belorussian and 1st Ukrainian) only as far as Zossen, in the southern outskirts. Konev's 3rd Tank Army reached Zossen first, and he turned it north into Berlin's southern suburbs. Zhukov's troops reached the city centre only to find Konev's tanks already there, just 300 metres from the Reichstag. Zhukov arrived, gave their commander, Rybalko, a tongue-lashing, and demanded that Stalin order Konev's forces to pull back.

It is unlikely that Zhukov would readily play second-fiddle to Vasilevsky, whatever the official status of 'Mars' relative to 'Uranus'. It was in his nature to drive at and for maximum intensity. However, that makes his remarks to Galitskiy, and his organisation of 'Mars' as a large number of small blows rather than a small number of large ones, out of character, and explainable only, as suggested above, by his perceiving a need to avoid, at least in the early stages, pressing the Germans to the point where they would abandon either or both salients. That Stalin did not consider Zhukov's conduct of 'Mars' a failure was evident not only from his promoting him, but from where he sent him after it was called off. From 2 to 9 January Zhukov was at Voronezh Front, then on 10 January he was sent to Leningrad, and stayed there until the 24th, overseeing Operation 'Iskra' ('Spark'), which restored the city's connection to the 'mainland' along the south shore of Lake Ladoga. After two weeks in Moscow his next assignment was to the North-West Front, from 6 February to 16 March, overseeing the unsuccessful 'Polar Star' and the liquidation of the Demyansk salient, before Stalin sent him to solve the problems Manstein's successful offensive had created for the Voronezh Front. So for almost all the first three months of 1943 he was busy overseeing operations against Army Groups North and South. These activities are not consistent with Dr Glantz's contention that throughout January and February Zhukov was arguing about the decisive importance of beating Army Group Centre.

At worst Zhukov can be said to have pushed 'Mars' harder and longer than a diversion required, and incurred larger than necessary losses partly because he did so, but, more importantly, because, unknown to him, the Germans had been deliberately forewarned. Stalin set the limits to what Zhukov could achieve, deciding not only where to send him, but also what reserves and reinforcements to give him, and Stalin decided the fate of 'Mars' well before it was mounted, basically on the grounds that more Germans killing Soviet troops at Rzhev meant fewer killing them at Stalingrad. That cold-blooded pragmatic judgement was soon to be confirmed by events.

Chapter Four

Victory at Stalingrad

Late on 12 November Zhukov and Vasilevsky flew back from Stalingrad to Moscow, and on the morning of the 13th reported to Stalin that preparations for Operation 'Uranus' were basically complete. Supplies of ammunition, fuel and winter uniforms had been somewhat delayed, but all should be delivered before the 18th. They recommended that the Don and South-West Fronts start the offensive on 19 November, and the Stalingrad Front, which had less distance to cover to the encirclement's intended meeting point, the bridge over the Don at Kalach, should join in on the 20th. Stalin agreed, then told them to fly back to Stalingrad next morning, and check once again that the Fronts and their commanders were ready. Zhukov spent the 14th with Vatutin; on the 15th, after consulting Vasilevsky, who was with Yeremenko, he endorsed the agreed dates, then on the 17th flew back to Moscow to make the final preparations for 'Mars' and for Galitskiy's linked operation to take Velikiye Luki and Novosokolniki.

Of the year's remaining 45 days after he left Stalingrad, Zhukov would spend 10 in Moscow and 35 with the Kalinin and Western Fronts. Operation 'Uranus' duly began on 19 November and in the next few days smashed the Romanian 3rd and 4th Armies. On the 23rd mobile forces of the South-West and Stalingrad Fronts met near the bridge at Kalach, closing the ring around 20 German and 2 Romanian divisions, plus several smaller units. Estimates of the numbers encircled vary from 250,000 to 300,000, but even the lowest figure is three times as many as the planners had expected to trap – an intriguing but unexplained failure of Intelligence, considering that the opposing forces had been fighting at extremely close quarters for three months. Consequently Stavka had to retain many more troops than planned in the Stalingrad area to contain them, and this necessitated some amendment of the second stage, Operation 'Saturn'. This was originally intended to be an advance along the Don to the Black Sea coast, to cut off Army Group A (1st Panzer and 17th Armies) in the Caucasus, but was modified into 'Little Saturn', a thrust by the South-West and Voronezh Fronts against the Italian 8th

115

Army, to threaten the rear of the newly created Army Group Don and Army Group B, and to terminate in the Morozovskaya area instead of continuing to the coast to cut off Army Group A.

After Zhukov returned to Moscow on 17 November he had no more direct involvement in 'Uranus', but retained an influential advisory role in its conduct and development. Vasilevsky and the General Staff kept him informed of progress, and on 28 November Stalin telephoned him at the Kalinin Front headquarters to seek his views on how to liquidate the forces besieged at Stalingrad, an enquiry probably prompted by the sudden realisation that they were far more numerous than expected. On the next day he provided his assessment, which was that the encircled force would not risk attempting a breakout on its own, but would hold its positions while a strike group was hastily assembled in the Nizhne-Chirskaya/Kotelnikovo area, tasked with attacking north-eastwards to open a corridor through which the besieged forces could be supplied and subsequently withdrawn. He therefore recommended attacking the Germans at Nizhne-Chirskaya and Kotelnikovo as soon as possible, establishing a densely defended westward-facing line, and maintaining two groups, each of at least 100 tanks, as reserves.

That Zhukov had yet again read German intentions accurately would be proved almost immediately. On 28 November, literally while Zhukov was compiling his assessment for Stalin, Manstein was presenting Hitler with a proposal to mount a relief operation, codenamed 'Wintergewitter' ('Winter Storm'), to be undertaken by Group Hoth, with the 6th (transferred from France), 17th and 23rd Panzer Divisions driving north-eastwards along the railway from Kotelnikovo to Stalingrad, while the 48th Panzer Corps, Army Detachment Hollidt and the Romanian 3rd Army attacked from Verkhne-Chirskaya along a shorter route to Stalingrad, so as to threaten the rear of the Stalingrad Front's 51st Army, which would be facing Hoth. Manstein's intention was, precisely as Zhukov had forecast, to establish a corridor through which to supply the beleaguered forces with food, ammunition and the fuel needed for withdrawing from the encirclement. Hitler agreed to 'Wintergewitter', but had forbidden Paulus to abandon Stalingrad; however, Manstein hoped to persuade him to change his mind, and was covertly also preparing Operation 'Donnerschlag' ('Thunderbolt') for complete withdrawal.[197] With that in mind, the supply vehicles accompanying Hoth's relief force carried not only food and ammunition, but enough additional fuel for the 6th Army to make a long withdrawal.

Operation 'Mars' was launched on 25 November. The troops were told that its objectives were for the right wing of the Western and left wing of the Kalinin Fronts to encircle the Germans in the Rzhev-Sychevka salient, liberate Rzhev and free the Moscow–Velikiye Luki railway. Certainly 'Mars' did not achieve these objectives, but whether they were its real targets has been discussed in Chapter Three. One Russian author[198] has suggested that if the forces used for 'Mars' had instead been sent to the south, the original purpose of 'Saturn', blocking Army Group A's withdrawal from the Caucasus, could have been achieved. However, it is questionable whether the Rear (logistical) Services could have handled the transportation and supply of even one or two, let alone six, additional armies – as noted above, the start of 'Uranus' had to be postponed from 15 to 19 November because of supply difficulties. Furthermore, the Intelligence information about the numbers that would be encircled by 'Uranus' would have had to be much more accurate than it was in reality, given that it was realised only after the trap was closed that the Intelligence assessments that had determined the original distribution of forces between 'Uranus' and 'Saturn' included some serious underestimates.

A further obstacle was Stalin's and the General Staff's continued preoccupation with the possibility of a renewed attempt to take Moscow, long after it had vanished from the German agenda. 'Mars' was the third attempt to eliminate the Rzhev salient, and it was only on 27 August, two months after the German summer offensive had begun, and ten days after it had reached the Volga, that Stalin authorised the dispatch of three armies of Stavka Reserve from the Moscow area to the vicinity of Stalingrad. On the same day he called Zhukov, who was then making his second attempt to remove the Rzhev salient, back to Moscow, appointed him Deputy Supreme Commander and ordered him to go to Stalingrad at once. Then, after Army Group Centre removed the most direct threat to the capital by abandoning the Rzhev salient in March 1943, Stalin had the rank of Marshal of the Soviet Union conferred on himself. As noted earlier, this was purely symbolic; he already had all the power he needed. However, his adoption for the first time of an actual military rank indicates the importance he attached to the removal of the direct threats to Moscow and Leningrad that the salients symbolised. After the war his official *Short Biography* perpetuated the myth that he had more than once saved Moscow from capture, claiming that he had foreseen and frustrated three German plans to outflank it from the east, in 1941 by an advance north from Tula, in 1942 by a drive up the Volga from the Stalingrad area, and in 1943 by a thrust north from Orel and Belgorod after the anticipated destruction of the Soviet forces in the Kursk salient.[199] Of these only the first had ever existed, he did not 'foresee' it, and it was frustrated not by any act of his, but by urgent redeployments ordered by Zhukov, which forced Guderian into an unauthorised retreat, for which Kluge dismissed him.

Hitler had forbidden the abandonment of Stalingrad, but it soon became clear that the airlift could not supply even the minimum requirement of 300 tons a day, and its task became even harder as the strength of Soviet fighter attacks on the lumbering transport aircraft increased, and as more and more anti-aircraft regiments were deployed along the supply route. There was no hope for the besieged without a relief operation on the ground, hence Manstein's 'Wintergewitter' plan to relieve them and the covert 'Donnerschlag' operation to bring them out.

   The relief force set off on 12 December and advanced about 30 miles on that day, but on the 13th became involved in what the 6th Panzer Division's commander, General Erhard Raus, later described as a three-day 'wrestling match' at Verkhne-Kumskiy, with Yeremenko's 4th Mechanised and 13th Tank Corps. The Germans won it, but the three days' delay had sufficed for two crucial Soviet decisions, the first to set 'Little Saturn' in motion on 16 December, and the second to send the 2nd Guards Army (under General, later Marshal, R.Y. Malinovsky) to confront Hoth's force at the Myshkova river, about 40 miles from the south-west edge of the encirclement. This was a full-strength army from Stavka Reserve, which Vasilevsky had requested on 12 December, origi-nally with the intention of reinforcing the Don Front so as to speed up the annihilation of the encircled forces. Rokossovsky argued strongly that he should retain and use it for that assignment, so that the relief expedi-tion would find nothing to relieve, but Stalin thought that 'too risky'. In addition, Vasilevsky and Yeremenko were apprehensive that Paulus might try to break out to meet the relief force, not knowing that he had only about 70 tanks left, hardly any fuel for them, and in any case would not even try to break out without a specific order from Hitler that was never forthcoming. The 2nd Guards Army was therefore dispatched to the Myshkova river, and arrived there just before Hoth did. Having outrun his fuel supplies, Malinovsky had what there was distributed evenly between all the tanks, so that as many as possible arrived at the river bank; even if out of fuel they could provide static fire support for the infantry, and emergency supply measures, including an airlift, remedied the situation before the Germans had a chance to realise, let alone exploit, their lack of fuel.

The signing of the Molotov-Ribbentrop Pact, 23 August 1939.

'Blitzkrieg': German tanks thrusting ahead.

The infantry follow-up: horses, bicycles and footslogging.

Hitler with his
closest military
subordinates, Keitel
and Jodl.

Stalin.

Zhukov.

Beria.

Timoshenko.

Malenkov.

Konev.

Mikoyan.

Mark IV tanks, the Panzers' workhorse. Early models with a short-barrel gun were outgunned by the KV-1 and T-34-76, but the long 75mm gun later fitted, as here, outranged Soviet tank guns until the T-34-85 medium and IS heavies came into service in early 1944.

Mark V Panther. Many Panthers failed to get into action at Kursk because of mechanical problems, but once they were solved the Panther staked a strong claim to be the war's best tank.

(*left*) Tiger I; (*below*) 'Ferdinand' self-propelled gun. The Tiger and Ferdinand outdid the T-34 and KV-1 in armour, gun range and firepower. The Tiger long dominated in tank-to-tank encounters, but Ferdinands, 90 of which were deployed at Kursk, were relative failures; in particular their lack of a machine-gun made them ineffective against infantry using anti-tank rifles or mines to disable them by damaging their tracks.

(*left top*) KV-1 heavy tank; (*left below*) T-34-76 medium tank. Production of these tanks began at the end of 1939, and a total of 1,475 were in service by June 1941. Their battlefield superiority was totally eroded by the Tiger and Panther, and regained only during 1944, when the KV was replaced by IS-series heavy tanks, and the T-34 upgraded with a more powerful 85mm gun, a larger turret to house it and an additional crew member, and thicker armour.

T-70 tank. The Soviet defenders had three times as many tanks as the invaders, but about half of them were these light tanks, thinly armoured and undergunned. Delays in production of T-34s and KVs caused by the evacuations meant that the T-70 continued to be made until mid-1943.

T-34s during the final stages of assembly.

'The Russian must die so that we live.'

Shortages of trucks and tractors meant that Soviet artillery was predominantly horse-drawn until Lend-Lease trucks became available in quantity during 1943.

Kiev soon after the Germans arrived. The poster is entitled 'Hitler the Liberator'.

Germans welcomed in the Baltic states . . .

. . . and in Ukraine.

Soviet soldiers were captured by the hundred thousand, and some of those pictured here don't seem to regret it.

Cossacks in German service. Anti-Soviet feeling among Cossacks was strong enough for the Germans to raise nine regiments and form a Cossack cavalry division from prisoners of war, defectors and volunteers from areas under German occupation.

The personal escort of General Helmut von Pannwitz, commander of the 1st Cossack Cavalry Division.

Another mass of captured Soviets, viewed from an aircraft.

In early winter Leningrad's 'Road of Life' over Lake Ladoga could only be used by horse-drawn carts . . .

. . . but eventually the ice became thick enough for lorries.

Following Stalin's 'scorched earth' order, retreating Soviet troops removed what they could and destroyed what they could not.

October 1941. Moscow women digging anti-tank ditches.

Barricades and a barrage balloon at the Bolshoi Theatre, Moscow.

To boost morale the traditional 7 November revolution anniversary parade was held as usual in 1941, but most of the participants marched on to the front line.

Even the local horses found the mud too much . . .

At last the snow came and the mud froze.

Germans not dressed for winter surrendering to Russians who were.

For lack of tanks and lorries Soviet mobile forces in the Moscow counter-offensive consisted largely of skiers.

Abandoned German equipment outside Moscow.

Paulus, promoted to field-marshal by Hitler but captured at Stalingrad.

The defenders of Stalingrad linked buildings by trenches.

Chuikov's leadership of the 62nd Army's defence of Stalingrad was inspired and inspiring.

Pavel Sudoplatov, the NKVD controller of
Agent Max for most of the war.

Manstein was generally considered the
most gifted of the German generals. He
was promoted to field-marshal by Hitler,
but dismissed by him in 1944.

Model, a master of defensive fighting
whose particular skills were more and
more in demand as the war progressed.

Guderian, the moving spirit behind the
creation of 'Blitzkrieg'; throughout his
career he was plagued by conservative
opposition and by his own reluctance to
obey orders with which he disagreed.

Another long chain of prisoners, this time German.

Preparing to fire 'Katyusha' multiple-rocket launchers.

Wrecking German supply trains was an important element in partisan warfare . . .

. . . and hanging was a regular German riposte.

Soviet tanks and
infantry advancing to
the Dnepr.

New tanks for
old. Wrecked
tanks awaiting the
furnaces.

The 'Big Three' at Tehran, November 1943.

The Germans who did get to Moscow. Some 57,000 of them were paraded through the streets in June 1944.

Apart from the launching of 'Little Saturn', 16 December was also notable as the day on which the Volga at Stalingrad finally froze solid. That, coupled with the severe reduction in German shelling of river traffic, because of the airlift's inability to deliver enough ammunition, greatly eased supply problems for the 62nd Army. In the first hours of 'Little Saturn' some of the South-West Front's units became disoriented in freezing fog and blundered into minefields, but momentum was soon regained. The Italian 8th Army was destroyed in two days, and on 23 December the 24th Tank Corps attacked the airfield at Tatsinskaya, the main base for the Ju52 transport aircraft that provided most of the airlift to Stalingrad. Some 124 aircraft managed to escape by taking off, but 60 were destroyed,[200] as were large amounts of supplies waiting to be airlifted and a trainload of unassembled brand-new aircraft. The airfield had to be abandoned; so, a few days later, had the other principal supply airfield, at Morozovskaya.

The 24th Tank Corps, spearheading 'Little Saturn', had advanced 300 kilometres (about 186 miles) in one week, and had far outrun its infantry support, so for five days it had to fight in encirclement, before finally breaking out on 29 December. Its feat earned it elevation to Guards status, and its achievements went far beyond the physical destruction of aircraft and supply dumps; it forced the Germans to shift the starting point for the airlift much further west, initially to airfields at Salsk and Novocherkassk, then even further. This increased the flight distance from 125 to 200 and eventually to almost 300 miles, the longer flights necessitating more fuel to be carried, hence smaller payloads, reducing the number of flights an aircraft could make in a day, and increasing the period it would be vulnerable to attacks from the 16th Air Army and the masses of anti-aircraft guns deployed along the flight path. To make matters even worse, five of the seven fields in the Stalingrad area were mere airstrips, and only one, Pitomnik, could handle night flights – a severe constraint in the short (and still shortening) daylight hours of winter. Maintenance of the aircraft, mostly in the open, clearing of snow and filling-in of bomb or shell craters on the runways became increasingly difficult in temperatures that were almost always below minus 30 degrees Celsius (minus 22 Fahrenheit), especially at the eastern end, where the ground staff were much weakened by cold and hunger – by mid-January the besieged troops' daily rations had fallen to 200 grams (7 ounces) of horsemeat, 75 grams (about 2.6 ounces) of bread, and 12 grams (less than half an ounce) of margarine or fat.[201]

Also on the day 'Mars' was terminated, Manstein ordered Hoth to abandon the relief attempt, because his forces would now be needed to cope with the threat 'Little Saturn' was posing to Army Group Don's rear. Even before Manstein issued that order the relief attempt had been forced to a halt, and four Soviet armies were about to counter-attack. By New Year's Day the front line in the southern sector was back where it had been before 'Winter Storm' began, and Hitler had had to agree to allow the 1st Panzer Army to withdraw altogether from the Caucasus and the 17th Army to pull back to positions along the Kuban river and in the Taman peninsula.

The very slow progress of Operation 'Kol'tso' ('Ring') in eliminating the Stalingrad 'pocket' led to some discussion at the State Defence Committee in late December. It was agreed that control by a single commander was desirable, but the question was whether it should be Rokossovsky or Yeremenko. Commenting 'I assess Yeremenko lower than Rokossovsky. The troops don't like Yeremenko . . . he's immodest and boastful',[202] Stalin ruled in favour of Rokossovsky, and left Zhukov to deal with an indignant Yeremenko, three of whose armies (the 62nd, 64th and 57th) were transferred from the Stalingrad Front (renamed the South Front on 1 January) to the Don Front, giving Rokossovsky a total of seven armies. Some units of the 2nd Guards Army were also brought back from the Myshkova river line. On 8 January Rokossovsky and Colonel-General Voronov (present as a representative of Stavka) sent Paulus an offer of surrender terms that blended twentieth-century psychological warfare (references to the failed relief attempt, promises of food and medical care, warnings of the hardships to be expected in the remaining months of winter, threats of annihilation if the terms were refused, etc.) with eighteenth-century punctilio ('senior officers may keep their swords'). The offer was rejected, so Operation 'Ring' began on 10 January, with a 55-minute bombardment by thousands of guns and mortars and hundreds of aircraft. By 17 January six of the seven airfields had been taken, including Pitomnik; the single remaining one, Gumrak, an improvised airstrip, could be used only intermittently. It, too, fell, on 21 January, and thereafter supply, such as it was, could be made only by dropping from the air. The final push began on the 22nd; on the 25th the 62nd Army's isolation ended when mobile forces of the 21st Army linked up with it at the 'Red October' factory housing estate in the north of the city and on the Mamayev Kurgan in the centre.

The determined German resistance Hitler ordered at Stalingrad could reasonably be held as serving a strategic purpose until 24 January, because it tied up Soviet forces that could otherwise have been sent south to cut off Army Group A's retreat from the Caucasus. However, by that date Army Group A had completed its withdrawal, retaining only positions from where evacuation across the narrow Kerch Strait to the Crimea could be easily undertaken if and when necessary. Surrender at Stalingrad on 24 January would therefore have been without detriment to Germany's overall strategic position, and on that day Manstein sought Hitler's agreement to it. Hitler again refused and instead sent yet another message to Paulus forbidding surrender, and also promoted him to field-marshal – an implicit invitation to commit suicide, as no German field-marshal had ever been captured. Instead Paulus surrendered on 30 January, and by 2 February 1943 all resistance at Stalingrad had ceased. Paulus was well treated in captivity, and returned to live in East Germany after the war. His troops were less fortunate; of the 91,000 who lived to surrender, only about 5,000 survived to return home after the war.

Comparison of Soviet and German losses at Stalingrad cannot be exact, partly because of differences in their methods of calculating casualties, partly through losses of documentation in chaotic phases of the battle, and partly through the total lack of published data about the numbers and fates of Soviet prisoners of war serving as *Hilfswillige* (volunteers) in encircled German units. Not all these were formally recorded on their units' nominal rolls; some, knowing the likely consequences of capture by the Red Army, managed to re-defect back to the Soviet lines, others sought to escape into the hinterland before their units were overrun, yet others to insist after liberation that they had been not volunteers but slave labour. Estimates of their numbers can be little more than guesswork. The average German infantry division had up to 1,000 of them, employed mainly as storemen, mess or stable orderlies, carters or driver-mechanics, but occasionally also trusted as sentries or even as ammunition carriers in gun crews; one source[203] estimates their total numbers at the end of 1942 as close to a million, so the twenty encircled divisions could easily have included 20,000 of them. Soviet sources, unsurprisingly, said nothing about how many there were or what happened to them.

The German rule of thumb for assessing 'irrevocable' losses was to add one-third of the wounded to the numbers killed, captured or missing, on the assumption that that proportion died during evacuation or in hospital or were rendered unfit for further service by their injuries. Soviet practice included only wounded who died before reaching hospital among 'irrevocable' losses, but the wartime Head of Red Army medical services noted that over 72 per cent of the wounded returned to service, and 90.6 per cent of those, i.e. 65.2 per cent of all wounded, took part in further fighting. The percentage that did not, 34.8, closely resembled the German one-third rule of thumb.[204]

Further problems are that the data for casualties do not cover identical periods, most Soviet wounded were evacuated across the Volga, and many German wounded were flown out only to die when their aircraft were shot down (488 transport aircraft were lost during the airlift, though many of those were destroyed on the ground). An OKH report compiled during 1943 gave total 'departures' (killed, captured, missing, and one-third of the sick or wounded) in the four months from November 1942 to February 1943 as 543,000, versus only 322,000 'arrivals' (replacements), an indication of how serious the German manpower shortages were becoming. Nor was the shortfall the full measure of the problem. The 'departures' were mostly of trained and experienced soldiers, the 'arrivals' a mixture of raw recruits and men previously rejected or classed as medically fit only for home garrison duty, and even to acquire these rather dubious assets Germany's overstretched industries had to be raided. For example, on 19 December Hitler ordered 200,000 industrial workers to be mobilised, in exchange for the release of 150,000 'elderly' soldiers to industry, and three weeks later ordered another 200,000 men previously rejected on medical grounds to be called up.

Soviet losses in killed, captured or missing during the counter-offensive period (19 November 1942–2 February 1943) were 154,885,[205] considerably fewer than the German 'departures'. However, the Soviet figure is for only 76 days, and includes none for the first 18 days of November, whereas the German data cover four months, and relate to the entire Eastern Front, not simply the Stalingrad disaster. Using the German rule of thumb on Soviet casualties, to make the data more comparable, in the defensive battle they were 430,518 (323,856 'irrevocable' plus 106,662, one-third of 'sanitary' losses), and in the counter-offensive 198,515 (154,885 plus 43,630) for a total of 629,033, or about 16 per cent more than German 'departures' in the same period.[206]

Despite these losses, the growing Soviet capacity to mobilise and supply larger forces now began to manifest itself in an ability to mount simultaneous offensives on more than one sector – precisely the strategy that Stalin had prematurely sought to implement at the beginning of 1942. January 1943, for example, saw three such operations additional to 'Ring'. On New Year's Day the South and Transcaucasus Fronts began Operation 'Don', on a front of 840 kilometres (about 525 miles). It continued for 35 days, with the North Caucasus Front joining in for its last two weeks, and when it ended, on 4 February, Soviet forces had advanced distances from 300 to 600 kilometres (roughly 185–370 miles). Although the prime objective, the destruction of Army Group A, was not achieved, the danger to the Soviet oilfields was removed, and so was any likelihood that Hitler could accomplish his fantasy of advancing through Iran to oust the British from the Middle East, or to meet the Japanese in India. Then on 12 January the Leningrad and Volkhov Fronts began Operation 'Iskra' ('Spark'), an attempt to lift the blockade of the city. This continued until the end of the month, and succeeded in clearing the Germans from the south shore of Lake Ladoga and opening a corridor to the 'mainland'. Efforts to enlarge it beyond a width of 8 kilometres (5 miles) at its narrowest and 11 kilometres (7 miles) at its broadest point were unsuccessful, so it remained vulnerable during daylight hours to German artillery fire as well as to air attack. However, the artillery fire could no longer be directed by spotters near the targets, so could not be pinpointed, and Soviet air force performance had much improved, so the corridor was sufficiently protected for a railway and oil pipeline to be laid quickly along it. The blockade would not be completely lifted for another 11 months, but the new land link enabled food rations and fuel allowances to be substantially increased from 23 February, improved the supply of weapons, ammunition, food and reinforcements to the city's defenders, and eased the evacuation of civilians, sick and wounded.

Calculation of Soviet losses in these operations on the same basis as those mentioned above produces the following results:

Operation	Losses: 'Irrevocable'	⅓ of 'Sanitary'	Total losses
Don	69,627	28,304	97,931
Iskra	33,940	27,047	60,987

Addition of these (158,918) to the Stalingrad figures (629,033) gives a total of 787,951, compared to 543,000 German 'departures', suggesting in round figures three Soviet losses for every two German. Compared to some battles at other periods of the war, especially in 1941, this is much less unfavourable to the Soviet side. Besides, these were the price for one major and two lesser victories, and more easily replaced than German losses that were incurred in one major and two lesser defeats.

The last offensive of the winter was at Voronezh and Kharkov, by the Voronezh Front and one army each of the Bryansk and South-West

Fronts, against Army Group B. It began on 14 January and continued until 3 March. Initially it was very successful, destroying most of the Hungarian 2nd Army and the remainder of the Italian 8th Army, together with several German divisions, and taking 86,000 prisoners. Operation 'Zvezda' ('Star'), proposed by Vasilevsky and Golikov and amended by Stalin and Zhukov, began on 2 February, aiming to take Kharkov and continue to the coast of the Sea of Azov, to cut off Manstein's Army Group Don. This soon created a serious enough situation for Hitler on 6 February to summon Manstein and Kluge to Rastenburg, where they at last secured his formal agreement to requests for shortening the front line that he had previously refused, Manstein's for a withdrawal to the River Mius, and Kluge's for abandonment of the Rzhev salient (Zeitzler had obtained Hitler's agreement to this latter on 25 January, but formal orders had not yet been issued). Hitler then abolished Army Group B, dividing the remains of its forces (the German 2nd Army and *Armeeabteilung* (Army Detachment) Kempf) between Army Groups Centre and Don (now renamed Army Group South).

Manstein also secured Hitler's agreement to a counter-offensive, spearheaded by the three experienced divisions of the 2nd SS Panzer Corps, just transferred from the west, and the Wehrmacht's elite 'Grossdeutschland' Division, redeployed from Army Group Centre. This offensive began on 19 February, and achieved complete surprise; by the second half of March, when the spring thaw imposed its customary pause on both sides, the 2nd SS Panzer Corps had retaken Kharkov, Grossdeutschland had captured Belgorod, the front line had been pushed back eastwards to the river line of the Seversky Donets, and most of the ground temporarily ceded north of the Don had been recaptured.

That Manstein's offensive took the Soviets so totally by surprise was mainly because the success of Operations 'Uranus' and 'Little Saturn' had convinced all the senior military involved, from Front commanders Golikov and Vatutin up to and including Stalin, that the Germans were engaged in a full-scale withdrawal to the Dnepr river. They interpreted events in the light of that assumption; when efforts to encircle westward-moving German formations failed, they were assumed to be in headlong retreat, whereas they were actually being regrouped and concentrated for the counter-offensive. Golikov admitted after the war that he had indeed misinterpreted the German moves, and Vatutin (who did not survive the war) obviously made the same mistake, urging his subordinate commanders on despite their reports that after three months of hard fighting their troops were exhausted, units were far under strength, equipment worn out, supply problems worsening as the distance from railheads increased (most supply columns still consisted of horse-drawn carts), and German resistance progressively stiffening. Stalin and therefore Stavka in turn were seduced by the possibility of driving the Germans out of all 'left-bank' Ukraine (east of the Dnepr) before the spring thaw, so the three Fronts – Voronezh, South-West and South (Malinovsky) – were ordered to keep pushing westwards, against German forces wrongly assumed to be incapable of striking back.

Hitler's reluctance to authorise retreats is frequently ascribed to his becoming obsessed by the belief that his 'stand fast' orders had prevented Army Group Centre's retreat in 1941 becoming a rout. However, an additional motive can be cited in this case. The German campaigns in western and southern Europe had all been concluded in a few weeks with the forces and equipment already in being, so the long-term industrial and economic production capacities of the adversaries had been irrelevant; the basis of the 'Barbarossa' plan had been the same, intended to destroy Soviet military power in five months, again before Soviet long-term industrial capacity could affect the issue. Germany had not 'geared' up for a long war, and had difficulty adapting when forced to face one. In 1941, except for a brief period in August–September when Hitler gave priority to seizing Ukraine rather than Moscow, the German offensive had not pursued economic objectives, but in 1942 its aims were specifically economic – to block Soviet oil supply, then seize the oilfields for German use, in the process also taking the major industrial and mining area of Donbass and the grain-growing lands of Ukraine. Stalin had always taken account of economic factors in relation to war, and had assumed that Hitler did too, wrongly in 1941, but rightly in 1942. Rokossovsky's post-war argument that the Red Army's best course of action in 1941 would have been to retreat, as Kutuzov did in 1812, ignored the differences in the situation. In 1812 the retreat did not hand over the country's industrial capacity to Napoleon; most of that was in and around St Petersburg, which was not threatened, and Moscow was then neither the capital nor Russia's major production centre. Mechanical transport, an essential component of an industrial society, did not exist in 1812, whereas in 1941 much of the rail system centred on Moscow. The uneasiness about loss of territory that prompted Hitler to fly to Manstein's headquarters on 17 February 1943 derived at least in part from anxiety about Manstein's apparent willingness to abandon the Donbass, the largest Soviet industrial and mining area still in German hands, and his apprehensions subsided only after Manstein explained that the retreat was a matter of '*reculer pour mieux sauter*', concentrating forces for a blow that would destroy many of the enemy and recover the temporarily abandoned territory – and that is precisely what his offensive achieved.

On the Soviet side, Stalin's refusal to sanction withdrawals in 1941 contributed to the enormous losses of the first six months, but the losses would have been great even without them, because soldiers on foot could not outrun soldiers in tanks or lorries, and the Red Army was not well supplied with lorries until the Lend-Lease trickle from the United States became a torrent in 1943. The attempts to stand firm at whatever cost, though catastrophic militarily, gained enough time to evacuate the machinery and work force of many factories in the European USSR. Anastas Mikoyan, who played a leading role in the evacuations, said in an interview in the 1970s that by December 1941 about 3,000 enterprises had been evacuated to the rear.[207] From the end of 1941 onwards they contributed greatly to Soviet war production from their new locations. As mentioned earlier, in the preamble to the notorious 'Not one step back' Order no. 227 of August 1942, Stalin justified its severity precisely in terms of the serious economic consequences of past retreats and catastrophic implications of any future ones.

Awareness of the importance of economic and industrial strength for waging a long modern war inevitably made national leaders such as Hitler and Stalin more sensitive to territorial gains and losses than their generals, whose main objective was to exploit terrain so as to preserve their own forces and destroy those of the enemy. The tensions that arose periodically between the dictators and their military professionals can probably be more readily understood as manifesting these conflicting priorities rather than by simply attributing a permanent 'stand fast' or 'attack at all costs' obsession to either dictator.

Manstein's successful counter-offensive did not counterbalance the disaster at Stalingrad, but it showed the Red Army that it still faced a formidable antagonist for the 1943 campaigning season. An incidental result of the fighting was the formation of the Kursk salient, which would become the focus of that year's German summer offensive. In the remaining weeks before the lull imposed by the spring thaw Stavka attempted to capitalise on the dangerous exposure of Army Group Centre's southern flank caused by the German 2nd Army's retreat of almost 200 kilometres (120 miles) to Rylsk following its breakout from encirclement at Voronezh. Rokossovsky's Don Front was renamed Central Front, and on 25 February began an attempt to get behind Army Group Centre with a thrust north-westwards by one tank army (2nd) and three infantry armies (21st, 65th, 70th), a cavalry corps, three ski brigades and a tank regiment. Kluge hastily brought in divisions released from the Rzhev salient by the first stage of its abandonment, and stabilised the situation, aided by Manstein's successful offensive. That created serious problems for the Voronezh Front, which Stalin attempted to solve by transferring the Central Front's 21st Army to it, thus weakening Rokossovsky's offensive to the point where in late March he sought and received the dictator's permission to discontinue it. The spring thaw then supervened.

As in 1941, Stalin's overestimation of the extent of German exhaustion had resulted in pressure for further advances, which now made his mobile forces vulnerable, outrunning their supply columns, thereby running short of fuel, ammunition and food, and of forage for their mostly horse-drawn transport, and lacking the strong air support they had had earlier because only a few of the newly captured airfields were as yet usable. His error of judgement cost the Bryansk, Voronezh and South-West Fronts 240,000 casualties (including 101,000 'irrevocable' losses), leading to retreats of 100–150 kilometres (62–95 miles), a second-time loss of the Donbass and third-time loss of Kharkov, before the spring thaw temporarily ended fighting.

Paul Carell's assessment of why Stalin and the Soviet General Staff so badly misread the situation puts it down to misleading information from Swiss General Staff reports, originating with a source named 'Werther', and passed to the Soviet-controlled 'Lucy' ring by Rudolf Roessler. The credibility of 'Lucy' will be examined in more detail later, in connection with the battle of Kursk. Here it is enough to note that, as Carell points out, reports sent after 11 February said that the Germans were retreating; specifically he cites Report no. 291 of 17 February, to the effect that 'German resistance . . . is now confined to covering the German withdrawal from the Donets bend, first of all to a line from the Dnepr bend to the Sea of Azov, in the second leap to the line Dnepr bend–Demyansk, in the third leap to the Lower Dnepr'.[208] Carell suggests that Stalin and his commanders believed information from 'Werther' because it was normally excellent, and that 'Werther', presumed to be a member of OKW or OKH in Hitler's East Prussian headquarters, was misled on this occasion because the important decisions were not being taken there but at Manstein's headquarters, and that Hitler himself was at his forward HQ at Vinnitsa. Carell argues that, precisely as did the Soviets, OKW staff officers remote from the action misread as retreats the westward moves by units that Manstein was grouping into a 'fist', and that

'Werther' reported accordingly in good faith. This thesis is perhaps supported by evidence that Hitler too was uneasy about them, until Manstein reassured him that they were only 'temporary'. However, the head of the 'Lucy' ring, Alexander Rado, said in his memoirs that he acquired Roessler only in November 1942. It seems unlikely that anyone as congenitally distrustful as Stalin would become in only three months so trusting of a new source as to base his own strategy on its reports, especially as during that period Operations 'Uranus' and 'Saturn' had had to be modified because of gaps in information that neither 'Werther' nor any other of Roessler's reports had filled. That the reports proved so misleading provides some ammunition for the argument of at least one contemporary Russian analyst that 'Lucy' was a German-controlled disinformation agent.

There is, in any case, no need to seek a foreign source for Stalin's euphoria. In January 1942 he had reacted to Zhukov's successful limited counter-offensive at Moscow by ordering its expansion to a general offensive, based on an assumption that the Germans were more weakened than they actually were, and overruling the objections of both Shaposhnikov and Zhukov. By the end of January 1943 he had far more to be euphoric about. The winter campaign's successes had far outstripped those of a year earlier, with six hostile armies (two German, two Romanian, one Italian, one Hungarian) destroyed, many other formations severely mauled, and the siege of Leningrad partially lifted; and this time the military too were euphoric, to the extent of interpreting all German westward moves as part of a general retreat to the Dnepr.

The blocking of Soviet oil traffic from Transcaucasus, one of the stated objectives of Germany's 1942 summer offensive, had required its forces to insert themselves somewhere along the Volga. They had achieved that objective north of Stalingrad in August, but then spent three months in fruitless attempts to capture a city they did not need and had virtually destroyed by bombing, thereby negating any use it might be to the Soviet enemy, before any of their troops even set foot in it. This was largely due to the symbolic importance of its name, but we should not overlook the willingness of generals such as Weichs and Paulus to pour more and more men and equipment into a fight they had no strategic need to undertake, and to do so at the end of a long flank defended only by the forces of less well-equipped and less motivated allies, whom German commanders and troops, influenced by Nazi 'Master Race' ideology, often alienated even further by displays of arrogance and uncooperativeness. As Yeremenko later put it, the German High Command's biggest error was 'to underestimate the power of the Soviet nation and its armed forces, at the same time overestimating its own ability'.

But the overestimation was not confined to Hitler and a handful of generals at OKW and OKH. Their errors were undoubtedly compounded by the appointment of Paulus to command the 6th Army. Almost his entire career had been as a staff officer and planner, and he had played a large part in drafting the 'Barbarossa' plan, but he had never previously commanded anything larger than a regiment – and that only temporarily, in a peacetime exercise in the 1920s, in which the directing staff had noted that he 'lacked decisiveness'.[209] In short, his experience as a field commander was almost as limited as that of Kirponos, Pavlov and Kuznetsov in the previous year; why Hitler selected him to command Germany's largest army and undertake one of the two main offensives of 1942 remains unclear. Paulus's main asset in Hitler's mind may simply have been that he was not 'von Paulus' – i.e. he did not come from the hereditary aristocracy that for so long dominated the senior ranks of the army, a practice that reached a temporary peak in September 1940 when seven of Hitler's nine newly created field marshals (all except Keitel and List) were 'vons'. However, Hitler frequently expressed dislike and contempt for that class, and chose no member of it for the military posts closest to him (Keitel and Jodl at OKW, successively Halder, Zeitzler, Guderian and Krebs at OKH). There certainly was a social and may even have been a security aspect – many military aristocrats took no pains to conceal their contempt for 'the Corporal' (Hitler's First World War rank), but only near the end of the war did it emerge that some of them, notably Henning von Tresckow and Claus von Stauffenberg, had organised several attempts to assassinate him. However that may be, Paulus's was a strange and ultimately disastrous appointment.

As noted earlier, Hitler's original plan was for the advances to the Volga and Transcaucasus to be undertaken consecutively, but in mid-July he made them simultaneous. This was a major strategic error, again based on serious underestimation of the enemy, and largely engendered by the apparent weakness of Soviet resistance to the German drive along the Don in early July. That, in turn, was due to the belief, wrongly but firmly held at that time by Stalin and the General Staff, that Moscow would be the main German target for 1942, which led them to retain reserves in the Moscow area for longer than necessary, at the expense of the front in the south; in a bizarre illustration of war as an interactive process, a rather large Soviet strategic error helped to create an even larger German one.

Although the Soviet preparations for the Stalingrad counter-offensive were masked as thoroughly as possible, their sheer scale meant they could not be totally concealed. German air reconnaissance discovered on 12 November that artillery was being moved into previously dug emplacements, and on that day Gehlen produced an assessment that, contrary to what he had reported on the 6th, suggested an attack across the Don to isolate Stalingrad was imminent. As mentioned earlier, in his post-war memoirs he claimed that this constituted a prediction of the counter-offensive, but he failed to grasp that the objective was not to compel the forces at Stalingrad to withdraw, but to encircle and destroy them, and he had no awareness of the intended follow-ups by 'Saturn' and 'Ring'. The outcome was a major failure of German Intelligence, and a major success for its Soviet counterpart, achieved by a skilful combination of measures, including disinformation conveyed through Max, deceptive use of radio traffic, and success in concealing the scale of movements of troops, equipment and supplies.

As the summer went on Hitler had taken control of the campaign more and more into his own hands. Having dismissed von Bock in July, he dismissed List in August and Halder in September. Then, in the last days of October, as the preparations for Operation 'Uranus' were nearing completion, he left his field headquarters and returned to Munich to prepare for the annual commemoration there of the abortive Nazi 'Beerhall' putsch of 1923. Events in places other than Soviet territory engaged much of his attention for the next three weeks. The first of these, the second Battle of El Alamein, began on 23 October, and the British soon forced the Afrika Korps into a retreat that would end only when it reached Tunisia. On 7 November Anglo-American forces landed in French North Africa, so Hitler ordered preparations made for invading unoccupied France and reinforcing the African theatre. After making his speech in Munich on 9 November, he did not return immediately to his headquarters in East Prussia, but went instead to the Berghof, his mountain retreat at Berchtesgaden, unaccompanied by any officer from OKH, the body responsible for the Eastern Front from Leningrad southwards. That suggests that, like Gehlen, he did not expect any major developments there in the near future. He stayed at the Berghof until 23 November, during which time his only reaction to the launch of Operation 'Uranus' on 19 November was to replace von Weichs by von Manstein in command of Army Group B, renamed Army Group Don, to order 6th Army to hold its positions in Stalingrad, and to promise to send two panzer, one mountain and two infantry divisions to reinforce it.

Only after the two pincers of 'Uranus' met at Kalach on 23 November did he prepare to return to Rastenburg. Before leaving, he rejected Jodl's suggestion of a withdrawal from the Volga, ordered Paulus to move his headquarters eastwards from Gumrak, west of Stalingrad, into the city centre, refused his request for 'freedom of action' (i.e. the freedom to decide whether or not to retreat westwards), and told him of possible supply by air. When he arrived back at his headquarters late on 23 November he spoke by radio to Paulus, repeated his 'stand fast' order, and again mentioned the possibility of supply by an airlift.

This had a precedent. In early 1942 the Luftwaffe had successfully supplied the troops in the Demyansk pocket by air for ten weeks, until Army Group North opened a corridor through to them. The encircled force, initially comprising 95,000 men, and besieged from 8 February to 21 April 1942, was supplied and maintained throughout by the Luftwaffe, including flying in 15,000 reinforcements and bringing out 22,000 sick and wounded, for a loss of 262 aircraft – a bearable average loss of fewer than four aircraft a day.[210]

Relying on this experience, on 24 November Goering undertook similarly to supply the forces besieged at Stalingrad. This undertaking was totally irresponsible, in that it ignored the major differences between the two situations. At Demyansk the worst of the winter was over before the airlift began; as time passed the days became longer, making more daylight flights possible, and the rising temperatures made living and aircraft maintenance easier. The Soviet air forces were so weak at that time that they never raided the airfields at the dispatching end of the route, and attacked those at the receiving end only sporadically. Last, but far from least, there were at that time no other substantial demands on the Luftwaffe's fleet of transport aircraft.

At Stalingrad, in contrast, the forces to be supplied were initially at least three times as numerous as those at Demyansk, and winter had just begun, so daylight hours would lessen and temperatures fall as time passed, making supply and maintenance more difficult. The encirclement was by Soviet ground forces much larger and better-equipped than those at Demyansk; during the year the Soviet air force had achieved qualitative near-parity in fighters and bombers, superiority in ground attack aircraft, and numerical superiority in all types; its aircrews had become much more proficient and willing to take on the Luftwaffe than previously; and large numbers of anti-aircraft guns were available to deploy along the flight path. Besides, Hitler's response to the British advance from Egypt and the Anglo-American landings in French North Africa had been to impose on the Luftwaffe unprecedentedly massive demands for transport aircraft to take troops and equipment to the African theatre.

Goering's undertaking was therefore completely beyond the Luftwaffe's capabilities. Chief of Staff Jeschonnek and Luftflotte IV's commander von Richthofen expressed strong objections to it at the time, but Goering's promise was what Hitler wanted to hear, so he overruled them. The same obstinacy prevented any attempt to save the besieged. Between 22 November 1942 and 30 January 1943 Manstein, Paulus, Jodl and Zeitzler between them made at least eleven requests for Paulus to be permitted to withdraw from Stalingrad, and at least three for him to be authorised to negotiate a surrender; Hitler rejected them all.[211]

The Soviet planning and execution of the counter-offensive indicated a high level of competence in the General Staff, and an increase in Stalin's willingness to heed military advice, in particular from Zhukov and Vasilevsky. Only towards the end of winter, when he yet again overestimated German exhaustion and pushed his forces beyond prudent limits, did his previous tendency to underrate the Wehrmacht manifest itself. And here he was not alone; Shtemenko noted that in respect of Manstein's counter-offensive the General Staff made the same mistake, which he attributed to faulty Intelligence reports.[212]

In human terms the Soviet side paid an enormous price for victory. Granted that the smallness of the 62nd Army's bridgehead in the city limited the number of troops that could be maintained there at any one time, more could perhaps have been done to relieve the pressure on the city's defenders, particularly by more and larger-scale attacks against the 6th Army's flank across the Don–Volga land bridge. However, the purpose of 'active defence' of the ruins was to wear down the enemy forces and distract their attention from the build-up of Soviet strength northwest and south of the city for the planned counter-offensive; and the fact of survival despite enormous losses in the first six months of the war had to a large extent conditioned commanders and troops alike to regard high casualty levels as normal and endurable.

It is not possible to disentangle the individual contributions of Stalin, Zhukov, Vasilevsky and the Front commanders (Rokossovsky, Yeremenko and Vatutin) to the battle, but some tentative points can be made. As already stated, in conceiving the plan for the counter-offensive Zhukov and Vasilevsky started from the knowledge that the process of forming new reserve armies would be complete by the end of October, and full- or near full-strength tank and mechanised infantry units with the latest equipment would be available by mid-November; they judged that in the meantime German attention must be kept fixed on Stalingrad by 'active defence'. Stalin decided what reserves to send to the front, and when and where to send them, but advice from Zhukov and Vasilevsky influenced many of his decisions. Comparison of the numbers involved and losses incurred in the Moscow battle, commanded by Zhukov, and that at Stalingrad, largely shaped by Stalin, shows common features. In both, units deployed in the defensive battle incurred very heavy losses, while reserves were accumulated for a counter-offensive, in which losses were far fewer, as Table 9 shows.[213]

The effect of the accumulation of reserves during 1942, mentioned by Zhukov, emerges from the contrast between the improvised counter-offensive at Moscow, for which fewer troops were available than for the preceding defensive battle, and the carefully planned one at Stalingrad, for which about twice as many were deployed as in the defensive phase.

Table 9. Ratios of losses between defensive and offensive battles

Battle	Numbers (A)	Losses* (B)	B as per cent of A
Moscow defensive	1,250,000	514,338	41.1 per cent
Moscow offensive	1,021,700	139,586	13.7 per cent
Stalingrad defensive	547,000	323,856	59.2 per cent
Stalingrad offensive	1,143,500	154,885	13.5 per cent
Kursk defensive	1,272,700	70,300	5.5 per cent
Kursk offensives	2,431,600	184,140	7.6 per cent

* Killed, captured, missing

The proportionally very high casualties in the defensive phases at Moscow and Stalingrad, compared to the counter-offensives that followed, suggest that in both cases available forces were deliberately reserved for the counter-offensive, a procedure that was perhaps militarily justifiable by the results, but for some units involved in the defensive battles amounted to a collective death sentence, and provided ammunition for post-Soviet attacks on Zhukov as seeking always to win at all costs and indifferent to casualties. The figures for Kursk are included to show how losses in the defensive battle could be kept down when, unlike at Moscow and Stalingrad, there was ample time to prepare the defences well in advance, and the experience of the earlier battles to draw on.

As mentioned earlier, one reason for uncertainty about the total numbers surrounded at Stalingrad is that many of them were captured Soviet soldiers serving as volunteers in German units. One post-Soviet account gives a figure of 'about 398,000' for Soviet nationals killed or captured while serving with the Wehrmacht or Waffen SS, but says nothing about the source of the figures,[214] nor whether they include auxiliaries who served with *Einsatzkommandos*, in security police units, as prison and concentration camp guards, or in anti-partisan operations. The same source claims that on average 10 per cent of the personnel of the German infantry divisions were Soviet *Hilfswillige*, and in the supply columns the proportion was as high as 50 per cent. If that is so, then there were at least 20,000 and maybe as many as 30,000 former Soviet soldiers in the 20 encircled German divisions.

Anecdotal evidence suggests that Soviet units quite often shot captured *Hilfswillige*, especially officers, in accordance with Stalin's Orders nos 270 and 227, but no figures are available. However, it is possible to put approximate figures to the numbers of civilians who were outside Soviet jurisdiction in Germany or German-occupied territory till the end of the war, and were not repatriated. A study of civilian losses during the war, published in 1995, tabulated the numbers of civilians taken from occupied territory to forced labour in Germany. These totalled 5.3 million; 2.2 million of them did not survive the war, 2.7 million were repatriated, and 451,000 stayed abroad. That means that one in seven of those still alive at the end of the war chose to avoid returning to the Soviet Union – and an unknown number of the 2.7 million who did return might have avoided doing so if they had had an opportunity.[215]

It is quite clear that the Soviet-era depiction of a nation and army totally united behind the Communist Party leadership contained a large fictional element, especially during the first 18 months. A wiser German regime could have exploited Soviet disaffection to much greater advantage. But a wiser regime would probably not have invaded, and would certainly not have gambled on defeating the world's largest country in just five months.

Post-Soviet official data record 3,137,673 'irrevocable' losses (killed, captured or missing) from 22 June to 31 December 1941, whereas German figures just for Soviet troops captured in the same period total 3,906,765.[216] The German figures may be inflated by the inclusion of non-military personnel such as police or railway workers taken into custody by troops unfamiliar with their uniforms, and of reservists captured before they could join their units, while the Soviet figures are widely considered understated, if only because many units' nominal rolls perished with the units in the series of encirclements that marked the first five months of the war. But comparison of German losses with the post-Soviet data is revealing. German 'irrevocable' losses from 22 June 1941 to 20 March 1942 were 276,550. Allowing for the German loss figures being for a longer period (272 days versus 193), the data translate into average losses of 16,257 Soviets and 1,017 Germans *per day*. And whereas the Germans several times made captures numbered in hundreds of thousands, the Soviets captured only 17,285 Germans in the first 12 months of the war (10,602 in 1941, 6,683 in January–June 1942). In the second half of 1942, which included the first six weeks of the Stalingrad counter-offensive, Soviet captures of Germans leapt to 172,143 (and, of course, large numbers of Italians, Romanians and Hungarians were also captured), and German losses from March to November 1942 almost trebled in total compared to the previous period, to 824,133, an average of 2,997 a day. Total Soviet losses ('irrevocable' and 'sanitary') for 1942, 3,258,216, averaging 8,927 a day, were still almost three times as high as the Germans', but even that was a marked improvement on 1941, where they had been sixteen times as high; and their daily average loss had been nearly halved, whereas Germany's had almost trebled.[217]

Soviet losses of weapons had also been staggering, as Table 10 shows.

Table 10: Soviet weapons losses in 1941 and 1942[218]

Type of weapon	Numbers lost (in thousands)		As per cent of total produced during entire war 1941–45	
	1941	*1942*	*1941*	*1942*
Rifles	6,290	3,310	40.7 per cent	21.4 per cent
Tanks/SP guns	20.5	15.1	21.2 per cent	15.6 per cent
Guns/Mortars	101	107.6	31.8 per cent	33.9 per cent
Combat aircraft	17.9	12.1	20.3 per cent	13.7 per cent

Direct comparisons with German figures for this period are complicated by the fact that the ones most readily available cover June 1941 to March 1942. In that period German army losses were 110,048 small arms, 3,492 tanks/SP guns and 17,377 guns/mortars. The easiest way to make comparisons with the Soviet losses tabled above is to divide the totals by the number of days covered, to give an average of each side's losses per day of war. The results are as follows:

Table 11. German and Soviet daily average losses

	German	Soviet
Troops (dead/missing)	1,017	17,120
Small arms	405	32,590
Tanks/SP guns	13	106
Guns/mortars	64	523

So per day of war in 1941, for every one German loss, Soviet losses were 17 soldiers, 80 rifles/pistols, 8 tanks/SP guns and 8 guns/mortars. Figures for aircraft are not included, but the scale of the debacle in the air can be illustrated from Soviet figures that of 1,200 aircraft lost on the first day, 800 were destroyed on the ground. By implication, the other 400 were shot down. By comparison, over 33 days of the Battle of Britain (13 August–15 September 1940) the RAF lost 915 aircraft and the Luftwaffe 1,741, daily average losses of 28 and 53 respectively. Soviet losses of 17,900 aircraft in 1941 averaged 93 a day, but that was cut by almost two-thirds in 1942 to 33 a day, reflecting experience, improved aircrew performance and direction, larger numbers of new and better aircraft, and increasing demands on the Luftwaffe in the Mediterranean basin and in defence of German airspace against British and, from mid-year also American, heavy bombers. However, of 62,600 Soviet aircraft lost from June 1941 to the end of 1943, only 31,400 were lost in combat. That means that almost exactly half the Soviet losses in that period were due to enemy raids on airfields, accidents, crew errors resulting from indiscipline or inexperience, or shortcomings in design, manufacture and/or maintenance of the aircraft. In 1944 the situation was even worse; 10,400 aircraft were lost in combat, but almost twice that number, 20,100, were lost in non-combat incidents.[219]

The improved performance of the Soviet armed forces was achieved despite a continued decline in the economy during 1942, the main features of which can be seen from the tables below.

Table 12: Some basic indicators of the Soviet economy, 1940–42[220]

Materials (million tonnes)	1940	1941	1942
Iron	14.9	13.9	4.8
Steel	18.3	17.9	8.1
Iron Ore	29.9	24.7	9.8
Coal	165.9	151.4	75.5
Oil (incl. gas condensate)	31.1	33	22

Comparing 1942 to 1940, production of iron ore and of iron dropped by two-thirds, of steel by almost as much, and coal by half. These falls mainly resulted from the loss of the Donbass. Oil production fell by about one-third, because of the loss of the Maikop-Grozny area in Transcaucasus, but liquid fuel supply fell by more, because from mid-August until the Volga froze in mid-December the Germans were able to interdict tanker traffic along it from their positions in the Stalingrad area.

Table 13. Key elements of Industrial Production[221]

	1940	*1941*	*1942*
Electric power (billion KwH)	48.3	46.7	29.1
Metal-working lathes (thousands)	58.4	44.5	22.9
Motor vehicles (thousands)	145.4	124.2	35
Ferrous metal sheet (million tonnes)	13.1	12.6	5.4

In 1942 compared to 1940, production of electric power was only 60 per cent, of lathes 39 per cent and of sheet metal 41 per cent. Yet tank and gun production increased, mainly through cutting vehicle manufacture to under a quarter of the pre-war level. This created further hardships not only for town-dwellers through problems of transporting food to them, but additionally for the peasants in the continually increasing demand for draft horses for the army, which had already taken most of their vehicles, a demand eased only in 1943 by the increased flow of trucks under Lend-Lease.

Table 14. Agricultural Stocks[222]

	1940	*1941*	*1942*
Sown area (million hectares)	150.4	108.1	67.3
Cattle (million)	54.5	31.4	28.4
Pigs (million)	27.5	8.2	
Sheep/goats (million)	91.6	70.6	61.8
Horses (million)	21	10	8.1
Tractors (thousands)	531	364	313
Combine harvesters (thousands)	182	141	119
Lorries (thousands)	228	66	43

This was a serious weakness. Compared to 1940, the sown area and numbers of draft horses were more than halved, livestock almost halved, tractors reduced by 40 per cent, and only one lorry available in 1942 for

every five there had been in 1940; and most able-bodied males had been
conscripted into the armed forces.

Table 15. Food Production (million tonnes)[223]

	1940	1941	1942
Meat	4.7	4.1	1.8
Milk	33.6	25.5	15.8
Grains	95.5	55.9	29.7
Potatoes	75.9	26.4	23.8
Sugar	2.165	0.523	0.114
Vegetable oils	0.798	0.685	0.253
Eggs (billion)	12.2	9.3	4.5

From a population of about 170 million in 1939, roughly 73 million,[224]
about 40 per cent, were in German-occupied areas in mid-1942. But, as
Table 15 shows, the fall in food supply was of the order of 60 per cent;
compared to 1940, supplies of meat and eggs in 1942 were little more than
one-third, of milk less than half, of cereals, potatoes and vegetable oils less
than one-third, and of sugar only 5 per cent. The falls reflected the loss
of much of the best farmland, particularly in Ukraine, and of tractors,
vehicles, horses and able-bodied male farm workers noted above.

In summary, industrial output in 1942 was just over three-quarters (77
per cent) of 1940, and food production just over one-third (38 per cent),
while expenditure on defence had risen in that period from 15 to 55 per
cent of the national income. The traumatic consequences for the population were extensively documented by the NKVD, but never made public
while the Soviet Union still existed. Extracts from one such report on
conditions in Vologda *oblast* (province) are enough to indicate the seriousness of problems in the rear areas, as this province was never invaded:

Centralised flour stocks for the first quarter of 1943 were reduced,
as a result of which a significant number of agriculture-associated
families of Red Army men, including forty thousand children, were
deprived of grain supply. As a consequence of the poor harvest in
1942 many of the soldiers' families did not receive grain as payment
for days worked on the collective farms, and at present have no food.
. . . in a number of areas there are numerous occurrences of substitutes (chaff, clover, straw, fur) and the corpses of animals that had
died being used as food . . . V.V. Kopylova, a soldier's wife, is

feeding entirely on substitutes. As a result her daughter has died of exhaustion. . . . A soldier's wife, M. Fedorova, who has five children, used the intestines of a dead horse as meat. As a result the entire family had serious poisoning.

Other extracts mentioned soldiers' wives preparing meals from horse-meat soaked on vet's orders in formaldehyde, or from dog meat, and in one case from a wolf shot by a hunter.

There had been at least one attempted suicide, by a soldier's wife with four children and no food, and 'many soldiers' families are in the same position . . . From the most backward section of collective farm members of soldiers' families, there are instances of expression of negative attitudes. Measures taken by the local organs are ineffective because of inadequacy of the grain stocks in the province.'[225]

Kobulov's superior, Beria, took the issue to an even higher level, in a report of early 1943 to the State Defence Committee and Stalin. This related to Chita oblast, in East Siberia, several thousand kilometres from the front line. 'In individual collective farms . . . the collective farmers are using dead animals and various substitutes as food. In a number of collective farms the workers do not come out to work because they have no bread . . .' The report went on to give particular details of different areas: in one 56 families, in another 112, in a third 360 individuals '215 of whom are members of soldiers' families' had 'no food whatsoever. Because of lack of bread and other food there are cases of illness and protein-deficient swelling among children of collective farm workers, especially in families of those mobilised into the Red Army.' Among other incidents mentioned in Beria's report were the November 1942 murder by a collective farmer of his mother, wife and six children, before shooting himself, leaving a note saying starvation had forced him to commit the crime, and in December a case of cannibalism, the murder of a 12-year-old boy, whose corpse 'was chopped up and used for food' by his killers.

As with Kobulov's report, Beria's was prompted not by concern at the hardships being experienced by soldiers' families working on farms far away from the front line, but by the possibility that they would engender disaffection. 'On the basis of difficulties with food, a growth in negative attitudes is observed among the unstable part of the collective farm workers. In collective farms in the frontier areas . . . a series of collective farm workers has been exposed as displaying emigrational attitudes. It has been established by investigation that a large section of them are experiencing insufficiency of food products.'[226] The only places to which these workers could 'emigrate' were Mongolia or the Japanese-occupied puppet state of Manchukuo, and that they could even fantasise about doing so indicates how serious the food situation had become; they were, after all, growers of food, with no reason to fear German occupation – the only Germans within 4,000 miles were prisoners of war.

There was also hardship among the urban population, especially in besieged Leningrad; at the lowest point in 1942 the daily bread ration for civilian non-manual workers there was three slices. But town dwellers had ration cards, which the rural population did not, and essentially the farm stocks were pillaged to feed the armed services and urban weapons producers. However, hunger did not bypass the towns, nor did the situation improve as the war turned in Soviet favour. There was another poor harvest in 1943, and as late as October 1944 incidents mentioned in a report by Beria on the situation in the Far East included cases of scurvy and dysentery among factory workers in Khabarovsk, numerous corpses being found in the streets of Komsomolsk, and infant mortality in Birobidzhan of 86.9 per cent (i.e. about seven of every eight infants dying within one year of birth). He noted that the increase in crime

> especially in the first half of 1944 results mainly from bad material conditions. The highest number of crimes are committed by workers employed by the large industrial enterprises of Khabarovsk and Komsomolsk . . . of 606 persons arrested for crimes in Komsomolsk, 583 are workers in defence plants and other enterprises in the town; 421 of them had no previous criminal record . . .[227]

If that was the situation in areas remote from the front line, and when the war was clearly being won, it requires little imaginative effort to grasp what life was like in areas where fighting took place and when the Germans still appeared to be winning. The food situation was to some extent alleviated by Lend-Lease shipments. They totalled about 4.7 million tonnes, small beer compared even to the poor Soviet harvests of 1941–43, but consisting largely of processed meat, dehydrated foods and powdered eggs, so of high nutritional value for their weight. They went mostly to the army, but at least reduced its demands on the civilian economy. Nevertheless, as the NKVD reports indicated, deaths from hunger were not a rarity even in remote areas of the country.

Conditions in the occupied territories were even worse. Of their pre-war population of about 88 million, 15 million were evacuated before the

Germans arrived; data put together in post-Soviet times indicate that 7.4 million of the 73 million who stayed were killed by the Germans and their collaborators or allies, some in accordance with General Plan 'East', which aimed to depopulate areas occupied by 'inferior' races to create room for German settlers, others as punishment for harbouring partisans. In addition it is estimated that 4.1 million died from hunger, infectious diseases or lack of medical care, and another 2.2 million while in forced labour in Germany. These add up to 13.7 million, more than half the estimated combined total of 26.6 military and civilian deaths, and 18.8 per cent of the population of the occupied areas; so almost one in every five Soviet citizens who came temporarily under German rule did not survive the war.[228] Not surprisingly, those who could escape increasingly took to the forests to become partisans, or joined underground Party organisations.

Chapter Five

Germany under Pressure

The repulse in December of Hoth's attempt to break through to Stalingrad enabled the Soviet command to reactivate one of the original elements of 'Saturn', the attempt to cut off the retreat of Army Group A from the Caucasus. The General Staff recommended that the Southern (formerly Stalingrad) Front, while directing its main effort towards Rostov-on-Don, should use some of its forces to take Tikhoretsk; by so doing it would cut off Army Group A from Rostov, and threaten the rear of its 1st Panzer Army. Simultaneously, the Black Sea group of the Transcaucasus Front was to thrust northwards to meet the Southern Front's forces at Tikhoretsk, and expand towards Krasnodar and Novorossiysk, while its Northern Group was to keep the Germans too busily engaged to break away or manoeuvre.

Shtemenko says anxiety was caused by information that the Germans had learned of the preparations for the Novorossiysk operation, but 'further investigation did not confirm that there had been a leak'.[229] This is rather disingenuous; as mentioned earlier, that a major offensive was intended in Transcaucasus was among the information on four such operations (including 'Mars' but not 'Uranus/Saturn') mentioned earlier as deliberately 'leaked' in Agent Max's 4 November 1942 message to Gehlen, composed in the General Staff and approved by Shtemenko himself. That the Germans knew what was coming is also indirectly confirmed by Shtemenko's own statement that 'the enemy did not wait for us to put our plans into practice. At the very moment when GHQ issued its directive concerning the attack on Tikhoretsk, the Nazi command began withdrawing its 1st Panzer Army from the Terek to the north-west', though he attributes this to the realisation 'that its rear was unavoidably threatened by Southern Front',[230] a dubious attribution, since on his own testimony the Directive to the Southern Front was not issued until 31 December, and by then Hitler had already authorised withdrawal from the Caucasus.[231] The 1st Panzer Army withdrew across the Don and held the vital crossings at Rostov until 14 February, while the 17th Army pulled back westwards, completing by 6 February its retreat to the 'Gothic Line' and Taman peninsula, from where further withdrawal into the Crimea could and would be made over the relatively narrow Kerch Straits. The withdrawals were skilfully conducted, as were those by Army Groups North and Centre from the Demyansk and Rzhev salients in the following few weeks, but, as Churchill said about Dunkirk, 'wars are not won by withdrawals'.

However, a withdrawal on one sector can provide resources for an attack elsewhere, and that is precisely what happened. About seven divisions-worth of German units, freed in the early stages of abandonment of the Rzhev salient, were dispatched to the southern end of Army Group Centre's line, to reinforce the 2nd Panzer Army. Five of them (two panzer and three infantry divisions) helped bring to a halt the poorly planned, inadequately supplied and over-ambitious offensives that Stalin insisted on the Western, Bryansk, Voronezh and Central (formerly Don) Fronts undertaking before the spring thaw in March–April.

Manstein's counter-offensive took the form of a strong strike by Army Group South against the left wing of Vatutin's South-West Front in the Donbass area, and was applied at full force on 19 February 1943. It achieved complete surprise; though Vatutin belatedly ordered his men on to the defensive, they were unable to hold their positions, and by the beginning of March had retreated to the line of the Seversky Donets river. This in turn exposed the left flank of Vatutin's northern neighbour, the Voronezh Front, which had recaptured Kharkov on 16 February and was still attempting to advance. The Front Commander, Colonel-General F.I. Golikov, was even slower than Vatutin to react to the danger, and hastily ordered his forces to take up defensive positions only on 3 March. They had no time to do this in an organised way, because on the next morning the 4th Panzer Army and Army Detachment Kempf attacked from south-east of Kharkov, driving the Voronezh Front back to the north and north-east, with heavy casualties, partial loss of control and several instances of troops fleeing in panic, abandoning their guns and tanks. By 14 March the Germans had encircled Kharkov, and they retook it two days later.

Stalin judged the situation serious enough to order Zhukov and Vasilevsky to the Voronezh Front on the day Kharkov fell, because, as Shtemenko delicately put it, 'it was impossible to compile an objective picture from Golikov's reports'.[232] They succeeded in 'not only uncovering but partially rectifying major inadequacies in the directing of our forces'[233] and also studied the situation at another danger point further north, the junction between the Western and Central Fronts. There had previously been another army group, the Bryansk Front, between them, but in order to centralise control over the forces attempting to take Orel this had been abolished and its forces resubordinated to the two neighbouring Fronts. However, since it was at the extreme flanks of both, neither Sokolovsky at Western nor Rokossovsky at the Central Front 'had been able to give it the necessary attention'.[234] Zhukov and Vasilevsky recommended reconstituting the Bryansk Front, sending Golikov to command it and replacing him at the Voronezh Front with Vatutin, who had previously commanded it in 1942. In view of their criticisms of Golikov, their recommendation that he command the recreated Bryansk Front was surprising, and Stalin accepted it only as a temporary measure; by 31 March Golikov had been replaced by Vatutin,[235] was in effect 'kicked upstairs' to head the Personnel Directorate of the General Staff, and was never again entrusted with a field command. Zhukov is unlikely to have shed any tears over that; during the 1937–38 purges Golikov, who at that time outranked him, had sought to have him investigated as a potential 'enemy of the people' (an episode described only in post-Soviet editions of his memoirs).[236] By 25 March, after the Voronezh Front had retreated 100–150 kilometres (about 62–93 miles), its line was stabilised, and the onset of the spring thaw then enforced a pause on both sides.

Despite the setback in the south, the increases in Red Army manpower and equipment that had made the Stalingrad counter-offensive possible were continuing, and shifting the balance further against Germany. To economise on manpower and create reserves, Army Group North between 15 and 28 February abandoned the Demyansk salient, until then held by 12 divisions, and between 2 and 31 March Army Group Centre abandoned in stages its positions nearest to Moscow (about 112 miles from the Kremlin), in the Rzhev-Vyazma salient, which it had successfully defended for over a year against repeated Soviet attacks. The heavy cost to the Soviets of Operation 'Mars' in November–December 1942 (discussed previously) has to be assessed against the fact that the successful German defence of the Rzhev-Vyazma salient had required 30 divisions,[237] at least three of which had already been packing to go south, and would have been joined by others if 'Mars' had not been mounted. Abandonment of the salient in March reduced the front line in that sector from 330 to 125 miles, releasing most of the divisions deployed there for Army Group Centre to use elsewhere or put into reserve; at least six of them subsequently fought in the battle of Kursk in July.

The evacuation of the two salients was presented to the Soviet public as the consequence of successful Red Army offensives. In fact both were well-organised and skilfully conducted withdrawals in stages behind strong rearguards, and the pursuing Soviet forces received at least as much damage as they inflicted. There was, nevertheless, an element of truth in the Soviet claims. Successful offensives had indeed prompted the evacuations, but they were those of Operations 'Uranus', 'Little Saturn' and 'Ring', where the destruction of 20 German divisions in the Stalingrad pocket, six more outside it, heavy losses in several others, and the virtual elimination of the Romanian 3rd and 4th, Hungarian 2nd and Italian 8th Armies had intensified the already manifest German manpower shortages. The strategic and psychological effects on both sides were also strong, in the obvious removal of any residual threat either salient might pose to Leningrad or Moscow, and the shortened line freed not only German but also Soviet forces for use elsewhere. At Leningrad the blockade would not be completely lifted for another year, but the effects of Operation 'Iskra' ('Spark') in January, achieving limited restoration of land links with the 'mainland', were also becoming tangible. Over two years the perilous 'Road of Life' over the frozen lake in winter, and ferries in the other seasons, had taken in 1.6 million tonnes of food, ammunition, fuel and equipment, and brought out 1.4 million evacuees, but now was no longer needed.[238] In the far south the North-Caucasus Front ended its Krasnodar offensive on 16 March, after advances of up to 70 kilometres (44 miles), and on 28 March the Central (formerly Don) Front did the same, after advancing about 150 kilometres (93 miles). In these areas, as at Demyansk and Rzhev-Vyazma, much of the action presented to the Soviet public as resulting from victories in battle was really pursuit of a skilfully withdrawing enemy, but that the Germans found it necessary to withdraw at all was a moral victory additional to those gained on the Volga-Don battlefields.

During the weeks of inactivity imposed by the spring thaw both sides began planning for the coming summer. In the interim, Zhukov secured Stalin's agreement to reinforce the Voronezh and Central Fronts with three entire armies (1st Tank, 21st and 64th) from Stavka Reserve. Granted a Soviet 'army' was much smaller than a German one, the contrast manifested the changing balance of forces; while Germany was having to abandon long-held positions to save manpower, the Red Army was fielding substantial new forces. Furthermore, it was also out-producing Germany in the tanks, guns and aircraft needed to equip them. The early trickle of Lend-Lease supplies was now becoming a torrent, almost doubling from 2.45 million tons in 1942 to 4.8 million in 1943.[239]

Supplies of American trucks and jeeps (118,000 during 1942 alone, over three times as many as the 34,900 produced by Soviet plants) gave the Red Army's infantry and artillery mobility on a scale Germany could not match, and enabled the Soviet vehicle industry to concentrate on producing tanks and self-propelled guns. American deliveries of transport aircraft similarly freed Soviet factories to produce fighters and bombers of new and improved types with which to take on the Luftwaffe.

When the situation stabilised, the Central Front was occupying the northern and Voronezh Front the southern face of an enormous salient, about 120 miles from north to south and over 60 miles from west to east, centred on Kursk, between two German salients, around Orel to the north and Kharkov to the south. The Kursk salient became the focal point of both sides' planning for the summer campaigning season.

In German planning the rivalries between OKH, responsible for the Eastern Front except for the Finnish sector, and OKW, in charge of that sector and of all other theatres, soon showed themselves. In the spring of that year 187 (67.5 per cent) of Germany's 277 divisions were on the Eastern Front,[240] and demand for manpower was increased by Hitler's insistence that OKW reinforce the North African theatre, to prevent or at least postpone collapse there, because if the Anglo-Americans were victorious, their next move would be a return to the European mainland.

Despite the reinforcements sent to North Africa, Axis resistance there collapsed in May, and the enhanced risk of an Anglo-American invasion prompted senior OKW officers such as Jodl and Warlimont[241] to argue for divisions to be withdrawn from the East to strengthen the Western and Mediterranean theatres. However, their chief, Field-Marshal Keitel, gave them no support, deferring, as ever, to Hitler's preferences. Guderian, recently restored to service as Inspector-General of Armoured Forces, strongly opposed mounting any major offensive at all in 1943. He saw such an undertaking as entailing the premature employment of the new Tiger heavy and Panther medium tanks, with their mechanical reliability yet untested, their crews not yet adequately trained or experienced to exploit their advantages and cope with any shortcomings, and their numbers too small to implement his maxim 'klotzen, nicht kleckern' ('downpour, not drizzle'), all factors likely to prove important when the expected Anglo-American invasion added pressure in the West to the Wehrmacht's increasingly heavy burdens in the East.

OKH, not surprisingly, saw things differently. Manstein later said in his memoirs that he had wanted to eliminate the Kursk salient at once, even before the spring thaw, but that proved impossible for lack of reserves. Hitler's general instruction for the war in the East in 1943, Operations Order no. 5 of 13 March, stated:

> It can be expected that after the end of winter and the spring thaw the Russians, after creating reserves of material resources and partially reinforcing their formations with men, will renew the offensive. Therefore our task consists of pre-empting them if possible in the offensive in different places, with the aim of imposing our will on them on even one sector of the front, as at the present time is taking place on the front line of Army Group South [i.e. Manstein's offensive at Kharkov]. On the remaining sectors our task amounts to bleeding the attacking enemy. Here we must create a firm defence in good time.

In the North Caucasus Army Group A was simply to hold its positions on the River Kuban and 'free forces for other fronts'. Army Group North was to prepare for another strike at Leningrad, while Army Groups Centre and South were to plan to destroy the Soviet forces in the Kursk salient. To achieve this Army Group South must 'strike northwards from the Kharkov region in cooperation with an assault group of 2nd Army, to destroy the enemy forces operating before 2nd Army's front', and Army Group Centre was to create 'an assault group to be used for an offensive in cooperation with forces of the northern wing of Army Group South. Forces for this are to be freed by the withdrawal of troops of 4th and 9th Armies from the Vyazma area to a shortened line . . .'. While Field-Marshal Kluge was arranging this, Manstein was to undertake 'formation of an adequately combat-capable panzer army, concentration of which must be finished by mid-April, so that it can go over to the offensive at the end of the spring thaw'.

So the general concept of the German offensive at Kursk had been decided by mid-March. However, the proposal to launch it before the end of April, immediately after the thaw, proved totally unrealistic; neither troops nor equipment, especially adequate numbers of the new tanks, could be made available so soon. Delays in tank production, and also the time taken to satisfy Model's needs for making up to strength divisions worn down in Operation 'Mars',[242] prompted Hitler to postpone the offensive several times, eventually to ten weeks later than originally intended; and, as will be seen, the Soviet forces in, around and behind the salient made good use of the time gained by the successive delays.

Hitler issued Operations Order no. 6, for the offensive, codenamed Operation 'Zitadelle' ('Citadel'), on 15 April. Army Group Centre's 9th Army (Colonel-General Walter Model), with forces made available by its withdrawal during February–March from the Rzhev-Vyazma salient, and the 2nd Panzer Army (General Rudolf Schmidt, soon replaced by General Erhard Raus) were to attack the Central Front at the northern neck of the salient, while the 4th Panzer Army (Colonel-General Herman Hoth) and Army Detachment Kempf of Army Group South attacked the Voronezh Front at the southern neck. Their aim was to break through and advance to link up near Kursk, then, in cooperation with the 2nd Army's foot soldiers on the salient's west face, to destroy the encircled Soviet forces. Success in 'Citadel' was to be followed by the transfer of the 2nd Army and units from High Command Reserve to Army Group South, for an immediate south-eastward offensive (Operation 'Panther') 'to exploit the confusion in the enemy ranks',[243] and to retake those parts of the Donbass industrial and mining area not regained by Manstein's March offensive or ceded by line-shortening tactical withdrawals.

Forces of both army groups were to be concentrated in rear areas well away from their start-lines, and to be ready any time after 28 April to start the offensive six days after receiving orders to do so, 5 May being set as the earliest possible date. In the meantime Army Group South was ordered to mislead the enemy by conducting ostentatious preparations for Operation 'Panther', including 'demonstrative air reconnaissance, movement of tanks, assembly of pontoons, radio conversations, agent activity, spreading of rumours, air strikes, etc.' Army Group Centre was not required to play such elaborate tricks, but should deceive by devices such as moving forces to the rear, making fake redeployments, sending transport columns back and forth in daylight hours, and spreading false information dating the offensive to not earlier than June. All real movements were to be by night, and all units newly arriving must maintain radio silence.

Germany's defeat at Stalingrad and the evident imminence of a strategically comparable debacle in North Africa was causing some urgent rethinking among her allies. Italy had not stood to gain any territory or much economic benefit from Germany's war with the Soviet Union, and Mussolini's main reason for committing the Italian 8th Army to that war was the hope of ensuring that Hitler would respond in kind, after the expected rapid crushing of the Red Army, by making major forces available to help achieve the Duce's primary ambition, victory over the British in the campaign to dominate the Mediterranean basin and North Africa. A quarter of a million Italians served on the Eastern Front; about 80,000 of them died in battle or captivity, and over 43,000 suffered wounds or frostbite;[244] the survivors cursed the Duce for sending them to Russia, and their German 'brothers in arms' for their arrogance and uncooperativeness. Mussolini had already in November 1942 begun urging Hitler to make peace with Stalin so as to concentrate Axis forces against the anticipated Anglo-American invasions, first of Italy and eventually of the rest of German-occupied Western Europe. An indication of senior Italian military opinion was that General Ambrosio, the Army Chief of Staff, who had been insisting since November that all remaining Italian troops in Russia must be brought home, was promoted on 1 February 1943 to head the Commando Supremo,[245] and before the end of May all the surviving members of the 8th Army had arrived back in Italy. With the surrender in the middle of that month of all German and Italian forces in North Africa, the Berlin–Rome 'Axis' effectively became a dead letter, with Mussolini's dictatorship under threat and Italy beginning to seek a way out of the war.

Equally strong effects on other sufferers from the Stalingrad debacle, Romania and Hungary, would soon become apparent. By the opening of the battle of Kursk all Romanian forces had been withdrawn from Soviet territory, except from Moldova and Transdnistria, adjacent to and claimed by Romania, and only two divisions of the Hungarian 2nd Army remained with Army Group South, which employed them on occupation and anti-partisan duties, not as front-line troops.

The 'Conducator' of Romania, Marshal Antonescu, and the 'Regent' of Hungary, Admiral Horthy, had both begun covertly seeking contact with the British and Americans, in hopes of making peace with the West while continuing to fight against the approach of Communism from the East. Mussolini, on the other hand, continued to advocate coming to terms with the Soviet Union in order to concentrate forces against the expected Anglo-American invasion of Italy, and again wrote to Hitler to that effect on 17 March.[246] But his grip on power and Fascism's hold on Italy were already loosening; on 25 July he was deposed and arrested.

At the other extremity of the Eastern front, Finland hitherto had been Germany's militarily most competent and reliable ally, but maintained that its war, unlike Germany's, was defensive, a continuation of the 'winter war' of 1939–40, aiming not to destroy the Soviet Union but merely to recover the territories lost by that war. Marshal Mannerheim, who had been a lieutenant-general in the pre-revolutionary Russian Army, was well aware of the dangers of over-provoking Finland's giant neighbour, and had agreed to resume the post of Commander-in-Chief only on condition that Finnish forces would on no account take part in any attempt to capture Leningrad. As early as August 1941 President Ryti, on Mannerheim's insistence, had twice rejected requests from Keitel for the Finnish Army to advance north and east of Lake Ladoga, to link up with German forces advancing along its south shore, and thereby isolate Leningrad. To exercise more pressure Keitel sent his deputy, Jodl, to Finland on 4 September 1941, but Mannerheim remained firmly uncooperative, so exasperating Jodl that he burst out, 'Well, do something, to show goodwill!' To get rid of him, and not pre-judice Finland's negotiations with Germany for 15,000 tonnes of wheat, Mannerheim agreed to arrange a small diversionary offensive, but in the event did not make even that limited gesture.[247]

The main constraint on Finland's independent posture was its depen-dence on Germany for food and fuel. This dependence became even greater after the United Kingdom, an important pre-war trading partner, bowed to Soviet pressure and declared war on Finland on 6 December 1941, a day ironically significant in two ways: first, it was Finnish Independence Day, and secondly, it was the day that Mannerheim ordered the Finnish Army to go on to the defensive on all sectors imme-diately after capturing Medvezhegorsk, which it was about to do. He had already begun demobilising older soldiers at the end of November, and by the spring of 1942 had released 180,000 of them. Coincidentally, Zhukov launched the counter-offensive at Moscow on the day before Mannerheim ordered his army to cease attacking, and the day after he did so, Japan brought the United States into the war.

The Soviet victory at Moscow made a prolonged war inevitable, hence even more straining Finland's limited resources, and this was further intensified after Stalingrad. On 3 February, the day after the last German units there surrendered, and four days after the end of Operation 'Iskra' at Leningrad, President Ryti took the prime minister and two other ministers to confer with Mannerheim about 'the general situation'. They all agreed that Finland must seek a way out of the war, but that it could not do so immediately because of its economic dependence on Germany. On 9 February, at the defence minister's request, Mannerheim's Head of Intelligence, Colonel Paasonen, addressed a closed session of Parliament, ending his speech by advising the members to 'get used to the possibility that we shall once again be obliged to sign a peace treaty with Moscow'. On the 15th the opposition Social-Democratic Party brought the issue into the open with a public statement that 'Finland has the right to get out of the war at the moment it considers it desirable and possible'. An American offer of mediation was conveyed through the US embassy in Helsinki, and Foreign Minister Ramsay was sent to Berlin to tell the Germans of the American approach and try to extract a promise that German forces in Northern Finland would withdraw voluntarily if Finland requested their removal. No such promise was forthcoming; on the contrary, Foreign Minister Ribbentrop demanded that Finland not only reject the American approach, but also undertake to conclude neither truce nor armistice with Moscow without German consent.[248] Ramsay conceded neither demand, so Ambassador Bluecher suggested applying pressure by restricting supplies of food and fuel, but for the time being Ribbentrop declined to go that far.

Hitler had already summoned the leaders of Hungary, Romania and Slovakia to meetings to pull them into line, and Bluecher demanded that President Ryti, re-elected on 15 February 1943, make the same journey, but Ryti refused. Germany showed its displeasure by temporarily recalling Bluecher, then, from the beginning of June, stopping all deliveries of food to Finland and halving deliveries of fuel and lubricants. However, Germany could not risk antagonising its only ally with proven ability to fight the Red Army successfully (and with a record at that better in some respects than Germany's own). So the restrictions were lifted at the end of June, even though Finland had still made no concessions.

Most Finnish political and military leaders resisted even the thought of a lost war until at least the end of 1942, but Mannerheim had recognised the possibility much earlier, and throughout the year the Finnish Army not only undertook no offensives of its own but also refused to participate in German ones, such as the attempt to cut the railway along which about a quarter of Allied Lend-Lease supplies were transported from Murmansk and Archangelsk to central Russia.

The Finnish government periodically sounded public opinion by surveys, the results of which were published only after the war.[249] The differences in results of two surveys, one in September 1942, the other in January 1943, indicated how public opinion shifted in response to the Soviet victory at Stalingrad and, on Finland's own doorstep, to the success of Operation 'Iskra' in partially lifting the blockade of Leningrad. The surveys asked simply 'Do you believe Germany will win?' The results, in percentages, were as follows:

Survey	Conservatives	Social-Democrats	Communists
September 1942	90–95	55	70
January 1943	40–50	19	14

Finland had been stressed by its war effort to the extent of calling up 45-year-olds, and continued throughout 1943 to explore, quietly, so as not to arouse German suspicions, the possibilities for negotiating a way out of the war. In July the Soviet embassy in Stockholm conveyed a message through the Belgian ambassador, indicating willingness to negotiate, provided the initiative came from the Finnish side, but that approach was not followed up. Unlike the UK, the USA had not yet declared war on Finland, so during the summer of 1943 the Finnish government made a desperate attempt to secure American rather than Soviet or German occupation by notifying the State Department, via the US embassy in Lisbon, that if American forces landed in northern Norway and invaded Finland from there, the Finnish army would not resist them. However, the United States military had no interest in such a diversion, so nothing came of this. Finland did not in fact leave the war until September 1944, but that its leaders began seeking a way out on the very day of the final surrender at Stalingrad was evidence of that event's impact on Germany's allies, even on one that had no forces involved in the disaster.

To add to the Germans' problems, the outcome at Stalingrad had important effects on the population of German-occupied Soviet territory. The Wehrmacht's inability to achieve the anticipated lightning victory, and the behaviour of German occupation forces, had already considerably cooled the enthusiasm with which many, particularly in the Baltic states, former Polish or Romanian territory and Ukraine, had initially greeted the invaders; support or at least acceptance of their presence was widespread as long as they appeared to be winning. However, the debacle at Stalingrad alerted the inhabitants of occupied areas, whether pro- or anti-Soviet, to the likelihood that ultimately Soviet rule would return, then those who had resisted the invaders would be rewarded, any who had not would be severely punished, and any who had actively assisted them could expect a rope or a bullet.

The consequence was a great increase during the first half of 1943 in the numbers joining partisan units behind the German lines – according to one account numbers doubled, so that by March there were up to 100,000 in 1,047 detachments, and by the opening of 'Citadel' the numbers had risen to 142,000. With so many men available, increasingly controlled and supplied by the regular Fronts, large-scale partisan operations became possible for the first time; on the night of 22/23 June, for example, the rail system in Bryansk province was attacked. It was claimed that 4,100 rails were blown up, but that is undoubtedly an exaggeration, as the same account described the main line along which German reinforcements and supplies came in as blocked only 'for three whole days'.[250] However, an indication of the extent of partisan activity is that these attacks took place only three weeks after the conclusion of a major anti-partisan operation, 'Zigeunerbaron' ('Gypsy Baron'), in precisely that area.

Partisan activity, small-scale and sporadic in 1941, had grown until guerrilla raids became too large and frequent to be countered solely by *Einsatzkommandos*, police battalions and (mostly Ukrainian) auxiliaries. It became necessary to use army units as well, and this diverted large numbers of German and allied troops from their front-line duties. Operation 'Zigeunerbaron' was a classic example. While preparations for 'Citadel' were in full swing, the entire 18th Panzer Division and other units, including Hungarian troops and Soviet 'volunteers', had to spend two weeks 'purging' the forest areas south of Bryansk of partisan forces estimated at 3,000–3,500 strong. The 18th Panzer Division alone claimed to have destroyed 207 'camps' and 2,930 'combat positions', killed or captured 700 partisans, killed 1,584 unspecified 'others', taken 1,568 prisoners and received 869 Red Army deserters, evacuated 15,812 civilians and burned down all villages in the area, thereby seemingly denuding it both of partisans and of all sources of support for them. Yet the partisans were able to mount substantial and coordinated attacks on the rail system only three weeks after 'Zigeunerbaron' ended.[251]

For 'Citadel' Army Group Centre had available three panzer (41st, 46th and 47th) and two infantry (20th, 23th) corps, totalling 6 panzer, 1 panzer-grenadier (motorised infantry) and 14 infantry divisions, with over 900 tanks, supported by 730 aircraft. At Army Group South Hoth had three corps (52nd, 48th Panzer, 2nd SS Panzer) and so had Kempf (3rd Panzer, 42nd and Corps Raus), totalling between them 6 panzer, 5 panzer-grenadier and 11 infantry divisions, with about 1,000 tanks and 150 assault guns, and 1,100 aircraft. In reserve Army Group Centre had two panzer and one panzer-grenadier divisions, Army Group South one of each.[252] The seven infantry divisions of the 2nd Army, on the salient's west face, were to form the west side of the encirclement that the mobile forces were expected to create, and until that happened were to do just enough to prevent the enemy moving troops to other sectors. The forces available for 'Citadel' therefore totalled 55 divisions (15 panzer, 8 panzer-grenadier and 32 infantry). All 23 mobile and 15 of the infantry divisions were at or near full strength,[253] and they totalled about 900,000 men.

Even after the Directive was issued, there was still disagreement among the generals about the form 'Citadel' should take. On 4 May Hitler held a meeting in Munich with Kluge, Manstein, Guderian and Zeitzler, at which a letter from Model was considered, raising objections to the operation as planned because he still contended the resources allocated to him were inadequate. Possible alternatives discussed included simply attacking the west face of the salient, or allowing the Soviets to attack first, weakening them in a defensive battle, and then mounting a counter-offensive; Hitler rejected the first as necessitating too complex redeployments, and the second as 'too passive'.[254]

Had Hitler but known it, the defensive option he then disdained was the very one that Stalin had already chosen three weeks earlier, on Zhukov's recommendation. Apart from one day (25 March) in Moscow, Zhukov was with the Voronezh and Central Fronts from 17 March to 11 April,[255] and Vasilevsky joined him on 1 April. On 8 April Zhukov sent a telegram to Stalin, in which he stated categorically that the Germans' summer offensive would be against the Kursk salient, that there were two options, to disrupt their preparations by attacking first, or to wear them out in a defensive battle then launch a counter-offensive, and that he favoured the latter course. This meant temporarily surrendering the initiative, something generals normally prefer to avoid unless absolutely sure they know what the enemy intends to do. Yet Zhukov, an anything but 'passive' commander, proposed to build the entire Soviet strategy around what he expected the Germans to do, only a few weeks after February's major Intelligence failure to foresee Manstein's offensive, and a full week before Hitler even issued the Directive for 'Citadel'. Why were he and Stalin so sure that they knew what the Germans would do?

Neither Zhukov nor Vasilevsky ever explained the reasons for their certainty. Zhukov said only that 'by agreement' with Vasilevsky and the Front commanders a 'careful reconnaissance' of the enemy facing the Central, Voronezh and South-West Fronts was conducted in late March and early April, using Intelligence Directorate and partisan resources to establish 'presence and deployment of enemy reserves in depth . . . the course of regrouping and concentration of forces redeployed from France, Germany and other countries'.[256] The main problem with this statement is that in 'late March and early April' there were few 'enemy reserves' for Intelligence to find anywhere at all, let alone deployed in positions that could be positively equated with an intended future attack on the Kursk salient. As already mentioned, Manstein's hopes of mounting an offensive against it in April had been thwarted by lack of reserves. Some would have become available after the abandonment of the Demyansk salient at the end of February. However, when Hitler issued Operations Order no. 5 his assignments of additional forces for 'Citadel' did not mention Demyansk at all, but specifically allocated troops from the 4th and 9th Armies that would become available by withdrawal from the much larger Rzhev-Vyazma salient. When he issued the Order, on 13 March, that withdrawal was still in progress. It was completed on the next day, reducing the length of the front line in that sector from 550 to 200 kilometres (from about 344 to 125 miles), and freeing 20 divisions, 15 of which were redeployed to block the offensive by the Bryansk and Central Fronts in the Orel area. However, by 8 April, the day Zhukov sent his message to Stalin, few of the units in question could yet have moved to locations identifiable by local Soviet reconnaissance as associated with anything beyond the local defensive battles in which they were engaged till the last days of March. In fact 27 March was the first day for several months on which the daily Sovinformburo bulletin announced 'no significant changes' in the front line.

As for 'regrouping and concentration of forces redeployed from France, Germany and other countries', movements involving more than routine replacement of casualties for units already on the Eastern Front would not be undertaken until that same Operations Order no. 5 was issued, so would not even begin until the second half of March, and only air force units could undertake them quickly (as mentioned below, Bletchley's first indications of German intentions related to Kursk came from Luftwaffe messages decrypted during the third week of March).

Vasilevsky was scarcely more forthcoming, commenting,

> although we didn't know everything about the German plans we foresaw much, and deduced much, relying both on information from the Intelligence organs and on analysis of current events. Documents in our possession fully reveal the mechanism of the German army's preparation for a new offensive . . . Despite all the contradictions and disputes, the German command's plans amounted to decisively weakening the striking force of the offensive by Soviet troops that they expected in summer, after that develop a

victorious offensive in the east, snatch the strategic initiative from the hands of the Soviet command and achieve a breakthrough in the war to their advantage.[257]

This passage is remarkable for two things. First, his use of the present tense 'reveal' may be a 'historic present' (somewhat more common in Russian usage than in English), meaning that the General Staff had the documents before the battle, or it may mean that they came into 'our possession' only after it, at some unspecified time before he wrote his memoirs. Secondly, his summary of the German plans as comprising a defensive battle followed by a counter-offensive is completely wrong. As noted above, Hitler had rejected that as 'too passive'. Furthermore, Vasilevsky contradicted himself in the very next paragraph, which correctly cited Operations Order no. 5 of 13 March as 'setting the task of pre-empting the Soviet forces on various sectors of the front after the spring thaw'. But here too he did not say whether the Order's contents were or were not known before the battle. So neither of the two main architects of the Soviet victory at Kursk shed much light on the question of where they got their information. There may therefore be some point in looking at possible sources that are known to have existed, but that neither would mention for security reasons.

The two principal Soviet Intelligence organisations, the GRU (Military) and NKVD (political), maintained large networks of agents abroad; before the invasion these had provided numerous warnings that it would happen, and some information about planning, but nothing precise enough to shake Stalin's erroneous beliefs that Hitler would not invade at all, or if he did, that his main purpose would be to secure resources for a long war. Up to and including the Stalingrad campaign, gaps in Intelligence continued to create problems for Stavka. As previously mentioned, one in particular, the failure to discover that the capture of Moscow was no longer on the German agenda, led it into serious errors, when von Bock's persistence in efforts to take Voronezh during July 1942 was misread as portending a subsequent northward drive to outflank Moscow, leading to retention in its vicinity of large reserves that, if sent south earlier, could have helped prevent the Germans reaching the Volga, Stalingrad and the Caucasus. It will be seen below that a persistent belief in the long-discarded German aspirations to capture Moscow continued to affect Soviet planning up to and including that for the defensive battle of Kursk in July, even though the Germans had abandoned the likeliest launching point for it, the Rzhev-Vyazma salient, during March.

Both the counter-offensives at Stalingrad (Operations 'Uranus' and 'Saturn') had to be extensively modified during their execution because of gaps in Intelligence information. The forces encircled proved over three times as large as expected, necessitating the temporary suspension of 'Uranus' and the modification of 'Saturn' into 'Little Saturn', keeping far more forces than originally planned in the Stalingrad area, and hence so much reducing those intended to cut off Army Group A in the Caucasus that that objective had to be abandoned. Another gap was closed only by chance. A German relief attempt was expected, but Intelligence could not discover where it would start. The answer was found only on 28 November when reconnaissance patrols of the 4th Cavalry Corps found the 6th Panzer Division, just transferred from France, detraining at Kotelnikovo, one of the two likely starting points that Zhukov had identified in the assessment he sent to Stalin at that time. Then in February 1943 Soviet Intelligence completely failed to detect the build-up for Manstein's counter-offensive that recaptured Kharkov, and forced the Voronezh, South-West and Bryansk Fronts to retreat to the Seversky Donets river, abandoning most of the just-reconquered Donbass.

Vasilevsky attributed this last failure to 'incorrect assessment of the strategic situation'[258] by the three Front commands, especially a misreading of Manstein's regrouping of his forces in early February. These involved westward movements from the Kharkov area, to Krasnograd by the SS Panzer Corps and to Krasnoarmeiskoe by the 40th and 48th Panzer Corps, and these were wishfully misinterpreted as the first moves in a major retreat to the Dnepr river line. Vasilevsky also admitted that Stavka and the General Staff compounded the error by setting over-ambitious tasks in pursuit of an enemy whom they wrongly believed so thoroughly beaten as to be incapable of mounting a counter-offensive. His explanation of his and Zhukov's confidence about German intentions at Kursk mentioned no sources of information higher than those available to the 'Fronts', i.e. prisoners, documentation at divisional or lower level, or reports of unit movements detected by partisans, cavalry patrols or reconnaissance aircraft. Otherwise he mentioned only unspecified 'information from the Intelligence organs', and 'analysis of current events', without specifying what information, or what 'current events' indicative of future German intentions could have been available as early as the first week of April.

An account provided by Anastas Mikoyan indicates that Stalin's mind was made up even before the end of March.[259] When the dictator summoned him to a meeting, at 2 a.m. on 27 March, he told him that

Intelligence information indicated the Germans were concentrating large forces for an offensive in the Kursk salient area: 'Seemingly they are trying to gain the strategic initiative having a long-range aim at Moscow.' He was wrong on that latter point, and on the first there cannot have been very large movements by 27 March. Withdrawal from the Rzhev-Vyazma salient had been completed only on 14 March, and not many of the units from there intended for the 'Citadel' offensive were likely to have moved in only 13 days, especially since the spring thaw was in full spate. It could be that Soviet Intelligence had gained some information about Operations Order no. 5 of 13 March, but no source so far has disclosed if or how they obtained it; and even if they had, it does not mention Moscow, so Stalin's reference to it must have derived simply from his reluctance to shed the belief that it must inevitably be the Germans' prime target.

On 8 April, a mere seven weeks after the complete Intelligence failure over Manstein's counter-offensive, Zhukov sought and obtained Stalin's approval for a plan based entirely on what the Germans were expected to do. Granted the salient stuck out as an obvious place to attack, but victory in war frequently rests on an ability to avoid the obvious, and German generals had often displayed considerable talent in that direction. Besides, a case could be made for other objectives. Operation 'Don', carried out by the Transcaucasus, North Caucasus and South Fronts from 1 January to 4 February, had forced Army Group A to withdraw to the Taman peninsula but had not evicted it from the Caucasus, and a German attempt to use the peninsula as a launch-point for a renewed attempt to retake the nearest oilfields, at Maikop, was not beyond the bounds of possibility. Nor was another assault at Leningrad, at least to close off the narrow corridor between the city and the rest of the country.

To discard all possible alternatives and identify the Kursk salient as the sole target for the German summer offensive of 1943 required more than inspired guesswork; so did the decision to fight a defensive battle rather than disrupt the German preparations by attacking first. Granted, the three previous major victories conducted or masterminded by Zhukov, in Mongolia, at Moscow and Stalingrad, had all involved a defensive battle followed by a counter-offensive, but in all three that sequence had been dictated by enemy offensives, whereas his proposal to follow the same pattern at Kursk was entirely voluntary. Completely reliable information about German intentions would have to be involved, and it is therefore reasonable to consider where he could have acquired it.

*   *   *

All the members of the 'Red Orchestra' networks of Soviet agents in Germany and occupied Europe had been executed, imprisoned or 'turned' to work for the Abwehr between August 1942 and January 1943, so none of them could have provided any advance information about plans for a future German offensive against a salient that came into existence only in March 1943.

Another possible source would be 'Lucy' in Switzerland, the codename of Rudolf Roessler, a German exile apparently with sources in the High Command. Moscow initially treated him with suspicion because he refused to disclose his sources (he never did), though it eventually came to regard him as highly reliable. Contrary to the fanciful account by Accoce and Quet, who claim Roessler was providing information to the Soviets from the spring of 1941, including the complete text of the 'Barbarossa' plan,[260] and that he met his Soviet controller, the Hungarian Communist Sandor Rado, at that time, all Soviet accounts agree that the details of 'Barbarossa' were not known in advance (if they had been, Stalin would not have made the erroneous assumption that the main assault would come south of the Pripyat marshes), and Rado wrote in his memoirs that he acquired Roessler only in November 1942.

Messages from Lucy from the first half of 1943, cited in Rado's memoirs or other sources, included nothing as high-level as plans for a major German offensive. Besides, the changes in Soviet plans necessitated by gaps in Intelligence between mid-November 1942 and mid-February 1943 suggest that Lucy did not provide especially valuable information in that period either. Even if he then began to produce much better-quality Intelligence, Stalin and Zhukov were hardly likely to have come to trust him so unconditionally by early April as to base their entire strategic plan on messages from him. Furthermore, the former NKVD/KGB general Sudoplatov pointed out[261] that many of Lucy's reports were similar or even identical to paraphrased Ultra material passed on officially by the British, and therefore concluded that he was a British 'plant'. The British had indeed succeeded in planting an agent in Rado's group, so Sudoplatov's claim is credible, but it is probably not the full story, especially as the most authoritative account of British Intelligence in the Second World War does not mention Operations Order no. 5 among the messages Bletchley decrypted during March.

Roessler also worked for Swiss Intelligence; Switzerland, then entirely surrounded by German or German-occupied territory, necessarily kept a very close eye on the Wehrmacht, and a tight rein over disclosing its findings. Roessler cannot have been its only source of information, and since

Switzerland's interests were better served by a Nazi defeat than a Nazi victory, it may well have passed information to Roessler, fully intending it to reach the British or any other of Germany's enemies. As noted in the previous chapter, Paul Carell's view was that Swiss Intelligence was the actual source of messages received from Roessler's sub-source 'Werther'. He noted that all messages received from Werther after 11 February 1942 gave misleading information that Manstein's forces were withdrawing rather than concentrating for his March counter-offensive, but claims this was because Manstein did not inform OKH or OKW, so officers there, including Werther, drew the same erroneous conclusion as the Soviets. It took a visit to Manstein's headquarters to dispel Hitler's misgivings on this issue, so Carell has a point; but an alternative possibility is that the source was a double-agent and the February messages were intended to disinform.

One Russian author has in fact suggested that Lucy was a German disinformation agent, basing his arguments mainly on manifest inaccuracies in some messages cited by Rado. For example, a Kursk-related message of April 1943, allegedly listing the divisions in the 4th Panzer Army of Army Group South, included five that were there and six that were not – the false identifications included one each then in Norway, Germany and with Army Group Centre, and three that did not exist then or ever.[262] If the purpose of the message was indeed to disinform, such an exaggeration of Army Group South's strength would aim at deterring the Soviets from attempting an offensive immediately after the spring thaw, but if it was not so intended, then Roessler's sources were clearly nowhere near as good as Accoce and Quet or Rado claimed.

Two other Lucy messages received in June also appear calculated to deceive. The first, on 17 June, said that the Germans considered an offensive at Kursk too risky in view of the Soviet strength, and the second, on the 21st, stated that Army Group South was regrouping so as to threaten the flank of an expected Red Army offensive. Both could only be attempts to dissuade the enemy from expecting an attack that in reality was only two weeks from launching.

Another ground for suspicion of Lucy is that not one of Roessler's alleged sources surfaced after the war ended. If they were really members of OKW or OKH, both defined by the victors as criminal organisations, their careers, incomes and prospects had been terminated by the Wehrmacht's defeat and disbandment, and they faced the prospect of at least a denazification hearing or possibly even a trial as war criminals. Their reception by Moscow would have been problematical; on returning there both Rado and Leonid Trepper, the Red Orchestra's 'Big Chief', were charged with having been German-controlled double agents, 'rewarded' with 10-year jail sentences, rehabilitated and freed only after Stalin's death. However, American or British Intelligence services would surely have welcomed Lucy's 'sources', and even have sought to recruit them as double-agents in the rapidly evolving Cold War, and that would have considerably improved their lives in devastated post-war Germany. Could it be that if Roessler had provided names, then the British, Americans or Soviets would have tried to contact them directly, and would then have found that they did not exist?

The contention that Lucy was a German-controlled double agent is inconsistent with the fact that it was German pressure that obliged the Swiss in October 1943 to locate Rado's transmitters and shut his ring down. However, there are at least three possible explanations for that. First, that it was a genuine espionage ring, to which the *Sicherheitsdienst* or Gestapo failed to apply the preferred counter-espionage solution of turning at least some of its members, as they did with the Red Orchestra, and as the British did with all German agents sent to the UK, and the Soviets did with agents sent in to support Max. Secondly, it may have been felt to have outlived its utility as disinformation, and that the Soviets were no longer reacting as expected. Thirdly, it could even be, as is not uncommon in espionage, that the right hand, Gestapo or *Sicherheitsdienst*, did not know what the left hand, the *Abwehr*, was doing. That no arrests in OKW or OKH accompanied the shutdown suggests that if Roessler had sources there, they were extraordinarily good at covering their tracks, or were indeed participants in a 'disinforming' operation shut down because it had outlived its usefulness. Or it could be that the information was, as Sudoplatov claimed, 'planted' by the British, or came from Swiss Intelligence, and that the Swiss complied with the German demand because by October 1943 it was clear that Germany's defeat, though not imminent, was inevitable. The ring was therefore no longer needed, and continuing risked exposing their own role, prompting a German blockade or even invasion. Evidence to establish the truth is not in the public domain, and probably never will be.

Advance Ultra information from Bletchley may have been among the factors influencing Stalin's decision of 12 April, but was not definite enough to have been the only factor. Its main utility was that later messages provided useful information about German preparations to the Soviet General Staff planners of the defensive battle. The British official history noted the first signs of German preparations in the third week of March 1943, from decrypted Luftwaffe messages 'about the movement of panzer divisions on the central sector of the eastern front, and a re-organisation of GAF [German Air Force] commands which brought Fliegerkorps VIII back to the Kharkov area for close support operations'. Then on 13 April another Luftwaffe message first used the codename 'Zitadelle' ('Citadel'), and on the 19th another disclosed that Luftflotte (Air Fleet) IV 'was sending forces allocated to Zitadelle to GAF Command East'.[263] If the messages from the third week of March were passed quickly to Moscow, officially in paraphrased form or unofficially by one of the 'resident's' agents, they could certainly have been taken into account in the Soviet decision-making, and may help account for what Stalin told Mikoyan on 27 March, but those of 13 and 19 April cannot have influenced the principal decision about how to fight the battle, because Stalin had already taken that on the 12th, when he endorsed the proposal Zhukov had made on the 8th.

The same reservation applies to the most comprehensive of the early indicators deciphered by Bletchley, a message from Field-Marshal von Weichs, commanding Army Group B, transmitted some time after 15 April and decrypted on the 25th.[264] The gist of it may have been passed on officially to the Soviets, but according to two post-Soviet publications the State Defence Committee received a translation of the actual text from the NKVD 'resident' in London on 7 May; one of the accounts says it had been passed to him by Philby, who had received it from Cairncross.[265] A post-Soviet account of Soviet Intelligence operations during 1941–45 devoted an entire chapter to Cairncross. It said that,

> in his new job at Bletchley Cairncross received access to a whole range of deciphered German documents, which were immediately passed to Moscow. Philby also had access to a range of such docu-ments – they were sent to him by the Chief of Intelligence. Blunt also sometimes managed to acquire some materials. But Cairncross had these documents in his own safe, and could use them as they arrived, i.e. without great delay. He passed on very important infor-mation about the offensive the Germans were preparing on the Kursk salient, indicated approximate dates for the offensive, the technical parameters of the new German 'Tiger' tank, and other information. By his self-sacrificing work he made a serious contri-bution to our victory at Kursk and on other fronts.[266]

The same post-Soviet account credited the NKVD 'resident' in London with 14 agents altogether; since MI5's post-war investigations did not, at least publicly, identify anything like that many, there may have been more than one still unidentified 'mole' passing on information.[267] Certainly the Weichs message and anything else the 'resident' obtained about 'Citadel' would be very helpful to the General Staff planners, but Stalin had taken the crucial decision two weeks before Weichs' message was deciphered, and four weeks before the State Defence Committee received its translated text. As for technical details of Tiger tanks, the Soviets did not need them; as noted below, they captured several between November 1942 and April 1943, and put them through comprehensive tests in April.

Although Ultra information from Bletchley cannot have been the sole or principal source of Zhukov's and Stalin's confidence as early as April about German intentions, information, particularly from Cairncross, about the methods employed in deciphering may nevertheless have played a role in the Soviet decision-making. When the Germans invaded the Soviet Union, the British decided not to share the Ultra secret, believing Soviet security to be German-penetrated, and expecting the Red Army would be speedily defeated. After both assumptions proved wrong, they took to passing on important information from Ultra, paraphrased and without disclosing the source, beyond dropping vague hints about an agent in the German High Command. The Soviets pretended to believe them, but obviously knew exactly what the source was, on information from Cairncross, Philby, Blunt and maybe others among the alleged 14 agents. Perhaps even more important than any information they passed on would be the messages' evidence that many Enigma-based systems (and, as with the Weichs message, even the more complex 'Tunny') had been broken, and that large numbers of messages were being deciphered daily, often within only a few hours of transmission, to the great benefit of the Anglo–American war effort. Even before the war the Soviet Union had had a large interception and decrypting organisation (Sudoplatov mentioned that they were deciphering messages to or from several foreign embassies, including those of Japan, Italy, Turkey and Bulgaria),[268] and the discovery from their British agents that the German cipher systems were breakable would justify a large commitment of intellectual and material resources.

In that connection the account mentioned above goes on to say:

Along with material of a military-operational character, Cairncross passed on data about the machine-cipher Tunny, which was used by the British to decipher German radio messages. On the basis of these data an analogous example of this machine was designed . . .

In the operational file there is a task set by the Centre to the London residency. In particular it is stated that the Germans have made some changes in the machine's design, and that therefore additional data are required, data that maybe are known to the British and accessible by Cairncross. The data were received from the source and sent on to Moscow. There is no information in the file about the further fate of this deciphering machine.[269]

Tunny was Bletchley's codename for the German SZ40 (*Schluesselzusatz*, 'key-adder') cipher machine and its derivatives, several versions of SZ42, used for communication at the highest military levels, such as between OKW/OKH and the headquarters of army groups, and including the message from Weichs, mentioned above. It was first observed in use in mid-1941, and by January 1942 Bletchley 'understood its design and method of operation'. It was far more sophisticated than Enigma, so decryption was 'normally too laborious to be undertaken by hand, and the first stage of mechanisation was the provision of a decyphering machine, delivered early in June 1942'.[270] As to the unknown 'further fate' of the machine, if the reference is to the British machine, it is quite wrong. The first machine-deciphering successes were achieved in early May 1943 by a machine codenamed 'Robinson', replaced in February 1944 by Colossus 1, the first programmable computer.[271] The reference must be to an attempted Russian counterpart to 'Robinson', otherwise why would Moscow ask its London 'resident' for data that could be obtained only from someone actually working at Bletchley? The most likely reason why there is nothing further on file is simply that they could not make the Soviet machine work, but that they even tried suggests a high level of cryptanalytical effort.

Bletchley could not acquire much Enigma traffic from German army units on the Eastern Front. Every division commander had an Enigma machine and radio transmitter in his command vehicle, but except when actually on the move most communication after December 1941 was via landlines, making use of radio too sporadic and the amount of traffic picked up by UK-operated intercept stations too small to decrypt on a regular basis. The best source of information about the Eastern Front remained the Luftwaffe general ('Red') cipher. 'Fish' messages, though taking longer to decrypt, were also valuable because the information they contained was more high-level, and consequently took longer to become outdated.

The Soviet situation was different. Landlines could be, and frequently were, tapped. During the Battle of Moscow for example, a German unit reported killing a Soviet officer who was doing so. General S.P. Ivanov, Vatutin's Chief of Staff at Stalingrad, mentioned in his memoirs both receipt of a decrypted message that had been transmitted less than 36 hours previously, and a successful tapping operation against the Romanian 3rd Army.[272] Line-tapping was also among the tasks set for partisans operating behind the German lines.

Radio interception of enemy traffic was frequently mentioned in Front commanders' reports from late 1942 onwards, though in most cases the references were to voice communication, especially between German aircraft and ground controllers. It is also relevant that Bletchley found Luftwaffe cipher systems easier to break than those of the army or navy. German army operations depended heavily on air support, and in early 1943 about 60 per cent of the Luftwaffe was on the Eastern Front. Luftwaffe liaison officers (*Fliegerverbindungsoffizieren*, or 'Flyvos'), each with an Enigma machine, were regularly attached to army units, and their messages frequently provided valuable clues about army operations.

The many secrets unveiled in the post-Soviet era have as yet included very little about the role of cryptanalysis in the Soviet–German war. That high-level Soviet communications were very secure is clear from the experience of Bletchley's German counterpart, the B-Dienst; it found Soviet low-level tactical military ciphers easy to break, but had no success above that level. Front or higher-level Soviet commanders used Baudot machines and landlines, so messages could not be regularly intercepted, and Soviet diplomatic traffic used codebooks plus one-time pads of randomly generated figures; if these are properly used, messages can be deciphered only by those holding both book and pads. It is therefore reasonable to assume that Soviet expertise in codes and ciphers was of a high standard; the simplicity of tactical ciphers was mainly because low-level transmission resources were often primitive, originators and receivers of messages were not highly trained cryptographers, and any action proposed or requested in tactical-level messages would usually be taken before any third party could decipher or act on them.

In addition to a massive intellectual and technological effort, the British mounted substantial operations (e.g. a commando raid on the Lofoten Islands, seizure of German weather ships in the North Atlantic, recovery of machines and documents from captured U-boats) in order to secure single Enigma machines and associated documentation such as key tables. The surrender of the German 6th Army and part of the 4th Panzer Army at the end of January must have provided Soviet cryptanalysts with a number of Enigma machines and associated documentation far beyond what any British or American operation acquired. Each of the 20 division and 5 corps commanders had one such machine; the 6th Army headquarters had at least one, and may have had a 'Fish' machine as well. Some Flyvos probably escaped on returning supply flights, but by 17 January the Soviets had taken six of the seven local airfields, and made the seventh unusable by artillery fire and air attacks, so there were no landings or take-offs in the remaining days before the final surrender, and most Flyvos must still have been in the city. Even if only five were still there, that brings the total of Enigma machines in Stalingrad to 30. The troops were freezing and starving, ammunition, explosives and fuel were almost all gone, the ground was frozen too hard and the troops too weak to destroy or bury the machines. They could at most take a rifle-butt to them, and in some cases not even that – one last message ended with 'the Russians are breaking in . . .'. It is also unlikely that key tables, operational documents and manuals were all destroyed, and it is entirely speculative, but not unreasonable to postulate that the haul of machines and documents at Stalingrad facilitated a 'last heave' by an already existing programme that had made progress, but not yet resolved all the problems.

This treasure-trove became available only in the first week of February, too late for much exploitation before Manstein's offensive at Kharkov, but during March it may have become possible to decipher some Enigma traffic, including messages between divisions and armies concerning preparations for 'Citadel'. Divisions on the move would sometimes have to resort to radio transmission – the order to observe radio silence applied to operator chatter and plain text messages, but not to enciphered traffic, because the Germans did not learn until 27 years after the war that the British had broken their ciphers. Interception of such transmissions could have been among the factors giving Zhukov the confidence about German intentions that prompted his message to Stalin on 8 April. Information from Front Intelligence and partisan observations of eastbound rail traffic would certainly also have been involved, but the most significant preliminary move, the German IX Army's withdrawal from the Rzhev-Vyazma salient, took place by stages between 1 and 14 March. As noted above, this released up to 22 divisions to IX Army reserve, and hence to eventual availability for 'Citadel'. However, with movement impeded by the spring thaw, and the need to employ several of these divisions to stop the attempted offensive by the Bryansk, Central and Voronezh Fronts, major redeployment into starting positions for 'Citadel' could not have been far enough advanced by the first week of April to account by itself for the confident tone of Zhukov's message to Stalin.

Bletchley's analytical effort naturally depended mainly on mathematicians, and although the relevance of chess-players is less obvious, work there did attract a number of them, including several of high international ranking. Russia was not short of mathematicians and chess champions, and given what it learned about Ultra from Cairncross and others, Soviet Intelligence must have devoted a large effort to Enigma-breaking. Intelligence failures up to mid-February 1943 suggest no or very limited success until then, but the least implausible explanation for the very marked improvement thereafter is successful exploitation of materials captured at Stalingrad.

No Russian account gives any details about where Stavka received the information that led it three times (on 2 and 20 May, and 2 July)[273] to notify the two Front commanders in the salient that the German offensive would begin within a few days. In fact Hitler first set the date as 3 May, but changed his mind on 29 April, because he considered the numbers of the new tanks, assault and anti-tank self-propelled guns so far available to the attacking divisions insufficient. He then set a new date of 12 June, but 'events in the Mediterranean' (specifically the surrender of all Axis forces in North Africa on 12 May)[274] forced another postponement, and even raised the possibility of abandonment. However, on 21 June he fixed the launching date for 'Citadel' as 3 July, then on the 25th changed it to 5 July. Stavka's warning to the commanders on 2 May fits with Hitler's original starting date of 3 May, and it is just possible that it was based on intercepted traffic. Hitler's original order specified that Army Groups Centre and South must be able to launch 'Citadel' on five days' notice. A launch on 3 May would therefore have to be ordered by, at the latest, 29 April, the date on which Hitler cancelled it. There is no information in the public domain to indicate whether any orders had been issued before the cancellation. The 20 May warning was simply wrong, but no Soviet or post-Soviet source has said on what it was based. The third warning, on 2 July, was absolutely correct, and its timing is interesting. It was only on 1 July that Hitler assembled at his Rastenburg headquarters the marshals and generals who would lead 'Citadel', Manstein, Kluge, Model, Hoth, Kempf and the commanders of the two air fleets, von Greim and Dessloch, and ordered them to start it on the 5th. The time of day of this meeting is not known, but since Hitler, like Churchill and Stalin, habitually worked into the small hours and then slept until at least mid-morning, it was unlikely to have taken place before

10 a.m. German summer time, which was 11 a.m. Moscow time. Stalin's message warning the Front commanders[275] that 'Citadel' was likely to be launched 'during the period 3–6 July' was transmitted at 2.10 a.m. Moscow time on the 2nd. That is 1.10 a.m. German time, at most only 15 hours after the meeting at which Hitler gave his generals their final orders.

This rapidity suggests two possibilities. One is that by then some Enigma traffic was being read. After the meeting, and before leaving headquarters, Manstein, Kluge, Model and Hoth, and probably also both air fleet commanders, would necessarily send orders to their own Chiefs of Staff to start alerting subordinate formations to prepare for battle, though without telling them the starting date. Messages from OKH to the headquarters of Army Groups Centre and South would probably use the more complex Fish machine cipher, and be sent by landline, but those from army headquarters to divisions or corps and to Luftwaffe units would be enciphered on Enigma machines,[276] and some of them would be transmitted by radio, therefore vulnerable to interception.

The other, simpler, possibility is that the Soviets could intercept but not decipher Enigma messages, but concluded from traffic analysis that action was imminent because of the sudden large increase in traffic caused by the messages that Army Groups Centre and South and the army and air force HQs under them had to send, to alert their subordinate formations. Either possibility fits the speed of Stavka's warning to the Fronts better than the idea of messages going from a source in OKW or OKH to Roessler in Switzerland, then through one of his intermediaries, Schneider or Duebendorfer, to Rado, who would then have to encipher it and contact one of his operators to have it transmitted to Moscow. Messages that Rado cited in his memoirs invariably took two or more days to be delivered.

Whatever the means that secured them, the improvements in Soviet Intelligence enabled Stavka's planning for the summer to proceed more or less in parallel with the German. However, the planners were soon confronted by the disconcerting discovery that the new German Tiger I heavy tank was far superior to their prized KVs and T-34s because of its thicker armour, superior binocular sights and much longer-range and greater-calibre 88mm gun. Tempting fate, the Germans in late 1942 had sent a small pre-production batch of the new Henschel Tiger Is to the Leningrad front, where one became bogged in marshland and was captured. However, the Red Army's tank and artillery specialists were preoccupied at that time with the situation around Stalingrad, so the encounter then attracted little attention. In December a battalion of Tigers was included in Hoth's force that attempted to lift the siege of Stalingrad, then in early April 1943 some damaged Tigers were captured near Belgorod.

Tests conducted on 25–30 April, using various calibre anti-tank, field, tank and anti-aircraft guns, showed that armour-piercing shells from the 76.2mm F-34 gun then standard on the T-34-76 and KV-1 could not pierce even the side armour of a Tiger at more than 200 metres, while the Tiger's 88mm shells could penetrate 110mm of armour at up to 2 kilometres (1.25 miles). The thickest frontal armour on Soviet tanks was 100mm on the KV-1 and 45–60mm on the T-34-76; therefore all would be vulnerable for the time it took them to get within killing distance of a Tiger.[277] Even if they could cover the 1.8 kilometres (about 1.1 miles) at full speed, it would take them over two minutes; a Tiger could fire several rounds in that time, with a good prospect that one of them would score a direct hit.

Nor was the Tiger the only threat to Soviet tanks. The Ferdinand assault gun had an even more powerful 88mm gun than the Tiger, and thicker frontal armour, while the new medium Mark V Panther tank and newer examples of the older Mark IV mounted a long-barrelled 75mm gun, shells from which could penetrate the frontal armour of a KV at 1 kilometre (0.62 miles) and of a T-34 at 1.5 kilometres (0.93 miles). In addition the late G and H models of the Mark IV had been fitted with extra sheets of armour-plate at the front and over the tracks, and even many of the obsolescent Mk III tanks had been retrofitted with a long-barrelled 50mm gun, shells from which could also penetrate the armour of a T-34 at over a kilometre. Furthermore, the Zeiss binocular sights fitted in the new and up-gunned older tanks ensured more accurate fire than Soviet tank crews could achieve.

The Soviet position was further eroded by the fact that only their commanders' tanks had radio transmitters. The rest had only receivers or nothing at all, so that if a commander's tank was knocked out, his entire unit became leaderless. Their German counterparts mostly operated from 'command tanks' equipped with a wooden dummy gun, with the liberated space in the turret used to mount superior radio equipment; tank crews subordinate to them could receive and transmit, enabling the second-in-command to take over if the command tank was knocked out, and crews to inform their superiors quickly of any changes in the local situation. Soviet accounts noted that the Germans were well aware of the Soviet lack of transmitters, and tended to concentrate their fire on any tank seen to have a transmitting antenna.

Stalin had further muddied the waters; in an attempt to exploit the superior speed and manoeuvrability of the T-34 he had issued a directive on 19 September 1942 ordering tank units to begin engagements by a storm of fire from their main armament and machine guns while on the move, carrying additional shells and bullets for that purpose, and enhancing mobility by mounting extra fuel tanks on their rear decks. Tank gun stabilisers had not yet been invented, so firing on the move was inaccurate and wasteful, while the additional ammunition created storage problems in the cramped turret, and the unprotected fuel tanks were a serious fire hazard.[278]

Although the claim that the T-34 was the best tank of the war in any army has cascaded from one post-war publication to another, that claim is tenable after mid-1943 only partially (once its mechanical problems were resolved, the Panther became a strong contender for the title) and in respect of the later version, the T-34–85, which did not start to arrive in units till March 1944. Apart from the inadequacy of its gun against the Tiger, Panther, Ferdinand or upgunned Mks III and IV, the T-34–76 as first manufactured had a number of other shortcomings, to which Timoshenko, when People's Commissar for Defence, had drawn attention well before the war. In a letter to Voroshilov (then Chairman of the Defence Committee of the Council of People's Commissars), dated 6 November 1940, he had recommended an increase in the crew from 4 to 5 to incorporate a gunner. The cramped nature of the turret meant the tank commander had also to be the gunlayer, and this distracted him from his command duties, creating serious problems, especially if he had to control other tanks beside his own (the Soviets did not follow the German use of 'command tanks' until well into 1944). Timoshenko also sought improvements to the view, especially from the turret, and to the communications system, and changes to the transmission and gearbox.[279] Manufacture was temporarily suspended, while work began on a modified T-34M, due to begin deliveries on 1 January 1942, but the outbreak of war and the need to evacuate much of the production base and workforce to the Urals or Central Asia delayed most of these improvements until they materialised in the shape of the T-34–85, seven months after Kursk, with an improved gun, a larger turret with room for an additional crew member, and frontal armour doubled in thickness.

Of all the shortcomings, the greatest in 1943 was the inadequacy of the 76.2mm gun, standard in the T-34-76 and KV-1, compared to those carried in the new and updated older German tanks. Clearly, all Soviet tanks would be completely outclassed unless more powerful guns could be provided. The most successful in the April tests was the 1939-pattern 52K 85mm anti-aircraft gun, shells from which penetrated the Tiger's frontal armour at a distance of 1 kilometre, so Stalin ordered development of a new tank gun based on this (similar to the German experience – their 88mm tank gun was based on the 88mm anti-aircraft gun that had proved exceedingly effective against ground targets) and four design groups began work in May. There was, however, no possibility that any of them could do more than produce testable prototypes before the German summer offensive, which would inevitably be spearheaded by the new tanks. To counter those would need a combination of measures, and closer than hitherto co-ordination between infantry, artillery, tanks and aircraft – in fact copying the German methods as closely as possible.

Stalin's initial reaction to Zhukov's proposal for a defensive battle at Kursk was to ask if he was sure that Soviet troops could withstand a German summer offensive – a reasonable question, since they had singularly failed to do so in the two previous summers. Zhukov assured him that they could, but he sought the views of the two Front commanders in the salient. Rokossovsky, commanding the Central Front on the north face, considered that the Germans would be unable to mount an offensive before the end of the spring thaw and floods, in the second half of May, and argued for a pre-emptive attack by the Central Front and the two Fronts north of it, Western and Bryansk, provided additional air and anti-tank regiments could be made available for support. Vatutin, commanding the Voronezh Front further south, where the thaw would be over somewhat earlier, expected the Germans would be ready for an offensive 'not before 20 April, but most likely in the first days of May', but unlike Rokossovsky, he did not express a clear preference between pre-emptive attack and premeditated defence. One post-Soviet source claims that both Vatutin and Malinovsky (commanding the Southern Front, due to mount a counter-offensive in August) favoured pre-emption;[280] this, however, appears to have been not in April but in June, when the successive postponements of 'Citadel' raised doubts among some Soviet generals over whether it was going to happen at all. In his April report, Vatutin also suggested that the German options might include a northward push to outflank Moscow, reflecting his past experience as Deputy Chief of General Staff, where, as previously noted, Stalin's preoccupation with possible threats to the capital persisted long after they had vanished from the German agenda.[281] References in his report to identification by 'radio intelligence' of locations to which the headquarters of two divisions had moved, may have come from the deciphering of messages, but were more likely based on direction-finding and intercepted operator chatter – orders to observe radio silence were easier to issue than to enforce. The references nevertheless show that interception of enemy radio traffic had now become an important tool of Soviet Intelligence, perhaps aided by the 35,000 radio transceivers and large quantities of cable supplied by the USA under Lend-Lease.

On the evening of 12 April, after receiving the views of Rokossovsky and Vatutin, and three days before Hitler issued the Order for Operation 'Citadel', Stalin held a meeting with Zhukov, Vasilevsky and Deputy Chief of General Staff Antonov. They agreed that 'the most probable aim of a German summer offensive would be to encircle and destroy the main forces of Central and Voronezh Fronts in the Kursk salient', but did not exclude the possibility that success in that area would be followed by thrusts in east and north-east directions, including towards Moscow. Shtemenko noted that 'on this matter Stalin displayed particular uneasiness'.[282] However, he accepted Zhukov's plan, and ordered both Fronts to prepare solid defences. The troops were to dig themselves in; no fewer than eight defence lines, one behind the other, were to be constructed, and an entire army group (first entitled Reserve Front, then Steppe Military District, and finally Steppe Front), with seven armies and eight tank or mechanised corps, would be positioned behind the two Fronts in the salient, to be used in the counter-offensive if the defensive battle went well, or to block any German advance if it did not.

Intriguing evidence suggesting Stalin knew about German intentions even earlier than mid-April is provided in the memoirs of Anastas Mikoyan, who was as much Stalin's ace troubleshooter on supplying the army as Zhukov was on using it to fight, and to whom he entrusted the establishment of this huge new force. When he sent for Mikoyan he told him 'according to data from our Intelligence the Hitlerites are concentrating major forces in the area of the Kursk salient', and 'a strong Reserve Front must be established urgently, capable of being brought into combat at the most acute and decisive moment of the battle, and for further transition to the counter-offensive'. It was to be formed of units that had fought in recent battles and were now in reserve for making up to strength in manpower and equipment. 'You . . . must take on the organising of this Reserve Front yourself, because all the material resources are concentrated in your hands. The General Staff will engage as usual in choosing the commanders, but everything else is up to you.'

The intriguing element in Stalin's remarks is that Mikoyan says the meeting at which he made them took place at 2 a.m. on 27 March, and, unlike with some other memoirists' recollections of dates of long-past events, there is substantial confirmation that Mikoyan's were correct. The task involved concentrating, equipping and supplying the largest reserve force Russia or the Soviet Union had ever yet put into the field and he set to work at once. First, on 29 March he met Colonel-General Shchadenko, head of the General Staff Directorate responsible for forming and manning units, and secured his agreement to constituting the new Front from units based in Moscow Military District. In those days it covered a large part of the European USSR and the conscripts it provided, one-third of the USSR's total, had mostly received good general or technical education, which made them especially suitable for service in the mechanised forces that would bulk large in the new Front. Then Mikoyan directed every armed service chief to submit plans for providing the armies of the new Front with all they would need, and timetables for delivering everything on time to eight principal locations. An example of the pace he imposed is that only six days after Stalin had first set him his task, he received the first report from an arm of service on 1 April, when Major-General Kalyagin, head of Engineer Troops, reported that three-quarters of the Reserve Front's needs for engineer equipment could be met from central resources, and the rest issued after deployment, from stocks held locally in Front or army depots.

Mikoyan decreed that the reinforcement and supply of the new Front's armies were to be completed between 15 April and 10 May. On 30 March he met the arm of service heads: Khrulyov (logistics), Karponosov (organisation), Yakovlev (artillery), Fedorenko (tank and mechanised forces), Peresypkin (signals), and Drachev (chief quartermaster). Transport presented particular problems, since much of the new Front's deployment area had been occupied until recently by the Germans, who had destroyed as much as they could of the rail and road infrastructure before leaving. In consequence transport of troops and equipment on the hastily and sketchily restored railways was frequently interrupted, and road transport could not be substituted for it because of the state of the roads and shortages of vehicles. Mikoyan dealt with this by frequent telephone calls to People's Commissar for Railways Kaganovich, the heads of the two most involved railways, local military commanders and Communist Party officials. Despite the difficulties the timetable was fulfilled; between 1 April and 24 May the railways shifted 2,640 train-loads, totalling 178,900 wagons, to the Kursk area, half of them carrying reinforcements and supplies for units of the Central and Voronezh Fronts already deployed in the salient, the other half bringing the new Reserve Front's forces and equipment to their positions directly behind it.[283]

While well-educated young Muscovites were being trained to operate complex equipment in the Reserve Front, the mainly peasant infantrymen and civilian populations within the Kursk salient were preoccupied with the simpler but no less important task of digging. This was a mammoth undertaking in itself. Realisation of the superiority of the German tanks, while for the time being ending disputes between tankers and gunners as to whether the best antidote to a tank is another tank or an anti-tank gun, and concluding both would be needed, had brought on an acute awareness that success in the oncoming conflict would need maximum coordination between tanks, aircraft, artillery, engineers and infantry, and best use of terrain, exploiting natural and creating artificial obstacles. The new tanks were the main threat, so anti-tank defence must be the focus of the entire system. This must use guns, mortars, tanks, obstacles artificial (ditches and minefields) and natural (gullies, ravines, rivers, hills), and air support, all linked by a fire control and communications system capable of switching guns and aircraft quickly between different sectors. Trenches must be deep enough for troops to move without being exposed to enemy machine-gunners or snipers, machine-gun and artillery positions camouflaged to prevent the enemy picking them off by aimed fire or bombing, and anti-tank ditches be dug so wide and deep that no tank falling into one could climb out under its own unaided power. The combination of defensive measures would include infantry in foxholes, armed with anti-tank rifles to fire at tank tracks, bottles of explosive mixture ('Molotov cocktails') to throw onto the rear deck over the engine compartment, and anti-tank mines to be pushed under immobilised tanks and set off by throwing hand grenades at them.

Nor were the '*osobisty*' (Special Sections of SMERSH, 'Death to Spies', of the NKVD) idle. Although morale had been raised by the winter's victories, it was still by no means unshakeable; desertion and defection to the German side were still problems. At the end of June, when battle was known to be imminent, orders were issued to remove all Estonians, Latvians and Lithuanians from combat units and send them to the rear. A few days later similar orders were issued concerning soldiers who had been prisoners until liberated by the winter counter-offensive. They were regarded with suspicion; it was well known that large numbers of captured soldiers were willingly serving in German units, and all liberated ones were suspected of having been indoctrinated while in captivity to serve as saboteurs or at least to infect their comrades with defeatism.

An example of the action taken was an order issued by the headquarters of the 5th Guards Army of the Steppe Front on 8 July. The men affected, 824 in all, were awakened and removed during the night of 9/10 July, immediately before the 5th Guards Army began moving to the salient.[284]

Head of Red Army Artillery Voronov insisted that the barrage of gunfire against oncoming tanks must start early and maintain high rates of fire, but his attempt to include tank guns in the barrage was vetoed, officially not only as wasting ammunition but because it would create excessive wear on the gun barrels, and hence reduce accuracy. The real reason was, of course, the discovery in April that the tanks' guns could penetrate the armour of the new German tanks only at close range, but to tell the crews that was not likely to improve their morale.

As to how these lines were to be manned and held, future Marshal of Artillery Kazakov wrote that 'one day' Voronov ordered his staff to do some hard thinking. He told them that the four SS motorised infantry divisions (Leibstandarte Adolf Hitler, Das Reich, Totenkopf and Wiking) were being converted into panzer divisions, each including a battalion of 45 Tigers, that the elite Grossdeutschland army division had also received a battalion of Tigers, and that all these formations, plus the 10th Panzer Brigade, equipped with Panthers, were being concentrated against the south face of the Kursk salient. The outcome of the deliberations was that the 6th Guards Army, on the expected main line of attack, was reinforced by 14 anti-tank artillery regiments, and reserves were deployed so as to be able to reinforce threatened sectors quickly to a density of at least 20 anti-tank guns per kilometre of front.[285]

Guderian's reservations about the premature use of the new tanks would be proved right as regards the Panther – some formations equipped with them did not get into action at all, because every one broke down en route. The mechanical faults would be corrected, making it one of the war's best tanks, but that all took time, and the only time available in 1943 was the few weeks of postponement decreed by Hitler. However, Guderian's strictures on the Ferdinand as 'unsuitable for close combat' because it did not have a machine gun and was therefore vulnerable to the Soviet infantry are not borne out by combat evidence. At Kursk Ferdinands were used only against the Central Front, and about 90 of them saw combat. Examination by Soviet artillery specialists on 15 July of 21 knocked-out Ferdinands showed 11 disabled by mines, 8 by gunfire, 1 by an aerial bomb, and only 1 by an infantry weapon – and that not an anti-tank rifle or grenade but a 'Molotov cocktail'.[286]

The Red Army used the weeks of postponement at least as well as the

Germans, constructing defence systems that took advantage of the experience of two years' fighting to combine the various arms of service more
closely than before, behind minefields both larger and more densely sown
with anti-tank and anti-personnel mines than previously possible.
Increases in the two sides' deployments between 10 April and 5 July were
as shown below in the table of strength in men and weapons on both dates.
The Soviet data are for the Central and Voronezh Fronts for both dates,
and for 5 July also the Steppe Front. The German figures are Soviet estimates for Army Groups Centre and South.

**Table 16. German and Soviet build-ups for 'Citadel',
1 April–5 July 1943**

	10 April		5 July	
	Soviet	*German*	*Soviet*	*German*
Troops	957,910	700,000	1,910,355	900,000
Guns/Mortars	11,695	6,000	30,880	10,000
Tanks/SP guns	1,220	1,000	5,130	2,700
Combat aircraft	1,130	1,500	3,200	2,050

As the table shows, the Soviets already outnumbered the Germans in all
but aircraft before mid-April, then up to the launch date of Citadel their
troop numbers more than doubled, guns and aircraft almost trebled, and
tanks quadrupled. The German increases were far smaller, so that by the
time 'Citadel' was launched the Soviets outnumbered the Germans by
over 2 to 1 in manpower, 3 to 1 in guns, almost 2 to 1 in tanks, and 1.6 to
1 in aircraft. The disparities became even greater as the battle progressed;
between 5 July and 23 August, i.e. in the period covering the defensive
battle and the two counter-offensives (Operations 'Kutuzov' and
'Rumyantsev'), additions from reserve totalled on the Soviet side 38
division-equivalents, with 658,000 troops, 18,200 guns, 3,300 tanks and
563 aircraft, while German reinforcements comprised only 2 panzer
and 1 mechanised corps, totalling 55,000 men, 550 guns, about 200
tanks and 300 aircraft.[287]

For the Soviets to outnumber the Germans in weaponry was no
novelty, but it had previously proved no guarantee of success. As
mentioned earlier, in 1941 they had had numerical superiority of 3 to 1 in
tanks, 2 to 1 in combat aircraft and about 5 to 4 in guns and mortars, but
nevertheless suffered a series of disasters on a scale unparalleled in the
previous history of warfare. The difference in 1943 was that the weapons-
users and the generals who directed them had learned from the defeats,

and had begun to match or even outdo the Germans in how they used their assets. On the most important sectors the five main and three intermediate defence lines in the salient stretched back to 190 kilometres (almost 120 miles) behind the front. During April–June troops and local civilians in the Central Front's area alone dug 5,000 kilometres (about 3,125 miles) of trenches, laid 400,000 mines and over 200 kilometres (125 miles) of barbed wire, a few kilometres of it even electrified.[288] These extensive preparations could not be concealed from the Germans, but the General Staff and NKVD utilised Agent Max and operatives sent to him who had been captured and 'turned', to inform the Abwehr that the Red Army intended to fight only a defensive battle, and credibility was added by making day and night rail deliveries of large quantities of cement, barbed wire, wood and metal beams on open flat trucks, while weapons and ammunition were moved in only at night and in covered wagons.[289]

Against the 55 German divisions deployed in 'Citadel', the Central and Voronezh Fronts had between them 77 infantry divisions, 9 tank or mechanised corps, 14 brigades and 3 'fortified zones' (garrison troops in fixed defences), the corps and brigades raising the total to about 110 division-equivalents, with 1,272,700 combat troops.[290] The Steppe Front, behind both, had one tank army (5th Guards), plus six tank and two mechanised corps, and six armies of infantry. It was meant as a reserve for the counter-offensive, but when the Germans appeared on the verge of breaking through the Voronezh Front, Stavka representative Vasilevsky on 9 July commandeered two of its armies (5th Guards and 5th Guards Tank) and parts of three others, totalling 19 divisions and one brigade of infantry, five tank and one mechanised corps. Manpower figures for them are not given, but they amounted to at least 30 additional division-equivalents, bringing the total to about 140, and the total Soviet manpower in the defensive battle to over 1.5 million. Granted that Soviet formations were smaller than their German counterparts, and that many of them were under strength,[291] the defenders outnumbered the attackers in manpower by about 1.7 to 1. In equipment, numbers favoured the Soviet side even more, by 1.8 to 1 in guns and mortars, 2.3 to 1 in combat aircraft, and 1.6 to 1 in tanks and self-propelled guns.[292] Compared to the defensive campaign at Stalingrad (37 divisions, 3 tank corps, 22 brigades, 547,000 men),[293] the manpower and resources defending the Kursk salient had considerably more than doubled. Germany's manpower, on the other hand, had fallen, and the contribution from its allies had dropped almost to nothing. The winter campaign of 1942/43 had involved Romanian, Hungarian and Italian as well as German armies, but at Kursk only

German units saw action, though a Soviet listing of forces present included the two Hungarian divisions. Clearly the strategic balance had tilted substantially away from Germany even in the few months since Manstein's February counter-offensive. Whether the tilt was decisive was still to be seen.

Both Zhukov and Vasilevsky later wrote that they (correctly) regarded the threat posed to the Voronezh Front as greater than that facing the Central Front,[294] but the distribution of forces suggests the opposite; the Central Front had 738,000 troops, versus the Voronezh Front's 534,000.[295] This meant that for each mile of front line on the sectors where the main German thrusts were expected, the Central Front had 7,200 men, 72 tanks and 166 guns, the Voronezh Front only 4,000 men, 67 tanks and 94 guns.[296] The discrepancy was never explained; it was partly due to Rokossovsky's being more successful in identifying the main German lines of attack and concentrating his forces there by stripping less threatened sectors, whereas Vatutin had to distribute them more evenly; but the principal reason for giving Rokossovsky substantially more resources in the first place must have been the continued preoccupation with possible threats to Moscow mentioned in Vatutin's April report and the 'particular uneasiness' in respect of it that Shtemenko mentioned Stalin as displaying at the meeting on the 12th. If such a threat were posed, it would obviously be posed by Army Group Centre, after destroying the Central Front on the salient's northern face, not by the much more distant Army Group South.

The scene was now set for the biggest trial of strength yet seen.

Chapter Six

The Battle for Kursk

On 2 July, after notifying the Fronts that the German offensive was imminent, Stalin sent Zhukov to the salient. He arrived at Rokossovsky's command post on the evening of the 4th. Later that evening the 13th and 48th Armies reported capturing German sappers who were removing mines, and who told their captors that the troops were in their forward positions for the offensive to begin at 3 a.m. It was then 2 a.m. local time. Rokossovsky's artillery, mortars and the M13 multiple rocket launchers that Soviet soldiers called 'Katyusha' (Katie) and German soldiers 'Stalin Organs' were already ranged on those positions, but Stalin's control of his generals was tight, and opening fire without his permission could bring down his anger. However, to seek it in the middle of the night would entail a delay, and the Germans might have vacated those positions and advanced before a reply was received. Possibly out of tact (Rokossovsky had been Zhukov's immediate superior until arrested in 1937), but more probably to divert Stalin's wrath if he disapproved, Zhukov told Rokossovsky, 'You're the Front commander, so you decide, with full responsibility for the decisions taken.' At 2.20 a.m., just 10 minutes before the German artillery was believed about to open up, fire from over 500 guns, 460 mortars and 100 Katyushas rained down on the enemy positions.

Rokossovsky claimed that confusion reigned on the German side, as losses were quite heavy; some of the German artillery was destroyed, and when it did open up, at 4.30, its fire was at first weak and disorganised.[297] However, Zhukov qualified this judgement:

> Of course the artillery counter-preparation caused the enemy great losses . . . but we expected greater results from it . . . I came to the conclusion that both Central and Voronezh Fronts began it too soon; the German soldiers were still sleeping in trenches, dugouts or gullies, and the tank units were concealed in waiting areas. It would have been better if the counter-preparation had begun about 30–40 minutes later.[298]

The most likely explanation is simply confusion caused by time difference. The German army kept Berlin time, two hours behind Moscow
time for most of the year, one hour behind in summer. Zhukov and
Rokossovsky either did not know this, or more likely mistakenly assumed
that the prisoners' interrogators had allowed for it. The time the sappers
mentioned would be when they were to be off the minefields to leave them
clear for the tanks and infantry, and Army Group Centre's combat reports
did not mention any disruption of the timetable. Sunrise at Kursk on 5
July 1943 was at 4.33 local time,[299] and that suggests the German
artillery's opening fire at 4.30 (3.30 Berlin time)[300] then tanks and infantry
advancing an hour later, were exactly as planned, and explains why the
Soviet gunfire fell largely on empty trenches; to have the infantry lose
sleep by occupying them for two hours before action was pointless and
bad for morale. If the offensive was really meant to begin 90 minutes
before dawn, it could do so only without the tactical air support integral
to all the Wehrmacht's major operations. It is most likely Rokossovsky's
belief that he had only 10 minutes to pre-empt the German artillery was
mistaken, and the alleged weakness of the German riposte was simply
because most guns were not yet manned, the pre-attack bombardment not
being scheduled to start for another two hours. Zhukov specifically
ascribed the below-expectation results to the darkness, which forced the
Soviet guns to shell by areas rather than at pinpointed targets, and also
mentioned that the Luftwaffe first appeared 'between five and six'[301]; that
too accords precisely with a timetable for air support of an advance
starting at 4.30 Berlin (i.e. 5.30 local) time. It would seem that 'disruption' of the launching of 'Citadel' simply did not happen. The *Soviet
Military Encyclopedia* claimed that the counter-bombardment postponed
the start of 'Citadel' by two-and-a-half hours on the Central and three
hours on the Voronezh Fronts; this is just another of the several legends
with which Soviet-era accounts adorned the Battle of Kursk.

Against the Voronezh Front 'Citadel' actually began at 4 p.m. local
time on the previous day, when 75 bombers attacked the lightly held
forward positions of the 6th Guards Army, followed 10 minutes later by
an advance of two infantry divisions supported by artillery, and 65 tanks
from the reconnaissance battalions of the 3rd and 11th Panzer Divisions
and of the elite Grossdeutschland Division. Fighting continued after
dark, and by the end of the day the Germans had reached the forward
edge of the first line of prepared defences. At 10.30 p.m. the artillery on
the 6th Guards Army's sector conducted a five-minute bombardment of
previously targeted German positions, but the main 'counter-

preparation' was not mounted until 3 a.m. on the 5th. It lasted for 25 minutes, and, as with the Central Front, the darkness resulted in its inflicting less damage than was hoped. However, on both Fronts the artillery barrages had an important psychological effect, showing the Germans, as their command ruefully concluded, that 'the date for starting the offensive had become known to the enemy, and therefore the element of surprise was lacking'.[302] Heavy rain halted ground fighting for the night, but planned air attacks on the German tactical airfields went ahead. They relied on surprise, but no effort was made to take out the radar stations beforehand, so the Germans were ready for them and took a heavy toll. For example, one Il-2 ground attack group dispatched 18 aircraft; only 14 reached their target, and 11 of those were shot down. The bad weather complicated matters further; only 8 of 40 Il-2s intended to attack Barvenkovo airfield actually reached it.[303]

On the Central Front's sector, the 9th Army attacked on a 40-kilometre (about 25-mile) front, Tigers and Ferdinands leading, medium tanks behind, and infantry following in armoured personnel carriers or on foot; they were supported by artillery and by about 300 aircraft attacking in groups of 50–100 over the entire tactical depth of the defence, trying in particular to knock out the artillery. One after another the leading tanks were destroyed or disabled in the minefields, but the following ones pushed on. By evening the Germans had advanced 6–8 kilometres, and Rokossovsky was told they had not yet committed the whole of their main force, so that he should expect strong attacks again on the next day. When he mentioned that in his evening report, Stalin at once promised to send him the 27th Army from reserve. But the next morning Stalin telephoned ordering Rokossovsky to send that army straight on to the Voronezh Front, where a dangerous situation had arisen, and warned him that he would not only have to get by with what he already had, but also defend Kursk with it if the Germans broke through the Voronezh Front. 'Bear in mind,' he said, 'your left-side neighbour's position is serious, the enemy may strike from there into the rear of your forces.'[304]

The situation at the Voronezh Front was indeed serious, and about to get more so. With fewer forces than the Central Front it faced a bigger threat, from four panzer corps and part of a fifth, versus three in the north, and Vatutin's staff had also identified the main lines of attack less precisely than at the Central Front. In part this was because the flatter terrain provided more possible lines of approach than on the north face, but Vatutin's deployment of the 40th Army, his strongest, on the west face of the salient, well away from the area from where the panzers posed the most likely threats, was certainly an error.

In his post-Soviet memoirs Lieutenant-General N.A. Antipenko, the Central Front's head of Rear (Logistics) Services during the battle, drew attention to the difference in the level of artillery support at the two Fronts:

> The weight of a combat allocation of ammunition for each Front was 20,000 tonnes. From four to five of these were offloaded at the artillery firing positions. The whole question is about how much ammunition was fired off during the defensive battle from 5 to 12 July. In other words, how much fire and metal rained down on the enemy's heads? For the stability of our infantry depended to an enormous extent on this. The intensity of the artillery fire can be judged from these data; in the period indicated, Central Front expended 1,079 freight-car loads of ammunition, Voronezh Front 417, almost two and a half times less . . .[305]

A 'freight-car load' was 20 tonnes, so in eight days the Central Front expended 21,580 tonnes and the Voronezh Front 8,340 tonnes. Antipenko's point is not that Vatutin had fewer guns at his disposal (Rokossovsky had more, but certainly not two-and-a-half times as many), nor that ammunition was in short supply. It definitely was not. Even the Voronezh Front's average of 1,042.5 tonnes a day testified to an enormous improvement in ammunition production and supply compared with the winter offensive of 1941–42, where Zhukov complained that on some sectors his guns had had only enough to fire one or two rounds a day. Antipenko's criticism implies that Vatutin could have had more if he had asked for it.

The Voronezh Front's situation at the end of the first full day of 'Citadel' was already critical, and its need for assistance would soon become urgent. The Germans resumed attacking at 6 a.m. local time on 5 July, and quickly broke through the first line of defences. Infantry then crossed to the east bank of the Seversky Donets south of Belgorod in rubber boats, followed by a company of tanks that forded the stream, and advanced to establish a line along a railway embankment about 3 kilometres from the river, while their sappers laid two pontoon bridges, one of them strong enough to bear the weight of Tigers. Soviet ground attack aircraft summoned from the adjacent South-West Front destroyed the pontoon bridges, but before they arrived the Germans had already put about 100 tanks across, in addition to those that had forded. Then 120 tanks and a regiment of infantry attacked, broke through the defences, and began to extend the breakthrough sector northwards. This attack began at 8.50 a.m., and the extent of the German gains after less than five hours of fighting must have come as a severe shock to Vatutin.

Relief came first from the weather; a cloudburst during the morning made the streams and rivers impossible to ford for almost half a day, thus delaying the reinforcement and supply of German units that had already crossed them, and hindering their attempts to expand the additional bridgehead they had made over the Psel river. Vatutin's orders and reports for 5 July prompt questions as to whether he grasped the seriousness of the situation at all, or whether he did, but feared to let Stalin know. At 4.35 p.m. he ordered the 2nd and 5th Tank Corps to take up defensive positions by midnight, tasked to provide 'stable defence' against any German attempt to 'spread out to north and north-east', and to 'dig in the tanks in defence'. But he also ordered them 'to be ready to go over to the counter-attack from dawn on 6.7.43'. Then at 5.40 p.m. he issued similar orders to the 1st Tank Army, to take up defensive positions to prevent a north-eastward enemy breakthrough towards Oboyan, with 'tanks in defence to be dug in and carefully camouflaged', and 'to be in readiness by dawn of 6.7.43 to go over to the counter-offensive'.[306]

These orders were confusing, because they imposed completely opposite dispositions within a very short time-frame. Establishing a defence required the tanks to be dispersed and dug in for infantry support over the entire front line of the sector, whereas for counter-attacking they had to be concentrated and free to move in whatever direction was needed. Vatutin's orders gave them about six to seven hours to disperse and dig themselves in, then they would need to spend the night repositioning to be ready to attack a mere five hours later. The 1st Tank Army had already suffered significant losses from the SS Panzer Corps' Tigers and Panthers, and was outmatched not only in numbers but in firepower, because of the longer range and superior accuracy of the German tank guns. Its commander, General Katukov, sent a report to Vatutin suggesting postponing the counter-strike and relying on the previously prepared defence in depth. Receiving no reply by dawn, he launched the counter-strike as ordered, and from the very first moments saw his T–34s being shot to pieces. He dashed back to his headquarters intending to telephone Vatutin and ask him to call off the attack, but by chance Stalin telephoned just as he arrived and asked for a situation report. The two knew each other well, as Katukov had distinguished himself in tank battles with Guderian during the Battle of Moscow, so he felt no need to mince words for fear of seeming to lack courage or initiative:

> 'In my opinion,' he said, 'we were too hasty over the counter-strike. The enemy has big unexpended reserves, including tanks.'
> 'What do you propose?'
> 'For the present it makes sense to use the tanks for stationary firing, after digging them into the ground or deploying them in ambushes. Then we could let the enemy machines approach to 300 metres and destroy them by aimed fire.'

After a brief silence Stalin replied, 'All right, you won't make the counter-strike. Vatutin will ring you about it.' Vatutin soon rang and confirmed that the counter-strike was cancelled.[307] But the very fact that Stalin's intervention had been needed casts further doubt on Vatutin's decision-making under pressure.

Before the battle Vatutin, with Vasilevsky's consent but over Zhukov's objections, had taken the controversial step of digging in many of the 1st Tank Army's tanks as fire support points to back up the infantry of the 6th Guards Army. The infantry naturally welcomed this tactic, and so did the tank crews; it was easier to camouflage or conceal the tanks, and made for more accurate fire. In the first few days they disabled or destroyed more of the SS Panzer Corps' tanks than Rotmistrov's Tank Army did in the so-called 'greatest tank battle in history' on 12 July (discussed later). The Grossdeutschland Division, for example, went into battle on 5 July with 350 tanks and assault guns; by the evening of the next day all bar about 85 had been destroyed or disabled. The losses can be divided in rough parity between Soviet action and German mechanical failure. The new Panthers proved particularly unreliable: Grossdeutschland took 200 of them into battle, and after two days' fighting only 40 were still service-able. Most of the others had suffered mechanical breakdowns,[308] justifying Guderian's reservations about the wisdom of committing new models of tank to a major battle, with crews still unused to them and initial design faults not yet rectified. When these defects had been overcome the Panther proved one of the best tanks of the war, but its debut at Kursk was not exactly triumphant.

Vatutin's reporting continued to bear little relation to reality. For example, on the evening of 5 July he informed Stavka that counter-attacks by the 7th Guards Army had driven the enemy back to the west bank of the Seversky Donets 'on the entire front', with German losses of 12,600 killed and 507 tanks and self-propelled guns destroyed. This was completely untrue. The first day's fighting had resulted in the German seizure of a bridgehead up to 12 kilometres wide and 6 kilometres deep on the east bank of that river, for casualties of about 700 dead and 5,300 wounded. These were their largest daily losses in the entire battle, but the dead were only one-eighteenth of the total claimed by Vatutin.[309] Losses in tanks and assault guns are harder to quantify because of incomplete reporting and the speed with which many knocked-out tanks were repaired on the spot, the Soviet anti-tank mines proving not powerful enough to do more than superficial damage to the new tanks.[310] However, Vatutin's figure of 507 tanks knocked out was sheer fantasy; it would have represented almost half of Army Group South's entire armoured inventory.

The Voronezh Front's problems increased when the Waffen SS divisions Leibstandarte Adolf Hitler and Das Reich broke through the 69th Army's first two defence lines on a sector where the existence of a natural obstacle, the marshes of the Psel river, had caused the third line to be constructed unusually far (about 18 miles) behind the second, and relatively thinly defended. Over the next few days Vatutin had to seek more and more help from elsewhere. First came the 27th Army, originally meant for the Central Front, then, on 7 July, some of the tanks and infantry and all the artillery of the 38th and 40th Armies from the salient's quiescent west face. On 9 July Vatutin received the Steppe Front's 5th Guards Tank and 5th Guards Armies, which after a 200-mile journey took up positions on 11 July near a railway station named Prokhorovka. Over the next few days they would be locked in battle with the 2nd SS Panzer Corps, and the name Prokhorovka would become part of the most widespread legend associated with Kursk, and one of the largest of the entire war – namely that on 12 July the 5th Guards Tank Army and the 2nd SS Panzer Corps fought the biggest tank battle in history, and Hitler's elite forces were so decisively defeated that he cancelled 'Citadel' altogether on the very next day. That he did cancel it on 13 July is true, but the rest is pure myth.

Let us look first at the opposing sides' tank strengths. On 1 July Army Group South had 1,269 tanks serviceable or due to be so by the start of 'Citadel' on the 5th. Its main striking force would be 102 Tigers, 200 Panthers and 377 Mk IVs. The guns of all the new tanks and of many of the Mk IVs very substantially outranged any Soviet tank gun; however, there were also 51 obsolete Mk IIs and 416 rather outdated Mk IIIs, and many of the Panthers would not get into action because they broke down en route. German forces directly involved in the fighting at Prokhorovka on 12–16 July had about 430 tanks and self-propelled assault guns (II SS Panzer Corps had 294, including 26 captured T-34s, and III Panzer Corps 135). Against them the 5th Guards Tank Army on 12 July deployed 642 tanks and 30 self-propelled guns, a 3:2 numerical advantage,[311] but nullified by the greater range and penetrating power of the German tank guns and superior accuracy of their binocular sights. Soviet-era depictions, including in the film *Osvobozhdeniye* ('Liberation'), of two tank armadas charging each other were completely fictitious. The Soviet tanks did indeed charge, because their crews were desperate to get as quickly as possible through the danger zone in which their guns were useless but the German ones lethal. The Germans, however, had no incentive to rush to close quarters where their advantage in gunnery would be lost, and their inferior speed and manoeuvrability would count against them. They remained stationary, because that way they scored more hits, and when the Soviet tanks did close in, they manoeuvred principally to keep their thicker frontal armour facing the enemy. Typical of the problems facing Soviet tank crews was a 1993 statement by a survivor: 'you see our shells bouncing off the German armour. They aren't penetrating. Contrary to all the rules you fire into the ground ahead of you, so you can get closer side-on to the German in the clouds of dust . . .'[312]

On the morning of 12 July the 18th and 29th Corps of the 5th Guards Tank Army attacked the Leibstandarte Division and parts of Das Reich and Totenkopf. The two Soviet corps had 368 tanks and self-propelled guns, the Germans not more than 150. A separate action between the 2nd Tatsinskaya Tank Corps and the rest of Totenkopf added at most 200 between them, making a total of around 700 in the actions on the so-called 'tank field' south-west of Prokhorovka. A third action, an attack on Prokhorovka from the south by III Panzer Corps with about 120 tanks, including 23 Tigers, was opposed by a hastily assembled group under General K.G. Trufanov, with 157 tanks and 11 SP guns. The totals would therefore be around 640 Soviet and 400 German tanks and SP guns, somewhere between 1,000 and 1,100 altogether, in three related but separate engagements – not the 1,500 or more in a single battle depicted in numerous Soviet accounts, and copied from a statement in the memoirs of the 5th Guards Tank Army's commander, Lieutenant-General (later Chief Marshal of Armoured Forces) P.A. Rotmistrov, that about 800 Soviet met 700 German tanks. As mentioned previously, it is likely that the title of 'the biggest tank battle in history' should go to an encounter in the first days of the war, an attempted counter-offensive on 26–29 June 1941 by six mechanised corps of the South-West Front, with at least 2,800 tanks, against about 1,000 of the 1st Panzer Group. The outcome for the Soviets was such a disaster that details of it were not published until the 1990s; however, the numbers engaged surely make it the biggest tank battle ever.[313]

Before going into action on 12 July the 5th Guards Tank Army had 368 T–34s (225 arrived, 143 en route or under repair), 236 T–70 light tanks (180 and 56 respectively), and 14 British Churchills. By 17 July no fewer than 222 (60 per cent) of its T–34s had been irreparably damaged, along with 89 (38 per cent) of its T–70s and all bar 2 of its Churchills. It claimed to have destroyed 552 German tanks, including 93 out of 100 Tigers, but that would be almost four out of every five German tanks and self-propelled guns engaged that day, and German documentation, though incomplete, indicates nothing like that many losses; most of the Tigers knocked out, nothing like as many as claimed, had suffered only track damage from anti-tank mines and were quickly repaired. Apart from the normal confusion of battle, in which several tanks and guns fire on an enemy tank and each claims in good faith to have destroyed it, an extra incentive to overstatement in the Soviet case was Stalin's introduction on 1 July of substantial cash rewards to tank or gun crews or anti-tank riflemen for each enemy tank knocked out. Army Group South's actual tank losses in the six days from 12–17 July were about 150, somewhat fewer than they had lost in the first week of 'Citadel', 5–11 July, at the hands of the Voronezh Front's 6th Guards and 1st Tank Armies; most of them could be, and were, repaired.

Soviet-era accounts, when they mentioned losses at all, tended to suggest that they were about equal, and to claim that the Soviet side won because the Germans withdrew, thus yielding control of the battlefield. Post-Soviet researchers with access to the archives have found a totally different picture. According to one set of calculations[314] the 5th Guards Tank Army lost 334 tanks and assault guns as total write-offs (54 per cent of its strength), and also had an unknown, but large, number knocked out but repairable. The 29th Tank Corps, for example, lost 153 of 199 tanks that took part, 103 of them write-offs.[315] The SS Panzer Corps lost at most 17 and the III Panzer Corps 37 tanks, a maximum of 54 – less than one-sixth of the Soviet losses. Other researchers put the ratios even higher,[316] at 70–80 German and 600–650 Soviet losses. Whatever the uncertainties in the actual figures, all assessments agree that Soviet losses were several times greater than the German, especially in write-offs. Contrary to post-war Soviet claims, the Germans kept control of the battlefield until 17 July, when they began an orderly withdrawal, and each night sent out engineer squads to tow away repairable German tanks and blow up repairable Soviet tanks.

Nor did the Germans withdraw because they had lost. Hitler cancelled 'Citadel' on 13 July because of two events elsewhere. The first of these was the Anglo-American landings in Sicily on 10 July, and signs that Mussolini's power was waning (he was deposed and arrested on 25 July); Hitler cited these events as necessitating the dispatch of the entire SS Panzer Corps to Italy. The second, of far greater credibility and more immediate importance, was the strong Soviet counter-offensive north of the salient launched by Zhukov on 12 July. This led Hitler to order the Grossdeutschland Division (not at Prokhorovka, but a little further south, with Army Detachment Kempf) to be sent north to reinforce Army Group Centre. That these decisions and the order to cancel 'Citadel' were taken together on 13 July disposes of any idea that the landings in Sicily three days earlier were the real trigger, rather than the events of the day before at the salient.

The lesser importance of the Sicilian events is further illustrated by the fact that only the Leibstandarte Division actually went to Italy, and it handed its tanks over to the other SS divisions before it left, receiving new ones while passing through Germany. Events on the Eastern Front prevented the intended departure of Das Reich and Totenkopf. They did indeed leave the salient, but not for Italy; Manstein had to send them further south, to join SS Wiking in resisting yet another Soviet offensive, by the South-West and South Fronts in the Donbass, which began on 13 August. Thus deprived of all his strongest units, and having no reserves with which to try for the still unachieved breakthrough, Manstein could only withdraw what was left to his 5 July start line, and await the inevitable Soviet counter-offensive. This withdrawal was conducted in good order, without major interference from the Voronezh Front's weary and depleted forces.

There are several other indications of how serious a defeat the Voronezh Front experienced in those few days of July. The first is that on hearing what had happened on the 12th (and, of course, unaware that Hitler was about to cancel 'Citadel'), Stalin at once ordered Zhukov to hand over to Voronov control of the major offensive he had launched just that morning, and go at once to the Voronezh Front headquarters to join, and within a few days take over from, Vasilevsky. Zhukov arrived at Vatutin's headquarters on the 13th; apart from one brief visit to the Bryansk and West Fronts and two to Moscow, totalling only 8 days, he stayed with the Voronezh and Steppe Fronts for over two months, until 24 September.[317]

The second sign of a crisis was that Stalin, who normally trusted

Vasilevsky completely, sent him away to the less threatened southern sector, to coordinate the preparations by the South-West and South Fronts for their offensive in the Donbass, due to begin in mid-August. This suggests that he thought the situation at the Voronezh Front, as at Leningrad and Moscow in 1941, too serious for anyone except Zhukov to handle. The third is that he contemplated dismissing and court-martialling Rotmistrov, though Vasilevsky managed to dissuade him.[318] The fourth was that on 12 July some Soviet infantry units had succumbed to panic, and mass flights from the front line had begun. In the 69th Army, for example, seven blocking detachments had to be hastily organised by its counter-espionage section of SMERSH and placed behind the troops in the line, where in just 11 hours (5 a.m. to 4 p.m. on 12 July) they detained 2,842 personnel who had fled from front-line units, including a number of officers. How they dealt with them is not stated. However, there is a possible clue in a recent publication based on research in the military archives.[319] It records the losses sustained by the 48th Rifle Corps of the 69th Army from 1–16 July. The corps had five infantry divisions, with a combined strength of 42,945 on 5 July and 38,152 on the 10th. By the 16th it had sustained casualties of 1,982 dead, 8,395 'missing', 3,828 wounded, 74 sick and 1,360 'other'. That there were over four times as many 'missing' as dead implies mass flights, surrenders or desertions. A strange feature of the 'others', a category not explained but counted among the 'irrevocable' losses, is that all bar one of the 1,360 were incurred in one division, the 89th Guards. A closer look at that division's casualty figures repays attention. First, its numbers had declined from 8,702 to 5,725 between 5 and 10 July, i.e. it had lost over one-third of its strength in just six days of defensive fighting. Secondly, its pattern of casualties was strikingly different from that of the rest of the corps.

Table 17. Casualties in the 89th Guards Division compared to the rest of the 48th Corps

Actual:	*Dead*	*Missing*	*Wounded*	*Sick*	*'Other'*	*Total*
89th Guards	796	962	1142	11	1359	4270
Rest of Corps	1186	7433	2686	63	1	11369
As Percentages:						
89th Guards	18.6	22.5	26.7	0.3	31.8	100
Rest of Corps	10.4	65.4	23.6	0.6	–	100

The percentages show that proportionally the 89th Guards had nearly twice as many dead and slightly more wounded than the other divisions, but only one-third as many 'missing'. However, almost one-third of its total losses were in the category 'other', i.e. not incurred in combat. Counting these as 'irrevocable' implies they were neither returned to their units nor sent to a penal battalion, and carries the implication that they were shot or hanged. The 69th Army comprised ten infantry divisions, two tank corps and a number of independent regiments as well as copious artillery and engineer support.[320] That the total of 1,359 'other' losses in a single division is almost half of the 2,842 mentioned above as detained in the 69th Army as a whole on 12 July suggests that, unlike in 1941, mass flight was confined to a few units. However, during the war the Red Army executed 157,000 of its own soldiers for cowardice or desertion,[321] so probably some of the fugitives were shot or hanged 'to encourage the others'. Whatever they did, it worked; the SMERSH commander reported on 17 July that the 69th Army had experienced no more mass flights.[322] Nevertheless, only two days later that army was taken out of action and transferred to the Steppe Front. On the same day the 7th Guards Army was also transferred, whether because of similar panic flights, heavy losses or a combination of both is not stated, but the only reason for taking both out of action would be that ten days of battle had worn them down beyond a capacity for further fighting. Apart from the 5th Guards and 5th Guards Tank Armies, the Steppe Front was still in reserve, and its losses for the whole of July were tabled as only 8,748, of which 2,490 were 'missing'. Figures for total losses are discussed below; they appear to have been 'rearranged' before publication, but are the only data available.

In round figures the Germans lost 1,500 tanks at Kursk and the Soviets 6,000,[323] including in the two counter-offensives, Operations 'Kutuzov' north of the salient and 'Rumyantsev' to the south of it. These continued until 18 ('Kutuzov') and 23 ('Rumyantsev') August, but even after both ended the Tigers continued to dominate wherever they appeared. For example, in six days of fighting from 5 to 10 September the 45 Tigers of Army Group South's 503rd Heavy Tank Battalion knocked out 501 Soviet tanks and 477 guns.[324]

The superiority of the new German tanks worried Rotmistrov enough that on 20 August he wrote in a memorandum to Zhukov 'our tanks . . . have lost their superiority in armour and armament over the enemy's . . . . in clashes with German tank units that have gone over to the defensive, we suffer enormous losses as a general rule, and have no success . . . On the basis of our T-34 tank . . . the Germans have been able in 1943 to provide an even better tank, T-V (Panther), that . . . stands significantly above the T-34, especially in the quality of its armament.'[325] In the light of this memorandum, published only in post-Soviet times, Zhukov's description as 'immodest' of Rotmistrov's post-war claim that the 5th Guards Tank Army had played the decisive role in defeating Army Group South's panzers appears the height of moderation.[326]

The Voronezh Front's defensive battle at Kursk was almost a major disaster. What converted it into an expensive tactical draw and contributed to an even bigger Soviet strategic victory than Stalingrad was the combination of tanks with minefields, anti-tank defences, artillery and air support, and perhaps above all Rokossovsky's successful defence of the salient's north face, which enabled the counter-offensive there to be launched on the date planned and at full strength. The Allies' landings in Sicily played a lesser role, and it seems more likely that in citing them Hitler was engaged in face-saving. By 12 July it was already obvious that 'Citadel' was failing. On the north face Model had been stopped in his tracks by the 10th, and was now threatened with encirclement by the counter-offensive Zhukov launched on the 12th. On the south face Manstein's substantial tactical victory had not resulted in the hoped-for breakthrough that would give it strategic status; to achieve that would need not only retention of the SS Panzer Corps and Grossdeutschland Division, but additional forces that were simply not available. For Hitler, to cite the Anglo-American landings in Sicily as forcing him to abandon 'Citadel', and blaming the necessity for it on the shortcomings of his Italian ally, was less humiliating than admitting that the despised *Untermensch* had beaten him yet again, this time in a battle at a time and place of his own choosing, and with no help from Generals Mud or Winter.

Rokossovsky had been a beneficiary of the only substantial Soviet miscalculation at Kursk: the belief that the German offensive, if successful, could be followed by a northward drive to encircle and take Moscow. He had made good use of the additional men and weapons, stopping Army Group Centre in only five days, after a maximum German advance of only 8–10 kilometres (5–6 miles), compared to the 35 kilometres (22 miles) they penetrated at the Voronezh Front. Better still, he had done it without needing reinforcements from reserve or other Fronts, or the wholesale commitment of his tank army, and with 'irrevocable' losses (15,336 killed, captured or missing) less than one-third of those suffered by the Voronezh and Steppe Fronts (official post-Soviet figures for them are given as 54,994, but do not include losses of the 7th Guards and 69th[327] Armies, which were taken out of the battle on 19 July). Furthermore, his success enabled Zhukov to open Operation 'Kutuzov' on 12 July, and the Central Front to join it on the 15th, whereas the Voronezh Front and the two armies from the Steppe Front engaged at Prokhorovka needed so many replacements of men and weapons that despite constant pressure from Stalin[328] they could not begin their counter-offensive (Operation 'Rumyantsev') until 3 August.

Operation 'Kutuzov', from 12 July to 18 August, took place on a front of 400 kilometres (roughly 250 miles) breadth. It was begun by three armies, the 11th Guards Army of the Western Front, heavily reinforced by tanks and artillery, and the 3rd and 63rd Armies of the Bryansk Front; the Central Front joined in with no fewer than five armies (13th, 48th, 60th, 65th and 2nd Tank) three days later. Initial progress was rapid, but Army Group Centre responded to the threat of the encirclement of the 2nd Panzer and 9th Armies by reversing the 9th Army's front and committing the Grossdeutschland Division to battle as soon as it arrived from Army Group South. The Soviet advance was halted but resumed on 20 July after three more armies (3rd Guards, 4th Tank and 11th) were brought in. Mussolini was deposed and arrested on the 25th, and on the 26th Hitler, who (rightly) did not believe the new Italian government's assurances of intent to stay in the war, ordered Army Group Centre to abandon the Orel salient altogether, in order to shorten its line and free units for dispatch to Italy and the Balkans. Field-Marshal von Kluge countered by proposing a staged gradual withdrawal, as had been done at Demyansk in February and Rzhev-Vyazma in March, to give time for the construction of proper defensive positions (the 'Hagen' line) in the rear. But on 29 July Hitler's suspicions that Italy was about to change sides were confirmed by interception of a radio-telephone discussion between Roosevelt and Churchill, so on 1 August he ordered the withdrawal to take place immediately.

To complicate matters even further for Army Group Centre, the weakened Army Group South was now also in difficulties. On 17 July the Soviet South-West and South Fronts mounted attacks against its right-flank armies (the 1st Panzer and the reconstituted 6th) on the Mius and Donets river lines. In a move that he later admitted was a 'disaster', Manstein responded by sending a substantial part of his remaining armoured forces to the south, believing the Voronezh and Steppe Fronts so weakened by their losses that they could cause no trouble for the present. But on 3 August the Germans were taken completely by surprise when Zhukov launched both those Fronts and the right wing of the South-West Front into Operation 'Rumyantsev', aiming in the first instance to recapture Kharkov and Belgorod. The initial assault, by four armies (5th, 6th and 7th Guards and the reconstituted 69th), quickly broke through the weakened German defences; the 5th Guards Tank and 1st Tank Armies were at once sent into the gap, and took Belgorod on 5 August. Hitler ordered Kharkov to be held at all costs, but the Steppe Front reached it on the 13th and the Germans abandoned it on the 23rd. The situation was stabilised, though only temporarily, by bringing back the Grossdeutschland Division yet again from Army Group Centre, and redeploying the 3rd Panzer Corps and the three Waffen SS Panzer Divisions, Das Reich, Totenkopf and Wiking, from Army Group South's southern flank.

Operation 'Rumyantsev' was terminated on 23 August, and marked the formal conclusion of the Battle of Kursk. However, the Germans received no respite. On 7 August the reinforced Kalinin and Western Fronts began Operation 'Suvorov', against Army Group Centre, and on the 13th the South-West and South Fronts, exploiting the success of Operation 'Rumyantsev' in drawing away the 3rd Panzer Corps and the three SS divisions, launched the Donbass Strategic Offensive. North of the former salient Operation 'Suvorov' continued until 2 October, with the Soviet forces advancing up to 250 kilometres (about 155 miles), entering eastern Belorussia and breaching the German 'Eastern Rampart' on the upper Dnepr. The Donbass operation ceased on 22 September, after the Soviet forces had advanced up to 300 kilometres (186 miles), retaken all of the important Donbass industrial area, and established a large bridgehead on the west bank of the lower Dnepr.

Nor was that the end of the Soviet autumn offensives. Their numbers and scale increased, and the pauses between them shortened. On 26 August, only eight days after the end of 'Kutuzov' and three days after the end of 'Rumyantsev', the Central, Voronezh and Steppe Fronts began the Chernigov–Poltava Strategic Offensive. This operation ended on 30 September, after advances of up to 300 kilometres (185 miles) and the seizure of two more bridgeheads west of the Dnepr. Even before it ended, the final phase of the battle for the Dnepr began on 26 September. It was for control of the lower stretch of the river, and was conducted by the 2nd, 3rd and 4th Ukrainian (the renamed Steppe, South-West and South) Fronts. The breadth of the front line, up to 800 kilometres (500 miles), and the weather (a rainy autumn followed by a snowy winter) combined with fierce German resistance to drag out this operation for almost three months. When it was formally ended, on 20 December, the Germans had been expelled from Ukraine east of the Dnepr, and their forces in the Crimea were cut off except for supply by air and sea.

Two smaller operations completed the account for 1943. From 10 September to 9 October Army Group A withdrew across the Kerch Strait from the North Caucasus to the Crimea. Soviet accounts depicted this exodus as the result of an offensive by the North Caucasus Front, the Black Sea Fleet and the Azov Flotilla, but in fact it was a phased withdrawal and did not experience much interference from the Red Army or Navy. However, the retreat removed the last residual threat to the Caucasus oilfields, and the Crimea did not exactly prove a refuge for the German forces; before the year ended they were cut off by land, and in April–May 1944 the Red Army reconquered the Crimea.

The other 'smaller' operation was the recapture of Kiev by the 1st Ukrainian (former Voronezh) Front. This began on 3 November; the city fell on the 6th, but the operation continued until the 13th and succeeded in establishing another bridgehead west of the Dnepr, over 300 kilometres (186 miles) from north to south and 150 kilometres (93 miles) from east to west. On 13 November Army Group South counter-attacked in force, and in 40 days of fighting succeeded in driving the 1st Ukrainian Front back about 40 kilometres (25 miles) before the front stabilised again. This 'Battle for the Dnepr' ended on 22 December, but the strategic superiority the Soviets now had was shown by their launching only two days later of the battle for 'Right Bank (i.e. west of the Dnepr) Ukraine' by all four Ukrainian Fronts, with 188 divisions, 19 tank and mechanised corps and 2.4 million troops. Another Front (the 2nd Belorussian) joined in during March, with an additional 33 divisions and 8 corps. By the time it ended, on 17 April 1944, Soviet forces had driven Army Group South out of Ukraine, entered Romania and were approaching the borders of Czechoslovakia and Poland. The operation compelled Germany to transfer 34 divisions and 4 brigades from the West, forces Rundstedt (Commander-in Chief West) must have sorely missed when the Anglo–American–Canadian landings in France took place only seven weeks later.[329]

Comparisons of these counter-offensives with that at Stalingrad indicate just how much the strategic balance had changed in Soviet favour in a few months. Operation 'Uranus' had been mounted with 74 divisions, 7 tank/mechanised corps, 34 brigades (17 of them infantry) and 9 Fortified Zones, with 1,143,500 troops. Operations 'Kutuzov' and 'Rumyantsev' between them fielded 132 infantry divisions, 19 tank/mechanised corps and 19 brigades (15 of them tank/mechanised), 3 Fortified Zones and 2,431,000 troops.[330] So in the defensive battle and associated counter-offensives the manpower and weaponry available for Kursk was more than double that of the Stalingrad campaign.

As discussed above, Soviet Intelligence performed much better than it had at Stalingrad, and considerably outshone its German counterpart, which detected the preparations for the defensive battle (that was easy: earthworks totalling hundreds of kilometres could not be concealed from aerial reconnaissance) but failed to foresee the ensuing series of counter-offensives, or their scale.

Other elements of the comparison with Stalingrad appear in Table 18.[331]

Table 18. Scope, gains and speed of advance, offensives of 1942 and 1943

	Uranus/Saturn	*Kutuzov*	*Rumyantsev*
Duration (days)	76	38	21
Breadth of front (km)	850	400	400
Maximum advance (km)	200	150	140
Daily advance (km):			
– infantry	1.5–2.5	4–5	7
– mechanised forces	4–4.5	7–10	10–15

What was the human cost?

Table 19. Official data, Soviet irrevocable losses at Kursk[332]

Front	*Defensive battle*	*Dates*	*Offensive*	*Dates*	*Total*
Central	15,336	5–11/7	47,771	12/7–18/8	63,107
Voronezh	27,542	5–23/7	48,339	3–23/8	75,881
Steppe	27,452	9–23/7	23,272	3–23/8	50,742
Bryansk	–	–	39,173	12/7–18/8	39,173
West (left wing)			25,585	12/7–18/8	25,585
Total	70,330		184,140		254,488

These *GSS* figures indicate that in the seven weeks from 5 July to 23 August 1943 Soviet losses (mostly dead) almost equalled all the British armed forces' deaths during six years of war. Furthermore, several Russian researchers in post-Soviet times have suggested that the *GSS* figures seriously understate the losses, particularly those of the Voronezh Front in the defensive battle. One, for example, cites reports from the Voronezh Front headquarters of 42,977 (18,097 dead, 24,851 missing) 'irrevocable' losses for just the 13 days from 4 to 16 July, whereas the Steppe Front reported only 8,748 (6,258 dead, 2,490 missing) for the entire month. The *GSS* data therefore appear to understate the

Voronezh Front's losses by about 50 per cent and to treble those of the Steppe Front, to produce almost identical figures (27,542 and 27,452) for the two Fronts. One reason for the discrepancy appears to be that most casualties incurred by the 7th Guards and 69th Armies were not included. Both were heavily involved in the defensive battle, but on 19 July Stavka transferred them from the Voronezh to the Steppe Front, so the Voronezh Front did not include their losses in its end-of-month report, because they were no longer on its strength, and Steppe Front included only figures for the 12 days after they became its responsibility. A partial clue about their losses is contained in yet another report from the Voronezh Front giving losses during July,[333] in this case including wounded and sick as well as dead or missing, but giving figures for the 15th as well as 31 July, and therefore including the 7th Guards and 69th Armies' losses for the first half of the month. The total, 148,349, is almost exactly double the 73,892 cited in *GSS* for the Voronezh Front's losses in the 19 days of the defensive battle. The apparent exaggeration of the Steppe Front's losses is similarly explainable. Its report for July did not include losses incurred by the 5th Guards Tank, 5th Guards and 27th Armies because they saw action only after they were transferred to the Voronezh Front on 9 July, but the table in *Grif Sekretnosti Snyat* counts them as still part of the Steppe Front until the defensive battle ended on 23 July. The effect of this is to make the Voronezh Front's losses appear less enormous by attributing a large part of them to the Steppe Front. If that Front's July losses are deducted from the *GSS* figures, and the difference (18,704) added, as it should be, to the Voronezh Front's, that Front's 'irrevocable' losses rise to 46,246, more than five times those of the Steppe Front, and three times those of the Central Front. Furthermore, if the ratio of 'irrevocable' to 'sanitary' losses was the same in the Voronezh Front staff report as in the *GSS* table, its losses during July were of the order of 92,000. However, Soviet manpower resources were more than adequate to replace casualties incurred at rates both allies and enemies considered excessive, but which the average Soviet infantryman bore with stolidity, if only because the early defeats had conditioned him and his commanders to regard heavy casualties as normal, inevitable and survivable. He had, after all, no opportunities to make statistical comparisons with German casualty rates, still less with those of the Americans or British.

German losses were much less extensive than the Soviets', but far harder to replace. In round figures the net loss (casualties minus replacements) at Stalingrad was a quarter of a million, and at Kursk half a million, and the losses were mostly of experienced soldiers, whereas the replacements were a mixture of raw recruits, rather elderly reservists or men hitherto rejected for medical reasons.

The battlefield value of Soviet tanks took until early 1944 to restore. The four competing gun design bureaus all produced prototypes in May 1943, and two of them, designated D5T and S-53, were accepted for further development. The first few D5Ts were produced in June. The gun functioned well but required many precision-engineered parts, and fitting it into even modified T-34 turrets proved difficult. It was planned to produce 100 T-34–85s armed with the D5T by the end of 1943, but the first batch rolled out only in January 1944.[334] In his memoirs Lieutenant-General Popel claimed the 1st Tank Army received its first T-34–85s some time between 10 September 1943, when it was withdrawn to reserve after suffering very heavy losses at Kursk, and early November, when it returned to the line, first seeing action on 23 December. Writing many years after the events, he may have got his dates wrong, or the 1st Tank Army may have received a pre-production batch of D5Ts sufficient to equip one of its corps, which at full strength would have around 130 T-34s. To train for a December offensive, the new tanks would have to arrive at the latest by the end of October; only 283 D5T guns were produced in 1943, and many of them were used in KV-85 and new IS-85 heavy tanks, so most, if not all, of the 1st Tank Army must still have been equipped with the T-34-76. It cannot have had the S-53 gun, because development of that was lagging behind, and it did not pass its final tests until the last days of the year.

The December offensive was supervised by Zhukov, who had strict instructions to report to Stalin by midnight of every day. The contents of his report for 23 December are not in the public domain, but must have included criticisms of the existing tank guns, because Stalin immediately sent the People's Commissars for Tank Industry (Malyshev), Armaments (Ustinov) and Ammunition (Vannikov) to Sverdlovsk in the Urals, where the S-53 was being developed. Their presence must have stimulated the design team, because the gun, reported as still seriously defective when they arrived on 26 or 27 December, was redesigned, recast and passed all tests in four days. The State Defence Committee accepted it for mass production on 1 January 1944, and on 23 January also accepted the modified T-34–85 tank with a larger turret and with frontal and turret armour doubled to 90mm thickness. The D5T programme was terminated on 1 March after only 543 had been made (most of them were put into self-propelled guns), and the first T-34–85s with the S-53 gun began reaching units in that month. The S-53 was much simpler and cheaper to make than the D5T, and over 11,000 were produced. There were some residual problems with its recoil mechanism, but the ZIS factory eventually solved them; from November 1944 to December 1945 over 12,000 of the modified ZIS-S-53s were manufactured. Some KV heavy tanks were also equipped with 85mm guns, but the type soon went out of production in favour of the new IS models with 122mm guns.

The improvement can be seen from the data about the April 1943 tests. The Tiger I's frontal armour was 100–110mm (about 4 inches) thick, the Panther's up to 120mm (about 4.5 inches). Shells from the T-34–76's F-34 gun had an 80 per cent chance of penetrating 102mm of armour only if fired from a mere 100 metres (110 yards) away and hitting at right angles, while even the Tiger's 80mm side armour was invulnerable to all types of Soviet 76mm armour-piercing shell at ranges above 500 metres.[335] Shells fired from the new 85mm guns proved capable of penetrating the Tiger's frontal armour from about 1 kilometre, cumulative and sub-calibre rounds from even further away, and they came to form an increased percentage of the tank's ammunition during 1944. Even larger guns (122mm) were soon available in the new IS-2 and IS-3 heavy tanks, but the T-34–85 remained in service until the mid-1950s.

The outcome at Kursk lacked the drama of Stalingrad, in that there was no siege, major encirclement or mass surrender on either side. However, it was strategically far more significant in several ways. For the first time the Germans could not blame their defeat on the weather or geography. They had mounted a set-piece offensive in the summer, at a time and place of their own choosing, but it had failed to achieve any of its objectives and had been followed by hasty withdrawals under pressure from a series of massive counter-offensives. Even though their new-generation tanks had proved their superiority, there had been no breakthrough, because the defenders had relied on a combination of elements, not simply on tanks, producing a credible facsimile of the Germans' own tactics but on a larger scale because they had more human and material resources.

On the planning side the only substantial Soviet error had been to assess the north face of the salient as needing more forces than the south face because of the lingering preoccupation with non-existent threats to Moscow. That made for some anxious times in the south, but the over-insurance in the north compensated for the under-insurance in the south, by enabling the Central Front to stop the Germans without needing help from elsewhere.

The Germans came nearer to success at Kursk than Soviet-era accounts admitted, but that does not mean they came close. To exploit the successes at Prokhorovka would have required substantial reserves, which they did not have. Granted the Voronezh Front had been badly mauled, but it still retained most of its fighting strength, and granted some of the Steppe Front's strength had had to be committed prematurely, but most of it had not. Even if Manstein had been successful, he would eventually have encountered Rokossovsky's forces, which could safely reverse their front to face him, because by then the Bryansk and Western Fronts were keeping Army Group Centre far too busy for it to take on the Central Front as well. From 13 August to 22 September Army Group South was also in full retreat on its southern sector; under severe pressure from the South-West and South Fronts, it was forced to abandon the Donbass and withdraw up to 450 kilometres (280 miles), proving unable to prevent the two Fronts establishing a bridgehead on the west side of the Dnepr and also cutting off all land connection to German and Romanian forces in the Crimea. These events are hard to reconcile with Manstein's post-war claim that but for Hitler's orders, Kursk would not have been one of his 'Lost Victories'.

Unlike the victories at Moscow and Stalingrad, the outcome at Kursk handed the strategic initiative permanently to the Red Army. Sheer professionalism would enable the Wehrmacht to conduct a skilful retreat, with numerous local successes, but at strategic level the rest of the war would consist of a series of Red Army advances, some less successful and more costly than others, but none of them total failures as had so often been the case in 1941–42.

The Red Army's remarkable acquisition from July 1943 of the ability to mount successful strategic-scale offensives simultaneously or in rapid sequence was due to several factors, among them hard-won experience, increased production of weapons and ammunition, and German over-stretch. However, these factors alone cannot account for the sudden development of the ability to overlap offensives or to mount new ones after very short pauses, such as Chernigov-Poltava, launched by three Fronts, the Central, that had just eight days previously completed five weeks of the 'Kutuzov' offensive, the Voronezh and the Steppe, both of which had ended the three weeks of 'Rumyantsev' just three days earlier.

The increased capability could result only from a spectacular rise in speed of resupply; that in turn would be possible only through widespread replacement of carthorses and footslogging by vehicles, and the primary source of vehicles was the United States. Altogether it supplied about 435,000 of these, and 1943 was a peak year for deliveries. Acknowledgements by Stalin and Zhukov of their importance are cited in the 'Conclusions' chapter. Here it need only be noted that reserves and reinforcements, ammunition, fuel and food could be transported faster and arrive in larger numbers and better condition than before, and the results, as indicated above, rapidly became apparent in a practically permanent switch of the strategic initiative into Soviet hands.

The surge in Lend-Lease deliveries from mid-1943 owed much to an event hardly ever mentioned in Soviet accounts, namely the Allied victory in the Battle of the Atlantic. As late as March 1943 the U-boats seemed to be winning it, sinking 600,000 tons of Allied shipping for a loss of only a handful of submarines, but the tables were turned so completely during the next two months that on 24 May Admiral Doenitz ordered all U-boats withdrawn from the North Atlantic. In September Churchill was able to announce that in the previous four months not a single ship had been lost.[336] This meant not only that more of what was sent reached its destination, but also that more was sent, because it was safe to do so.

Even the lack of a Second Front made no strategic difference, except as something for Stalin to complain about. In over ten-and-a-half months, from the start of Operation 'Kutuzov' on 12 July 1943 to the landings in Normandy on 6 June 1944, the Red Army was almost continuously on the offensive, usually on several sectors simultaneously. 'Kutuzov' (12 July–18 August) was overlapped by 'Rumyantsev' (3–23 August), 'Suvorov' (7 August–2 October), and the Donbass operation (13 August–22 September), and the latter two were overlapped by the Chernigov–Poltava offensive (26 August–30 September). Two more offensives began before it ended, the final operation to remove Army Group A from the Caucasus (10 September–9 October), and the Lower Dnepr offensive (26 September–20 December). The Caucasus operation was more pursuit than battle, as Army Group A withdrew in generally good order, ending with evacuation of the 17th Army's last units across the Kerch Strait to Crimea. The Lower Dnepr offensive retook almost all of Ukraine east of the Dnepr and isolated 14 German and 7 Romanian divisions in the Crimea. A separate operation from bridgeheads north and south of Kiev began on 3 November, recapturing the city on the 6th and ending on 13 November, by which time the autumn rains were well advanced and movement of both sides was temporarily constrained by mud. As noted above, successive offensives followed, first for the Ukraine, then the Crimea, and continued until May 1944.

The likelihood that the Voronezh Front's casualties in the defensive battle at Kursk were much heavier than the official figures was discussed earlier. Some of the Soviet offensives mentioned above also incurred very heavy casualties. For example, 233,300 troops of the left wing of the Western Front took part in Operation 'Kutuzov'; in 38 days of fighting 102,441 (43.9 per cent) of them were killed, captured or wounded. The whole of that Front, some 824,200 troops, then participated in Operation 'Suvorov'; over its 57 days 333,188 of them (40.4 per cent) suffered the same fates.[337] Even Stalin found these casualty levels unacceptable for the results achieved, and dismissed the Front's commander, General Sokolovsky. He was not punished, but returned to the staff work at which he excelled – he had been Zhukov's Chief of Staff in the battle of Moscow, and would be again in the battle of Berlin. In the Lower Dnepr offensive the 2nd Ukrainian (formerly Steppe) Front's casualties (including wounded) were even heavier, 65.5 per cent, but the commander, Konev, was not replaced, even though his 'irrevocable' losses (17 per cent) were far higher than Sokolovsky's (11 per cent in 'Kutuzov', 9.7 in 'Suvorov'), because he achieved more impressive results.

The very high casualty rates accepted in the Red Army owed much to the indifference to human life of a regime that had murdered millions of its citizens in peacetime. They also owed much to geography, as dwellers on plains lacking natural barriers of seas, mountains or deserts, subject to invasion in times of weakness and to their rulers' expansionist ambitions in times of strength, and in either case required to fight and die en masse. This in turn engendered an appeal to tradition that emphasised fighting to the death. The casualties also constituted a macabre testimony to the professionalism of the Wehrmacht, vastly outnumbered and outgunned, the delusion of invincibility long since lost, but to the end able to make antagonists pay dearly for even small gains.

However, lessons that Soviet generals learned in the first 18 months of war, mostly from the Germans, about cooperation between tanks, infantry, artillery and aircraft, the increasing mechanisation of the army, and gradual acquisition of air superiority by the air force, did lead to a reduction in casualties as a proportion of the troops engaged. The figures in Table 20 are from *GSS*. As noted above, the losses of the Voronezh and Steppe Fronts at Kursk appear to have been 'redistributed' between them, but this does not affect the totals except for the omission of the losses of the 7th Guards and 69th Armies before they were taken out of action and transferred to the Steppe Front.

The method adopted in the table – adding the percentages together and dividing them by the number of operations – is a very crude device for measuring average loss rates, because the numbers involved, circumstances, ratios and compositions of opposing forces differed greatly from one operation to another. However, the differences between pre- and post-Kursk results are large enough to be considered significant. The average 'irrevocable' Soviet loss in the pre-Kursk operations listed was 39.6 per cent, but at Kursk and after it was only 7.2 per cent.

Totalling the numbers involved indicates another great difference between pre- and post-Kursk. The nine pre-Kursk operations listed involved a total of 7,096,100 soldiers, of whom 2,551,645 (36 per cent) were 'irrevocably' lost. The fourteen from Kursk onwards involved 23,355,100, with 'irrevocable' losses of 1,459,421, or 6.2 per cent. So the

Table 20: Soviet irrevocable losses as a percentage of those in combat

Operation	Total involved	Lost	Percentage
Baltic 1941	498,000	75,202	15.1
Western 1941	627,300	341,073	54.4
W Ukraine 1941	864,600	172,323	19.9
Kiev defensive	627,000	616,304	98.3
Leningrad defensive	517,000	214,078	41.4
Moscow defensive	1,250,000	514,338	41.1
Moscow offensive	1,021,700	139,586	13.7
Stalingrad defensive	547,000	323,856	59.2
Stalingrad offensive	1,143,500	154,885	13.5
Kursk defensive	1,272,700	70,330	5.5
Kursk offensives	2,431,600	184,140	7.6
Lower Dnepr	1,506,400	173,201	11.5
Dnepr-Carpathian	2,406,100	270,198	11.2
Leningrad-Novgorod	822,100	76,686	9.3
Belorussian	2,331,700	178,507	7.7
Lvov-Sandomir	1,002,200	65,001	6.5
Yassy-Kishinev	1,314,200	13,197	1.0
Baltic	1,546,400	61,468	4.0
Budapest	719,500	80,026	11.1
Vistula-Oder	2,112,700	43,251	2.0
East Prussia	1,669,100	126,464	7.6
Vienna	644,700	38,661	6.0
Berlin	1,906,200	78,291	4.1
Manchuria	1,669,500	12,031	0.7

Source: *Grif Sekretnosti Snyat*, pp. 162–223.

average number of troops involved in an operation increased from 788,456 to 1,668,221, i.e. by 46.7 per cent, but average losses fell from 283,516 to 104,244 or from 36 to 6.2 per cent; in round figures, after Kursk the average Soviet operation had almost half as many more troops as before it, but the losses were only just over one-third of the pre-Kursk average. In other words a Soviet soldier's chances of avoiding death or capture were almost six times as good after Kursk as before it.

German manpower losses at Kursk are harder to determine, but some idea of them can be gained from OKH assessments that the forces under its control (the whole Eastern Front, except the small number on the Finnish sector), totalled 3,100,000 on 1 July 1943, and 2,564,000 on 1 October. The latter figure included replacements for half the losses, so those losses were presumably twice the difference (536,000) between the July and October figures, or 1,072,000, including, under the German system of reckoning, the dead, captured, missing and one-third of those wounded, injured or sick. There are no reliable separate figures for these last in the public domain.

On the Soviet side the period 5 July to 2 October saw the defensive battle at Kursk, then five complete counter-offensives ('Kutuzov', 'Rumyantsev', 'Suvorov', Donbass, Lower Dnepr), and parts of two others (21 of the 30 days of the Novorossiysk-Taman and the first 5 of the 86-day Lower Dnepr operations); allowing for proportional daily losses in the two offensives still in progress at the end of September, the 'irrevocable' losses came to 645,000, the 'sanitary' losses to 1,554,457. Adding one-third of the latter to the former puts the Soviet figures of 'irrevocable' losses for July–September onto the same basis of calculation as the German, and the results, 1.072 million German and 1.162 million Soviet, differ by only 8 per cent. The Soviet side had at least 50 per cent more troops in the field than the Germans, and was attacking for almost all the period, so 'irrevocable' losses only about 8 per cent more than the Germans' tend to indicate that, contrary to beliefs still widely held and argued outside and (particularly) inside Russia, many Soviet commanders had learnt by mid-1943 how to wage war as economically in lives as the enemy, and thereafter their overall loss rates were comparable to, and often lower than, the German ones. It is probably impossible to assess how much of this improvement was due to experience, how much to increased availability of weapons, fuel and ammunition, and how much to the increased mobility conferred by American-supplied trucks, but all three were essential to it. Having survived disasters on an unprecedented scale, coming close to fulfilling pessimistic British and American forecasts that Leningrad and Moscow would fall in a matter of weeks, the Red Army became a juggernaut; Churchill became worried that it might not stop, and in 1945 even ordered the Chiefs of Staff to prepare a plan to start a Third World War on 1 July 1945 by attacking with 47 Anglo-American and 10 German divisions. The plan (Operation 'Unthinkable') was presented to him about two weeks after the end of the war, but rejected as beyond the capability of the Allied forces. Soviet allegations of malicious Western intent, long dismissed as Cold War propaganda, received some post-mortem justification by the publishing of details of Operation 'Unthinkable' in 1998; they are accessible on the Internet, including the entire text of the report presented to Churchill in May 1945. Given the powers of recovery the Soviet Union had displayed in 1941 and 1942, 'Unthinkable' was a well-chosen title.

Granted that in many places the Germans were initially welcomed as liberators, and a Soviet-era joke among Russian dissidents was that if Russia had not won its wars with the Swedes in the eighteenth century, the French in the nineteenth and the Germans in the twentieth, it might have acquired their political freedoms and high living standards; however, the Russian language also has a proverb, '*pust' khuzhe da nashe*' – 'never mind if it's worse, provided it's ours'. Stalin did not hesitate to invoke symbols of Russia's past; the title 'Stavka' chosen for the supreme headquarters of the armed forces was that of Tsar Nicholas II's headquarters in the First World War. He named major offensives and awards for success after victorious Tsarist generals, and in October 1942 abolished the institution of military commissars and reintroduced the gold braid and rank badges that in 1917 soldiers had ripped from their officers' shoulders. Communist values were not set aside, and communists were expected to set an example to their comrades-in-arms, but in appeals to the 'masses' Lenin, if mentioned at all, followed Alexander Nevsky, Suvorov or Kutuzov. And the war itself became the 'Great Fatherland War' (usually mistranslated as 'Great Patriotic War'; patriotism is a feeling, so a war cannot be patriotic any more than it can be cowardly or treacherous). The 'masses' responded, and after mid-1943 the war in the east turned into a succession of Soviet advances, a remarkable reversal for a Red Army that less than two years previously had appeared about to disintegrate.

Conclusions

The 26 months from the day of invasion to the formal end of the battle of Kursk in August 1943 can be summarised roughly as follows.

On 22 June 1941 German and German-allied invaders attacked Soviet western border forces that had slightly less deployed manpower, but were equipped with three times as many tanks, twice as many aircraft and 25 per cent more guns and mortars than the invading forces. Despite their large numerical inferiority in weapons, the invaders achieved in just four months a series of victories a whole order of magnitude greater than those of their First World War predecessors that had sufficed to bring about the Tsarist regime's collapse in 1917 and force its Bolshevik successor to sign the humiliating peace treaty of Brest-Litovsk. In the first six months Soviet losses in manpower alone were on a scale unprecedented in the history of warfare; official figures released for the first time in 1993, and widely considered to be understated, conceded 3,137,673 'irrevocable' (killed, captured or missing) and 1,336,147 'sanitary' (wounded, injured or sick) losses by the end of 1941.

These figures were not disclosed in the Soviet period because they did not match the image of an army of 'mass heroism' that the regime chose to project; on the contrary, they showed that in 1941 every two Soviet casualties resulting from wounds or illness were accompanied by five dead or 'missing' – a complete reversal of 'usual' warfare ratios, in which the wounded or sick outnumber the dead, captured or missing by at least two to one. Further examination of the details of 'irrevocable' losses shows that for every one definitely known to have been killed in action (totalling 465,381) during the first six months of the war, five had gone 'missing' (2,335,482), most of whom had surrendered, deserted or defected.[338]

However, though many Red Army units simply collapsed, others resisted with a determination the Germans had not encountered in their previous campaigns. Fulfilment of the 'Barbarossa' plan to achieve victory in five months was delayed by long-drawn-out fighting at Smolensk and Kiev, and it foundered in front of Leningrad, Moscow and Rostov-on-Don. Soviet counter-offensives began in early December, and continued until the spring thaw in April 1942. They secured no great encirclements comparable to those the Germans had achieved earlier, but inflicted considerable losses of men and equipment, recovered substantial territory, subjected the Wehrmacht to its first major defeat on land, and exposed Germany to a prolonged war for which it had not been prepared.

In 1941 all three German army groups had mounted major offensives, covering the entire eastern front from the Baltic to the Black Sea. German planning for the summer campaign of 1942 already implicitly acknowledged an adverse shift in the strategic balance, in that only Army Group South would mount an offensive, and to bring it up to full strength necessitated the transfer of some forces from Army Groups North and Centre.

The 1941 campaign had been based on a strategy of forcing the Red Army to battle and destruction by threatening targets that it would have to stand and defend rather than preserve itself by retreating. The concept survived into 1942, but its focus shifted, by posing a threat not to the major urban centres but to Ukrainian grain, coal and iron ore and Transcaucasus oil, first by seizing a vast expanse of Ukrainian territory including the Donbass (Donets basin) industries and mines and cutting the main Soviet oil supply route by advancing to the Volga, and secondly by driving into the Caucasus and seizing the oilfields. The operations were to be consecutive, and Army Groups North and Centre were to undertake no major offensives until Army Group South's operations had succeeded.

Gaps in Intelligence information led each side to misread the other's intentions. Stalin's conviction that Moscow was still the main target in 1942 caused him to reject as 'disinformation' captured documents that showed it was not. Believing the first stage of the German offensive, an onslaught at Voronezh, to be the prelude to a northward drive against Moscow, he sent some reserves there and retained others nearby, instead of deploying them against the German advance to the Volga. Field-Marshal von Bock in turn misinterpreted the increased Soviet resistance at Voronezh as the prelude to an intended push into the rear of Army Group South. To counter this, he retained so many of his mobile forces at Voronezh that no major and few minor encirclements were achieved during the Soviet retreat along the Don. Hitler thereupon dismissed him, and at the same time divided Army Group South into Army Groups B, to continue the drive to the Volga, and A, to advance forthwith into the Caucasus.

This decision, to make simultaneous two blows originally specified as consecutive, can be explained only by the wishful-thinking belief that the

Red Army was at the end of its tether, and perhaps also by an over-estimation of the effects of Axis successes in North Africa and Japanese advances in South-East Asia and the Pacific. The morale of Soviet troops in the south was indeed adversely affected by the long retreat, but by the end of July Stalin had at last accepted that Moscow was not currently endangered, and had begun dispatching reserves to the narrow land bridge between the Don and the Volga. However, Soviet attempts to hold positions west of the Don bend failed, and in mid-August the Germans reached the Volga north of Stalingrad. That should have constituted 'mission accomplished' for interdicting Soviet oil supplies, but the symbolic value of a city named after Stalin prompted a strategically unnecessary German campaign to take it, and a determined Soviet effort to defend it. The outcome was a concentration of major German and some Romanian forces in a potentially vulnerable forward projection of the front line, with a long exposed flank on the west–east stretch of the Don, which German manpower shortages and gross underestimation of Soviet recovery potential caused to be entrusted mainly to Hungarian, Italian and Romanian armies. After the failure of Soviet attempts to relieve the situation in early September by southward attacks from north of the city, Zhukov and Vasilevsky devised, and Stalin approved, a major counter-offensive, to cut off and destroy the enemy forces in the Stalingrad area, then to drive south along the Don to the Black Sea coast, thereby isolating Army Group A in the Caucasus. This last objective had to be abandoned, and most of the forces intended for it retained in the Stalingrad area, when the enemy forces besieged there were found to be at least three times larger than expected, but achievement of the other objectives obliged Army Group A to withdraw from all of Transcaucasus except the Taman peninsula, thus removing any direct threat to the Soviet oilfields.

An offensive against Army Group Centre (Operation 'Mars') was mounted to coincide with the Stalingrad counter-offensive (Operation 'Uranus'). Dr David Glantz has postulated that 'Mars' was intended to be the main Soviet offensive of the winter, and was subsequently ignored or described as merely a 'diversion' in Soviet accounts only because it was a disastrous failure. Similarly, Dr Aleksey Isayev has argued that 'Mars' was meant to be interdependent with 'Uranus' and of at least equal status with it. I examined these contentions in Chapter Three, and concluded that the evidence against both hypotheses greatly outweighs that for them, in particular because neither author has taken the differences in context of the two operations into account, nor considered why the three men ultimately responsible for both (Zhukov, Vasilevsky and Stalin) deliberately devised totally different solutions for them, 'Uranus' as a small number of large-scale assaults and 'Mars' as a large number of much smaller ones; nor apparently was either author aware that Agent Max, who gave the Germans advance notice of 'Mars' but not of 'Uranus', was a Soviet-controlled double-agent, whose message, composed in the Operations Directorate of the Soviet General Staff, was precisely intended to distract German attention from the preparations for 'Uranus' in the south, by providing four apparently credible alternatives elsewhere, including major threats to Army Groups Centre and North.

In early 1943 Stalin repeated his error of the previous winter by again overestimating German exhaustion, and pushing the offensive further than was sustainable. Manstein exploited this with a counter-offensive in March 1943 that inflicted severe losses and recaptured much territory, including Kharkov and most of the Donbass, before the spring thaw imposed a lull. The front line then stabilised with a large Soviet salient centred on Kursk, and Operation 'Citadel', the plan for the German summer offensive, was for Army Groups Centre and South to eliminate the two Soviet Fronts in that salient. The Soviet side came to know well in advance what the Germans planned, and as early as 8 April Zhukov recommended to Stalin that they counter it by fighting a defensive battle from prepared positions followed by a series of counter-offensives. Stalin accepted this recommendation on 12 April, three days before Hitler issued the actual Directive for 'Citadel'. Precisely how the Soviets so soon became so sure of the German plans that they built their own strategy entirely around them remains only sketchily described; some possible explanations were discussed in Chapter Five.

Hitler expected victory to be achieved mainly through new and improved older tanks and self-propelled guns that decisively outgunned and were better-armoured than the previously dominant Soviet KVs and T-34s. He several times postponed 'Citadel', mainly so as to have as many of the new tanks available as possible, though also to some extent because of the time needed to replace losses in the divisions of Army Group Centre that had fought in 'Mars', and it did not begin until 4–5 July. The Soviets used the time to strengthen and diversify their defences, especially after tests on captured Tigers in April showed them the threat they posed to Soviet tank forces. They arranged their defensive systems in from five to eight belts in depth, combining natural obstacles such as gullies, rivers and marshes with trenches, barbed wire, minefields, artillery, tanks, infantry and air support, and in addition deployed an entire third army group (the Steppe Front) behind the two in the salient.

The defensive resources proved less than ideally distributed, with the weaker Voronezh Front in the south facing a stronger German threat than the Central Front in the north. This mis-distribution was probably based in Stalin's residual fear that if Army Group Centre's offensive succeeded, it would be followed by a northward drive against Moscow. His miscalculation did not, however, prove fatal, mainly because Rokossovsky made excellent use of his assets, stopping Army Group Centre's advance by 10 July, then five days later joining, as planned, in the counter-offensive launched under Zhukov's control on 12 July by the two Fronts north of the salient.

However, by then the situation on the south side of the salient had become serious. Three additional armies (the 27th from Stavka Reserve, the 5th Guards and the 5th Guards Tank from the Steppe Front) had to be committed, and on 12 July the 5th Guards Tank Army and the 2nd SS Panzer Corps clashed in a series of engagements in the Prokhorovka area. These were subsequently presented in Soviet-era accounts as the largest tank battle in history, and as a Soviet victory so decisive that it forced Hitler to cancel 'Citadel' completely the very next day.

The reality was very different. The action around Prokhorovka comprised not one battle but a series of engagements, and the numbers committed on both sides did not make it the largest tank battle in history. That dubious honour goes to the deployment, so disastrous that details were disclosed only in post-Soviet times, of six Soviet mechanised corps against the 1st Panzer Group of Army Group South in the first week of the invasion. Nor was Prokhorovka a Soviet victory; on the contrary, it was a near-disaster. Accounts of the numbers engaged and their losses differ in details, but all agree that Soviet tank losses were extremely heavy, several times greater than the Germans', and that the Germans retained control of the battlefield until they began a planned withdrawal five days later. Hitler did indeed cancel 'Citadel' on 13 July, but because of events elsewhere. He gave two reasons, first the Anglo-American landings in Sicily on 10 July, and secondly, the Soviet counter-offensive launched north of the salient on 12 July. These, he claimed, necessitated his sending Army Group South's strongest elements elsewhere, the 2nd SS Panzer Corps to Italy and the elite Grossdeutschland Division to Army Group Centre. Hitler's first reason was probably mere face-saving. By 13 July 'Citadel' was clearly in trouble; blaming its failure on a problem elsewhere and the shortcomings of an ally was less humiliating than admitting defeat by racial 'inferiors'. In fact only one of the SS Panzer Corps' four divisions was sent to Italy; the others had to be retained and deployed further south against another Soviet offensive launched in mid-August.

However, unaware that 'Citadel' was about to be cancelled, and clearly shaken by the 5th Guards Tank Army's debacle, Stalin on 12 July judged the Voronezh Front's plight so dire that he ordered Zhukov to hand over coordination of the offensive (Operation 'Kutuzov') which he had launched that day to a competent but lesser light, Voronov, and go to the Voronezh Front's headquarters at once. He arrived there on 13 July and stayed for most of the next seven weeks. On 17 July Army Group South began withdrawing to its original starting line, pursued somewhat desultorily by the Voronezh Front, which was then mainly preoccupied in replacing its heavy manpower and equipment losses, and preparing for its own counter-offensive, Operation 'Rumyantsev'. How radically the strategic balance had changed in Soviet favour can be seen by listing the offensives undertaken during the second half of 1943. Some of these offensives proved expensive in casualties and losses of equipment, but unlike most of those attempted in the first half of 1942 some were very successful, and none was a total failure.

Table 21: Soviet offensives launched in July–December 1943[339]

Operation	No. of Fronts	Dates	Maximum gain km (miles)
Kutuzov	3	12/7–18/8	150 (94)
Rumyantsev	2	3–23/8	140 (88)
Suvorov	2	7/8–2/10	250 (156)
Donbass	2	13/8–22/9	300 (188)
Dnepr	3	26/8–30/9	300 (188)
N Caucasus	1	10/9–9/10	150 (94)
Lower Dnepr	3	26/9–20/12	300 (188)
Kiev	1	3–13/11	150 (94)
West Ukraine	5	24/12/43–17/4/44	450 (281)

The momentum was sustained for the rest of the war, with eleven Soviet strategic-scale offensives mounted during 1944, and eight in the four months of 1945 that preceded the German surrender early in May. The tempo of offensives in the last year of the war increased somewhat, due in part to the additional demands placed on the Germans from June 1944 by the Second Front, but also because Lend-Lease vehicles enhanced the Red Army's mobility while that of the German forces was reduced by fuel shortages, especially after the loss of the Ploesti oilfields following Romania's change of sides in August, and by Anglo-American bombing of Germany's synthetic fuel plants. As the table above shows, the sequence of continuous Soviet advances began in July 1943, and had been under way for almost 11 months before the Allies landed in France. Soviet claims to have overcome the German threat without the military aid provided by the Second Front are therefore justified, but their subsequent downplaying of the importance of the material aid they received from the Allies, especially the United States, is not. Both Stalin and Zhukov, in statements discussed below, and published only in post-Soviet times, admitted that without the American 'Lend-Lease' deliveries they would have lost the war.

The answers to the questions raised in the Introduction are as follows:

1. To what extent did Stalin's purge of the military in 1937–38 really 'decapitate' the Red Army and bring about the disasters of 1941?

It was only one of several factors that made the early disasters inevitable. It encouraged Hitler to go ahead with his invasion plans, and aggravated problems created by the large increases in the size of the Red Army between 1935 and 1941. The boastful doctrine of 'beating the enemy on his own territory', and experience of poorly conducted offensives in the 1939/40 'Winter War' with Finland, led to a concentration before the invasion on training in offensive fighting, with the concomitant neglect of training in defence, and early post-invasion attempts at instant counter-offensives were mostly catastrophic failures. However, post-Stalin Soviet criticisms of the failure to create fixed defences along the new post-1939 frontiers seem overdone, given the relative ease with which fixed defences were overcome or by-passed by both sides during the Second World War. Stalin's early refusal to permit retreats led to huge encirclements and surrenders, but also facilitated the mass evacuation of industrial plants and their labour forces to the Urals, Siberia and Central Asia, where they contributed enormously to the war effort from 1942 onwards. Orderly withdrawals would have been difficult, given the greater pursuit speed of German mobile forces, and would also have rendered the mass evacuations impossible. Also, as Zhukov admitted, the General Staff, himself included, simply had not realised beforehand how large, fast-moving and hard-hitting were the German mechanised forces. Suggestions that the Red Army would have fared better if the purged generals had survived cannot be proved or disproved, but the one most often cited, Tukhachevsky, believed until the day of his death in the doctrine of instant counter-offensives that had proved so disastrous when attempted in the first weeks of invasions, and all Germany's unpurged previous opponents had been defeated in a few days to a few weeks. For lack of experience, vehicles, trained drivers and adequate air support the Red Army could not in any case emulate German mobile warfare in 1941.

A major error of military planning was the attempt to do too much too quickly. The reforms begun by Timoshenko in mid-1940 envisaged the creation of 31 mechanised corps, each with 1,025 tanks. On paper these far outweighed the Wehrmacht's 20 panzer divisions, which had between 150 and 300 tanks each, and its 16 mobile infantry divisions, which then had no tanks, but in reality the Soviet mechanised corps fell far short. By the day of invasion 29 had been formed, but only one of them was fully equipped. Nor does the record of the survivors from the pre-war cohort of military leaders inspire confidence; Voroshilov, Budenny and Kulik all very quickly proved failures as field commanders, and were replaced.

Inadequate military communications were another important factor. Initially reliance was mainly on the civilian telephone system, which in frontier areas was effectively disrupted by German sabotage squads and bombing raids in the first hours of the invasion. Even as late as mid-1943 Soviet tank formations were not as thoroughly equipped with radios as the panzer divisions were in 1941.

However, it was also largely due to Stalin that the initial disasters did not prove decisive. He had specifically defined the industrialisation pursued throughout the 1930s as designed to improve defence capacity; between 1935 and 1941 he greatly increased defence spending and more than trebled the size of the armed forces. As pointed out earlier, the defenders outnumbered the invaders by three to one in tanks, two to one in aircraft, and five to four in artillery. Responsibility for the military's initial inability to utilise its resources as well as did the Wehrmacht rested mainly with the professional soldiers, though Stalin's choice of the inadequate Voroshilov as People's Commissar (Minister) for Defence from 1925 to 1940 was an important contributing factor. However, German superiority did not suffice to produce the victory in five months postulated by the 'Barbarossa' plan. When that period expired, at the end of November, Army Group South had already been forced into retreat, and Army Group Centre was about to suffer Germany's first major land defeat of the war.

2. Why was Stalin so convinced that Hitler would not attack the Soviet Union while the British remained undefeated, that until the very last moment he apparently ignored all warnings about the imminence of invasion, and even after it had begun, continued to maintain, until the official declaration of war arrived, that it was a 'provocation' by German generals, undertaken without Hitler's knowledge?

In the nine months preceding the invasion Stalin received many warnings. Some were imprecise, others gave dates on which nothing happened, and after receiving so many false warnings scepticism would not be unwarranted. It has also been suggested that Stalin's insistence that war would not come in 1941 was wishful thinking, derived from his fear that his purges had deprived the Red Army of its best officers. However, the internal effect of the purges should not be exaggerated. The figure of 40,000 dismissed, cited by Voroshilov, included routine dismissals on non-political grounds, and the review Beria instituted after becoming Interior Minister in November 1938 resulted in more than half the 'purged' officers being reinstated during 1939–40. Shortages of officers owed more to the rapid expansion of the armed forces after 1935 than to the purges, but the latter created shortages at the top because they fell most heavily on the senior military.

The Russian military still contends that the alleged conspiracy claimed as the reason for the purge did not exist. This is certainly true of the charges of spying, planning for defeat, restoring capitalism, etc., brought against the victims. However, there was serious discontent among the military. It was mainly directed at Voroshilov, but Stalin was likely to take criticism of his appointee as questioning his judgement, and therefore as disloyal. Only after the Finnish debacle did Stalin replace Voroshilov with a qualified professional soldier, Timoshenko, and the German invasion came before most of the reforms he initiated could take effect.

Three further explanations advanced for Stalin's refusal to believe invasion imminent are that he expected Hitler would: (1) observe the Molotov–Ribbentrop Pact, or (2) not invade without an ultimatum or a set of demands, e.g. for increased food or raw material deliveries, or (3) not fight a war on two fronts. The first assumes that Stalin trusted Hitler more than he trusted even his own entourage, and also goes against his belief in the ultimate inevitability of war with the capitalist world that he gave signs of shedding only in 1952, shortly before he died. The second ignores the reality that Germany had already invaded nine countries without any forewarning, and he had no reason to think the Soviet case would be any different.

However, he does seem to have seriously believed the third, that Hitler would never undertake a two-front war, and was undoubtedly encouraged in that belief by a German deception campaign, which included claims that German units were sent to the east to be out of range of British bombers while training for the forthcoming invasion of England. Nevertheless, his persistence in this belief raises questions.

First, should not the Soviet Intelligence 'resident' in London have reported that from late October 1940 the British had observed the invasion barges dispersing, Bletchley had deciphered messages indicating abandonment, and that from 31 October 1940 the Defence Committee, chaired by Churchill, assessed the likelihood of invasion as 'relatively remote'. And should not the Soviet embassy in Berlin have reported that British bombing in 1941 was neither large-scale nor specifically aimed at military targets such as barracks, airfields or training grounds?

Secondly, although officially Operation 'Sealion' was only postponed until the spring of 1941, it was widely known in Germany that it had been abandoned, and this was reported to Moscow. Nor was it a secret that Hitler admired the British Empire, and would have preferred the British as allies, not enemies.

Stalin's persistence in the belief that Germany would avoid a two-front war ignored both First World War experience and the circumstances of 1941. Stalin could surely remember that after failing in 1914 to knock France out before Russia mobilised, Germany had fought a two-front war so successfully that during 1917 the Russian front and regime collapsed, and the French army experienced large-scale mutinies. Then, having succeeded in 30 months of a two-front war, Germany lost the ensuing one-front war in only 20 months. As a beneficiary from Germany's defeat of Tsarism, Stalin must have been well aware of all this.

Another factor that should have qualified his belief is that in mid-1941 there was no Western Front, and no possibility of re-establishing one soon. The British could not invade Europe single-handed; invasion would only be possible if the United States joined the war, and in mid-1941 there was no prospect of that. In mid-May Stalin again told Timoshenko and Zhukov that Hitler would not fight a two-front war, and vetoed their request to disrupt Germany's ominous preparations by pre-emptive attack. He later told Churchill that he knew invasion was inevitable, but had hoped to postpone it for another six months or thereabouts.

Another likely reason for his rejection of a pre-emptive attack was political. In Western eyes the Molotov–Ribbentrop Pact made him and Hitler accomplices. Since signing it Germany had invaded nine countries, the Soviet Union six, and the Soviet attack on Finland even raised the possibility of war with Britain and France, though the 'Winter War' ended before their expeditionary force could be dispatched. If the Soviet

Union attacked first, the world might see the war as just a dispute between gangsters – it was politically necessary for it to be seen as a victim.

Finally, Stalin believed German generals capable of defying Hitler's wishes and 'provoking' a war by attacking on their own initiative; he clung to this belief even into the first hours of the invasion. This belief too had no basis in historical experience, and ignored the tensions between the adventurist Hitler and his cautious generals, few of whom were Nazi by conviction, and some were anti-Nazi enough to make several attempts to assassinate him. In the end Stalin's major error was to assume that Hitler was more rational, therefore more predictable, than he really was.

3. Why did Stalin believe that if Germany did nevertheless invade, its main objectives would be not the 'political' targets of Leningrad, Moscow and Kiev, but the 'economic' targets of Ukrainian coal, iron ore and grain, and Caucasian oil?

He believed that the invasion's purpose would be to secure economic resources for a long war, and did not realise that Hitler aimed to avoid one by winning before the first winter. Hitler's Directive no. 32, issued on 11 June 1941, described intended operations against the British in North Africa and the Middle East, and continued:

> This situation, which will be created by the victorious conclusion of the campaign in the East, can confront the Armed Forces with the following strategic tasks for the late autumn of 1941 and the winter of 1941/2.
>
> 1. The newly conquered territories in the East must be organised, made secure and, in full cooperation with the Armed Forces, exploited economically . . .

In short, Hitler expected to achieve complete victory over the USSR by the end of November 1941 at the latest.

Stalin's reasoning led to a mis-distribution of the forces along the western border, with more troops south of the Pripyat Marshes than north of them, whereas the German deployment was the converse, with two army groups north of the marshes and only one south of them; only in 1942, when it was abundantly clear that the war would be prolonged, did Hitler's strategy shift to seizure of economic resources.

4. Did the German invasion pre-empt by only 15 days a Soviet attack on Germany, scheduled to begin on 6 July 1941, and aimed at taking

*over not only Germany but all of German-occupied Europe, as
Victor Suvorov has claimed?*

No. The deployments of troops, tanks, guns and aircraft in the forward
areas was consistent with the vapid official doctrine of 'beating the enemy
on his own territory' by immediately driving out any invader. This could,
of course, have served as cover for a war of aggression, but in this case
deficiencies in training and deployment and shortages of equipment
remove all credibility from the contention that these forces were only 15
days from initiating a major war of aggression against the strongest
possible antagonist. Besides, Stalin's insistence on not 'provoking' the
Germans extended to giving their reconnaissance aircraft complete
freedom to violate Soviet airspace, which he would scarcely have done if
preparations for invading Germany in two weeks' time were then under
way.

5. *Was the attempt, in the first weeks of invasion, to use the Bulgarian
   ambassador to convey peace proposals that offered the Germans
   substantial territorial concessions a genuine, panic-induced offer, or,
   as Soviet sources subsequently asserted, simply an attempt to 'disinform' the Germans and gain time?*

According to Sudoplatov, two hints were received in mid-July 1941 that
the time might have come for Germany and the USSR to prefer settling
their relations by mutual concessions. It is possible that, writing many
years after the episode, he got his dates slightly wrong, or was not told of
the true origins of the initiative. There is some evidence from another
source that Stalin, Molotov and Beria met the Bulgarian ambassador
Stamenov on 28 June and discussed a peace offer under which the Soviet
Union would cede the three Baltic States, Moldavia and parts of some
other republics (e.g. Ukraine) to Germany, but that Stamenov insisted
that the Soviet Union would win. Sudoplatov may have been brought in
to try to persuade Stamenov. He says that Beria ordered him to tell
Stamenov, a Soviet agent since 1934, of 'alleged rumours' about possibly
ending the war by ceding Soviet territory, in the expectation that
Stamenov would pass the information to King Boris, who would tell the
Germans. Molotov added a promise to provide a job for Stamenov's wife.
However, Stamenov believed so strongly that the Soviets would win that
he never passed the information on.

Sudoplatov explained the episode as intended to gain time and
strengthen the position of German diplomats and generals who still hoped
to end the war by compromise. This is not very convincing. Time would

be gained only if negotiations included a cease-fire, and the Germans at that time had no incentive to grant one. They were encountering problems from dust, heat and mileage, and from gaps opening between formations as they moved from the relatively narrow frontier area to the broader expanses of the European USSR, but by mid-July they had covered well over a third of the distance from the frontier to Moscow, captured almost half a million Soviet soldiers, destroyed several thousand tanks and aircraft, taken Minsk, the capital of Belorussia, and, though held up in the Battle of Smolensk, were about to close the trap there; on 5 August the 'Smolensk pocket' surrendered, with over 300,000 soldiers captured, 3,200 tanks and 3,000 guns taken or destroyed. It is more likely the initiative was born of desperation. The situation at the end of June warranted it. On 28 June, the date of the alleged meeting that Stalin, Molotov and Beria had with Stamenov, Minsk fell; the Germans had covered one-third of the distance from the border to Moscow in just seven days. On the next day Stalin's turbulent visit to the General Staff mentioned in Chapter One took place, following which he expressed despair, withdrew to his villa at Kuntsevo, and had all communication with him cut off. Then on 30 June, when a group of senior men led by Molotov went to him to suggest he form and head a State Defence Committee, he at first thought, according to Mikoyan, that they had come to arrest him.

However, the moment of deepest desperation passed. President Roosevelt had already announced on 26 June that the Soviet Union would be eligible for US aid, and by 8 July the Soviet Union had submitted an enormous shopping list. Roosevelt then sent his special representative, Harry Hopkins, to Moscow, where he met Stalin on 29 and 30 July. His report to Roosevelt was favourable, so it was already abundantly clear before mid-August that substantial US aid would eventually be forthcoming, and an agreement to provide British aid had already been signed on 12 July. Although the Germans were still advancing, and would score some more major victories in September and October, they were already finding it impossible to sustain the headlong pace of the early weeks. The success of 'Blitzkrieg' in Western Europe had largely depended on an abundance of excellent roads and of short distances; the Soviet reality provided neither.

6. Was Operation 'Mars', against the German Army Group Centre in November–December 1942, a diversion, intended only to prevent it sending troops south to counter the Soviet counter-offensives at

Stalingrad (Operations 'Uranus' and 'Saturn'), as Zhukov's and other Soviet-period accounts maintained, or was it meant to be either the main assault of the 1942/43 winter campaign, as David Glantz has claimed,[340] or as Aleksey Isayev contends, of equal status with 'Uranus', and, as both argue, subsequently ignored or played down only because it was a disastrous failure?

Zhukov's economy with the truth in his memoirs and the ignoring of 'Mars' in most Soviet accounts of the Stalingrad victory certainly seem to indicate that more was expected of 'Mars' than it delivered. However, consideration of the greatly differing context of the two operations, of the very different plans for conduct of the two, as devised by their main architects, and of additional evidence that these two authors apparently had not seen (discussed in detail in Chapter Three), points to its indeed being a diversion, with advance information about it deliberately leaked to the Germans to mislead them into believing it the main offensive, thereby distracting their attention from 'Uranus'.

7. *What are the most likely reasons for the improvement in Soviet Intelligence about German intentions between mid-February 1943, when a major German counter-offensive took them completely by surprise, and 8 April, when Zhukov was (rightly, as it proved) so sure of their intentions that he proposed, and Stalin agreed, to base the Soviet strategy for the summer campaign entirely around the German plans?*

The Soviet Union possessed a large analogue to Bletchley, intercepting and deciphering foreign diplomatic and military traffic. At least three of the 'Cambridge five' had access to decrypted Ultra messages, and knowledge that German traffic enciphered on Enigma machines was decipherable would justify a large commitment of Soviet resources. The forces that surrendered at Stalingrad at the end of January 1943 had about 30 Enigma machines plus key tables and operating manuals, far more than the British or Americans captured in all their operations during the entire war, and this may have provided the final impetus for an already existing programme.

At a meeting with Operation 'Citadel's commanding generals on 1 July, Hitler ordered them to launch the offensive at Kursk on 5 July. Stavka's message notifying the Fronts that the launch was imminent was transmitted at the latest only 14 hours after this meeting. There are two possible explanations for this. One is that some Enigma messages from armies to divisions ordering preparations for combat were deciphered quickly. The most vulnerable would be messages from air fleet HQs to airfields in the Luftwaffe 'Red' cipher, which Bletchley often broke 'quite early in the day'.[341] Alternatively, if they could not decipher messages, they could deduce action was imminent from the sudden increase in the numbers of transmissions. Either explanation implies a high level of radio intercept activity. From Kursk onwards radio intercepts figure frequently in reports by Fronts to Stavka; they mostly relate to communications between aircraft and ground controllers, but they show that the Red Army considered radio interception as important a tool of warfare as did the other major belligerents.

8. *Was the tank battle at Prokhorovka on 12 July 1943, during the battle of Kursk, the biggest tank battle ever, and was it, as Soviet-era accounts unanimously claimed, a Soviet victory so decisive that it forced Hitler to abandon the entire German summer offensive on the very next day?*

No. Two Soviet tank armies (1st and 5th Guards) were defeated that day, not in a single battle but in several separate engagements, because they were comprehensively outgunned by the new or updated older German tanks and self-propelled guns. A combination of defensive measures prevented the Germans from breaking through, but at a heavy cost in casualties. Hitler did indeed cancel 'Citadel' on 13 July, but this was due to events elsewhere, specifically the Allied landings in Sicily on 10 July, and (more importantly, though he did not say so) the major Soviet counter-offensive against Army Group Centre that began on the 12th. Despite Manstein's objections, Hitler deprived Army Group South of its strongest elements, ordering the 2nd SS Panzer Corps to Italy and the Grossdeutschland Division to Army Group Centre, and cancelled 'Citadel' forthwith. Hitler's citing of the invasion of Sicily as a reason was probably mere face-saving; in fact only one SS division was sent to Italy, but to blame events there and an ally's shortcomings was less humiliating than admitting defeat by an 'inferior' race. However, both Soviet claims were unjustified. The Germans retained control of the battlefield at Prokhorovka until they began an orderly withdrawal five days later; every night they sent out engineer squads, who towed out repairable German tanks and blew up repairable Soviet tanks.

The most likely candidate for title of 'largest tank battle' was the attack by six (some accounts say five) Soviet mechanised corps against the 1st Panzer Group of Army Group South in the first days (23–29 June) of the invasion. Precise numbers of tanks engaged are not known, but were at least

3,000, more than twice as many as at Prokhorovka. The outcome was such a disaster for the Red Army that details emerged only in post-Soviet times.

9. How important were Lend-Lease supplies to the Soviet war effort?

Between February 1941 and September 1945 the United States provided $50.1 billion in Lend-Lease supplies to its allies, including $31.4 billion to the United Kingdom and $11.3 billion to the Soviet Union. Russian use of 'Lend-Lease' to describe all Western aid is strictly inaccurate, because the Soviet Union granted no leasing rights to bases in Soviet territory in return for the aid. However, 'Lend-Lease' is a conveniently brief description, so will be used here.

Supplies were delivered by three routes, in round figures a quarter each via the Persian Gulf and north coast ports (Murmansk/Archangel), and half via the Pacific and Trans-Siberian railway. Many aircraft were also flown or shipped via the Pacific and Siberia, the safest route as the Soviet Union was not at war with Japan until 1945; the Japanese Navy sometimes harassed or delayed Soviet ships, but only two ships were sunk, both by an American submarine in the mistaken belief that they were Japanese masquerading as Soviet. Lend-Lease included the handover of 90 merchant ships for the trans-Pacific route, and of 302 small warships for the brief Soviet–Japanese war in August 1945.

All Soviet-era and some post-Soviet accounts either ignored Lend-Lease altogether or played down its importance, concentrating on deliveries of aircraft, tanks and guns, emphasising how few they were compared to Soviet production, and that the tanks were inferior to their own. This was true of the T-34 medium and KV and IS heavy tanks, less so of those produced before the war, and not true at all of the light tanks they went on producing up to late 1943.

Table 22. Soviet production and Lend-Lease supply of weapons

	Soviet production	Lend-Lease supply
Tanks/Self-propelled guns*	92,595	10,000
Guns/howitzers (37mm and above)	516,648	8,218
Aircraft, all types	157,261	18,700

*Medium and heavy, gun of 75mm or greater calibre.

The figures cited were correct in themselves, but the emphasis on them was misleading because weapons were only a very small part of the aid provided by the Western Allies. For example, the USA supplied 435,457 motor vehicles (jeeps, trucks and tractors), over twice the 197,100 manufactured in Soviet plants in the war years. The supply included over 50,000 jeeps, but most of the deliveries were of 1.5- and 2.5-tonne trucks. How necessary they were can be judged from a table listing the numbers of lorries allocated to the Fronts at 22 May 1942; they totalled only 32,786, an average of one vehicle for every 88 men, and ranged from 998 vehicles per army in the Southern Front to only 250 in the Karelian Front.[342] Lend-Lease vehicles began arriving in quantity towards the end of 1942, and not only improved the rear services' ability to move supplies from railheads to the front line, but vastly enhanced the mobility of infantry and artillery, enabling reserves or reinforcements to be moved much faster and arrive in much better shape than if, as previously, they had marched most or all of the way. Furthermore, the Soviet vehicle industry's feat in producing almost two-and-a-half times as many tanks and self-propelled guns as Germany (92,595 versus 37,794) owed much to three elements of Lend-Lease. First, the availability of American/Canadian-built 'soft' motor transport enabled it to concentrate on producing tanks and self-propelled guns; secondly, by value over 10 per cent of Lend-Lease supplies ($1.8 billion) to the Soviet Union comprised machinery, most of it machine tools, lathes and generators. Thirdly, supplies included large quantities of sheet steel, including armour-plate. Similarly, the Soviet aircraft industry's ability to produce 83 per cent as many aircraft as Germany (157,261 versus 189,307) was partly due to American supplies of machine tools, non-ferrous metals (802,000 tons), and trainer aircraft – the Soviet aircraft industry manufactured only 4,061 trainers, just 2.6 per cent of its total output, versus 6.1 per cent of German, 17.7 per cent of American and 24.2 per cent of British aircraft production. The rear services also benefited from receipt of almost 2,000 steam locomotives and over 11,000 goods wagons, and of about 3.8 million rubber tyres for its new fleets of American lorries. At the end of the war the Soviet armed forces had 665,000 motor vehicles, roughly 1 vehicle per 17 men, a low level of mechanisation compared to the Western armies, but higher than the German. Even allowing for losses, for use of captured German vehicles, and for Lend-Lease vehicles sent to the civil economy, between 50 and 60 per cent of the Red Army's transport comprised American- or Canadian-made trucks or jeeps.

The food supply situation was at its worst during the first two years of war. Towards the end of 1942 substantial quantities of Lend-Lease food began arriving. They were mostly supplied to the armed forces, but reduced the military demand on domestic production. Altogether Lend-Lease food deliveries from the USA, Canada and the UK totalled 4.3 million tonnes, equivalent to 11 per cent of the armed forces' consumption over the entire war period.[343]

In 1941 only 361,000 tons of aid were received, and in 1942 just under 2.5 million tons. It can therefore be reasonably claimed that the Red Army survived its most testing period, and achieved two of its most important victories, at Moscow and Stalingrad, before the trickle of foreign aid became a torrent, of 4.8 million tons in 1943 and 6.2 million in 1944. However, there is a definite correlation between the growth of the aid and the increase in number, scale and speed of advance of Soviet offensives over the two years and ten months from mid-July 1943 to the end of the European war in May 1945. Following the decisive victories at Kursk and in the counter-offensives that followed it, Stalin told Churchill and Roosevelt, at Teheran in November 1943, that the successes had been due to the ability to move Supreme Command Reserves quickly between different sectors of the front. That ability could not have been achieved without motor transport on a scale that Soviet industry could not have provided without drastically cutting tank production. The vehicles supplied did not necessarily make the difference between defeat and victory, but without them victory would have taken much longer to arrive.

However, other forms of Lend-Lease supply appear to have had even more decisive effects on the war's outcome. Extracts from a study relating Lend-Lease supplies to the total Soviet war effort can be summarised as follows. Lend-Lease accounted for 59 per cent of aviation fuel, 33 per cent of explosives, 45.2 per cent of copper ore, 55.5 per cent of aluminium, 27.9 per cent of machine tools, 15.1 per cent of meat, 29.5 per cent of sugar, 30.1 per cent of tyres, and over 80 per cent of railway locomotives and rolling stock.[344]

Soviet-era denigration of Lend-Lease as a whole was not based on a genuine belief that it was unimportant, but was for cold-war propaganda purposes, to maximise Soviet (and Communist) prestige by conveying the idea that the Soviet Union won the war virtually single-handed, and that its former Allies (by then its principal current antagonists) devoted more effort to delaying the opening of a Second Front than to aiding the country fighting on the First Front. Censorship deleted even passing references in memoirs. For example, a passage in which Zhukov attributed the shift of much of the Red Army's artillery from horse to mechanical traction to 'receipt from the USA under Lend-Lease of Studebaker vehicles with increased cross-country capability' was deleted. And not until post-Soviet times was the text published of a toast to Roosevelt, proposed by Stalin at a dinner during the Teheran Conference (28 November–1 December 1943). It ran:

The absolute main thing in this war is machines. The United States has demonstrated that it can produce from eight thousand to ten thousand aircraft a month. Russia can produce at least three thousand aircraft a month. England produces from three thousand to three thousand five hundred a month, mostly bombers. Therefore the United States is the land of machines. Without the use of those machines, with the aid of Lend-Lease, we would have lost the war.[345]

Zhukov was even more categorical, and can perhaps be permitted the last word on this issue. In May 1963, in private conversations, bugged by the KGB and detailed in a Top Secret report sent by its then head, Semichastny, to Nikita Khrushchev, he criticised the just-published six-volume Soviet *History of the Great Fatherland War* as

absolutely untrue. Now they say the Allies never helped us . . . But it can't be denied that the Americans rushed us so many materials without which we couldn't have formed our reserves and couldn't have continued the war . . . We received 350 thousand motor vehicles, and such vehicles! . . . we didn't have explosives or gunpowder. We didn't even have anything to power rifle bullets . . . The Americans really baled us out with gunpowder and explosives. And they rushed us so much sheet steel. Could we have organised tank production so quickly if we hadn't had American help with steel? And now the affair is presented as if we had all this ourselves in abundance . . .[346]

10. Need the price of Soviet victory have been so high, namely more lives lost than the combined total for all the other major belligerents on both sides?

First, there is still considerable disagreement over how high the price was. The most detailed official figures for 'irrevocable' losses (killed, captured or missing) in the armed forces are contained in the 1993 publication *Grif Sekretnosti Snyat*. They totalled 11,444,100, but 939,700 called up on Soviet territory recaptured during the war, and 1,836,000 prisoners of war repatriated in 1945 must be deducted from that, giving a net loss of 8,668,400. However, these figures are widely criticised as understated. For example, one reputable source has claimed that a card index of losses kept in the Central Archive of the former USSR Ministry of Defence contains cards for dead totalling 16.2 million soldiers, 1.2 million officers and '3 to 4 million missing', and a representative of the Main Archive of the Russian Federation stated that computerised research had found irrevocable military losses totalling 19.5 million.[347] However, the figures in *GSS* will be used here because they are the most detailed and comprehensive; even if understated they indicate initial catastrophe and recovery through self-sacrifice on an unprecedented scale. Their distribution by years, and the relationships of 'irrevocable' to 'sanitary' (wounded, injured or sick) losses were as follows:

Table 23. Red Army casualties, 1941–45

	1. Irrevocable	2. Sanitary	Ratio of 1 to 2
1941	3,137,673	1,336,147	2.35:1
1942	3,258,216	4,111,062	1:1.26
1943	2,312,429	5,545,074	1:2.40
1944	1,763,891	5,114,750	1:2.90
1945	800,817	2,212,690	1:2.76

Of particular note is the very high ratio of irrevocable to sanitary losses in 1941; in round figures seven out of every ten casualties were killed, captured or missing, versus only three wounded or sick. The irrevocable loss rates are also revealing bearing in mind that in 1941 the Soviet Union was at war for only 193 days, and in that time lost manpower equivalent to over 200 full-strength divisions. Irrevocable losses were even heavier in the first three months; in the 101 days to the end of September they totalled 2,129,677, a daily average of 21,086. In that same period sanitary losses, at 687,626, were less than a quarter of total losses; for every one who was wounded, three died, surrendered, deserted or defected. In the last three months of the year, during which Army Group North was thwarted at Leningrad and Army Group Centre at Moscow, the daily rate of irrevocable losses was more than halved, and the ratio of irrevocable to sanitary losses improved to 1.55 to 1. This improvement, however, still meant three dead, captured or missing for every two wounded or sick.

Whether the losses of 1941 could have been much reduced is questionable. In passages restored in the post-Soviet edition of Rokossovsky's memoirs he argued that the proper course would have been to preserve the forces by an orderly withdrawal, such as he managed to conduct with his own corps. However, he and several other memoir writers describe so many instances of panic flight as to raise doubt about the possibility of a general orderly retreat, especially since almost all the troops were on foot and vulnerable to being overtaken and encircled by the German mobile forces, as happened on a number of occasions in 1941.

Nor were all the surrenders involuntary. Conscripts from the recently annexed Baltic states, eastern Poland and Moldavia had no incentive to defend the first invader against the second, and for many others, especially Ukrainians and Cossacks, the Germans and their allies were at least initially welcomed as it was believed they offered a chance to cut loose from Soviet oppression. Besides, Rokossovsky's successful conduct of the retreat was so exceptional that it earned him promotion in just 45 days to command of an army; furthermore, his preferred course of action would have left insufficient time to load up the equipment and labour force of the many defence plants that were evacuated from areas about to be occupied. Some indication of the scale of evacuation can be gained from a few figures. For example, by the end of 1941 the labour force and equipment of 2,593 industrial plants had been evacuated to the east by rail alone. Although this was only a small proportion of the 31,850 plants located in German-occupied Soviet territory, it included most of the major defence-oriented industries, and dismantled turbo-generators from many power stations. However, metal or power-station furnaces were too large to be moved, and the need to build replacements for them was the biggest constraint on the speed at which the evacuated undertakings could resume production. Nevertheless, by the end of 1941 no fewer than 1,910 of the evacuated plants, 412 of them manufacturing weapons and ammunition, the rest providing metals, chemicals and machinery, had begun producing in their new locations, and by March 1942 the combined production of weapons by previously existing and relocated plants in the east already equalled the entire USSR's pre-invasion output. Even that was small compared to the potential; by the summer of 1942 only 1,200 of the relocated plants were yet at or near full production.[348]

The losses of 1941 were probably necessary and unavoidable. Their worst consequence was that, since the Red Army survived the disasters, the high casualty levels incurred came to be regarded as normal and acceptable by generals and troops alike, and even after the strategic balance turned irreversibly to Soviet advantage their operations were sometimes attended by human costs that both enemies and allies regarded as excessive.

Until Stalin's death post-war accounts glossed over the early disasters, presenting the retreats as deliberate, meant to lure the Germans on as Kutuzov had lured Napoleon in 1812. The losses too were glossed over; not until the first post-war census, in 1959, did some idea of their true dimensions begin to reach the public domain. That census showed that among those born before the war 20 million fewer men than women were still alive in 1959. It was inevitably an underestimate of war losses, as it took no account of female deaths, but in the absence of more specific data this figure was cited for decades afterwards as the Soviet wartime loss. Not till the post-Soviet release of suppressed data from the 1937 and 1939 censuses could assessments be made of total losses, and even then different methods of calculation produced different results, especially about civilian deaths. Studies published in 1995 put the totals within a range from 21.2 to 26.6 million, including the 8.7 million military of *GSS*, i.e. from 11 to 14 per cent of the pre-war population, compared to British losses of 375,000 (0.9 per cent of population), American 405,000 (0.3 per cent), or Japanese, 2.5 million (3.4 per cent).[349] Even at the lowest estimate, Soviet losses were proportionally higher than those of any other Second World War belligerent except Poland (6 million, 17.2 per cent).

The price of victory can be assessed another way. For the entire duration of the war, 22 June 1941 to 9 May 1945, Soviet war losses averaged 20,900 *a day*, of which 7,900 were 'irrevocable'. The worst period for losses was from 22 June–4 December 1941, i.e. from the first day of the war to the day before the start of the winter counter-offensive outside Moscow. In that period 'irrevocable' losses totalled 2,841,900, averaging 17,120 a day, and 'sanitary' losses 1,145,800, averaging 6,900. So during 166 days the Red Army lost an average of 24,200 a day, for a total of 3,987,700, or 82.6 per cent of the 4,826,907 it had in its ranks on the first day of the war. The next heaviest period for losses was from 1 July to 31 December 1943, covering the defensive battle of Kursk and the series of counter-offensives that followed. Here over 184 days the losses totalled 5,020,600 (1,393,800 irrevocable and 3,626,800 sanitary), giving daily averages of 27,286, 7,575 and 19,711 respectively.[350]

The differences in the two sets of figures reflect changes in the situation. In 1941 irrevocable losses were approximately 2.5 times sanitary, whereas in 1943 the ratio was almost exactly reversed, with sanitary losses about 2.6 times irrevocable ones. Furthermore, in 1943 total daily losses were about one-eighth higher than in 1941, but irrevocable losses were well under half. The reason is that in 1941 most irrevocable losses resulted not from deaths but from mass surrenders, desertions and defections, whereas in 1943 potential deserters were fewer because the surrenders at Stalingrad and in North Africa had put paid to the image of Germany as the winning side, and the Soviet authorities, taking no chances, had reduced the number of potential defectors even further by, for example, ordering all Estonian, Latvian and Lithuanian soldiers and all ex-prisoners of war to be removed from units about to go into battle at Kursk. Besides, the Germans achieved no substantial encirclement in that battle, and then had to retreat to avoid being encircled themselves.

The enormous losses in human lives were parallelled by losses in equipment. Soviet attempts to present the early disasters as resulting from being outnumbered have been shown to be false by figures unearthed in the post-Soviet period. According to official data released in 1993, the Red Army had 22,600 tanks on the first day of the invasion, over 10,000 of them with the field armies on the Western borders, more than three times as many as the 3,350 in the invading force. In the rest of 1941 some 5,600 more were produced, but 20,500 were lost, so that on 1 January 1942 only 7,700 were available. During 1942, mainly through activation of the plants evacuated to the Urals and Siberia, 27,900 tanks were produced, but 15,000 were lost; the total, 20,600, available at 1 January 1943 was almost three times that of a year earlier, but still fewer than on the day of invasion. However, it comprised mostly T-34s and KVs, much superior to the types in service in 1941, though inferior in armour and firepower to the new, and upgunned older, German tanks just coming into service. Production during 1943 was lower, at 22,900, through ending production of T-70 light and KV heavy tanks, and because of time consumed in retooling before starting production of the modified T-34-85 medium and new IS heavy tanks, while losses, at 22,400, were higher than in 1942, reflecting the superiority of the new German Tiger and Panther tanks. On 1 January 1944 the Soviet tank park, at 21,100, was only 500 more than a year earlier; it took until mid-1944 for tank numbers to regain the mid-1941 level, and to restore battlefield superiority through the upgunned T-34–85s and then the IS series heavy tanks, perhaps not quite the equals of the Panther and Tiger, but available in much greater numbers.

A similar pattern was observable in other weapons systems. On the first day of invasion the Soviet air forces had a fleet of 32,100, some 20,000 of which were combat aircraft (fighters, bombers, ground attack aircraft). Another 11,000 were produced or received from allies in that year, but 21,200 were lost, and it was late 1942 before pre-war numbers were regained. Throughout the war losses in combat were less than half of total losses; the authors of *GSS* attribute the high accident rates to 'pilot training with reduced training times, especially for mastering new equipment, and also indiscipline of aircrew and flight leaders in carrying out flight-training tasks . . . and also design or construction shortcomings of the machines'.[351] Though the Soviet air forces acquired air superiority from mid-1943 it does not seem to have been on the crushing scale attained by the Anglo-American air forces. Until the end of the war, it remained standard Luftwaffe practice to send newly trained fighter pilots first to the east, to get some experience of aerial combat before being required to take on the Anglo-Americans.

Losses of small arms in the first six months were especially great – in round figures three out of every five rifles, and two of every three machine guns had been lost by the year's end.[352] Then, despite having lost in less than six months most of the troops and weapons of all kinds with which it had begun the war, and with evacuated arms plants not yet producing at their new locations, the Red Army nevertheless inflicted Germany's first major defeat of the war on land, thereby ensuring a prolonged war in which superior Allied industrial capacity, particularly that of the United States, would prove decisive (the vital importance of $11.8 billion's worth of Lend-Lease to the Soviet war effort is duly noted above, but it was dwarfed by the $31.8 billion's worth the USA provided to the smaller British war effort).

The extraordinary power of recovery the Red Army and Soviet economy displayed suggests that, as Field-Marshal Lord Montgomery said in a speech in 1962, 'Page 1, Rule 1 in the Book of War is – "Do not march on Moscow".'

Notes and Sources

1. In *Voyenno-Istoricheskiy Zhurnal* (*'Military-Historical Journal'*), no. 9 (1965), p. 74.
2. Zhukov, G.K., *Vospominaniya i Razmyshleniya* (*'Recollections and Reflections'*), 11th edn, vol. 1 (Moscow, Novosti, 1992), p. 340.
3. For example, Jones, M.K., *Stalingrad: How the Red Army Triumphed* (Barnsley, Pen & Sword, 2007).
4. Glantz, D., *Zhukov's Greatest Defeat* (University of Kansas Press, 1999).
5. Isayev, A., *Georgiy Zhukov* (Moscow, Yauza-Eksmo, 2006), p. 354.
6. For example, against a paper war establishment of 14,483 men, the infantry divisions of the 16th Army in January 1942 were all down to 1,200–1,500, but still kept in action, and the neighbouring armies were in the same state. Rokossovsky, K.K., *Soldatskiy Dolg* (*'A Soldier's Duty'*) (Moscow, Voyenizdat, 1997), p. 139.
7. *Voprosy Istorii* (*'Questions of history'*), no. 8 (1990), pp. 54–5.
8. Rokossovsky, *Soldatskiy Dolg*, pp. 30, 33.
9. Figures from Zamulin, V., *Prokhorovka, Neizvestnoie Srazheniye Velikoi Voyny* (*'Prokhorovka: Unknown Battle of the Great War'*) (Moscow, Khranitel', 2006), pp. 24–7.
10. Figures of Front and troop numbers taken from Krivosheyev, G.F. (ed.), *Grif Sekretnosti Snyat. Poteri Vooruzhennykh Sil SSSR v voynakh, boyevykh deystviyakh i voyennykh konfliktakh* (*'Secret Stamp Removed: Losses of the USSR Armed Forces in wars, combat actions and military conflicts'*) (Moscow, Military Publishing House, 1993), pp. 219–20. Hereafter *GSS*.
11. *GSS*, pp. 162–213.
12. D'yakov, Yu L. and Bushuyeva, T.S., *Fashistskiy Mech' Kovalsya v SSSR* (*'The Fascist sword was forged in the USSR'*) (Moscow, Sovietskaya Rossiya, 1992), pp. 162–205 and 279–80.
13. Kolpakidi, A. and Prudnikova, E., *Dvoinoi Zagovor* (*'Double Conspiracy'*) (Moscow, Olma-Press, 2000), pp. 49–50.
14. D'yakov and Bushuyeva, *Fashistskiy Mech' Kovalsya v SSSR*, p. 23.
15. *Photoalbum, I Kh Bagramyan* (Yerevan, Ayastan, 1987), p. 39.
16. Zen'kovich, N., *Marshaly i Genseki* (*'Marshals and Communist Party General Secretaries'*) (Moscow, Olma-Press, 2005), p. 417.
17. For a more detailed treatment of the issue, see Bullock, A., *Hitler and Stalin: Parallel Lives* (London, HarperCollins, 1991), pp. 629–53, and Jukes, G., 'The Red Army and the Munich Crisis', *Journal of Contemporary History* (April 1991), pp. 195–214.
18. Zolotarev, V.A. and Sevost'yanov, G.N. (eds), *Velikaya Otechestvennaya Voyna* (*'The Great Fatherland War'*) (Moscow, Nauka, 1998), vol. 1, p. 76.
19. Banac, I. (ed.), *The Diary of Georgiy Dimitrov* (New Haven, Yale UP, 2003), p. 115.

20. Fest, J.C., *Hitler* (New York, Harcourt Brace Jovanovich, 1974), p. 641.
21. Hinsley, H., Thomas, E.E., Ransom, C.F.G. and Knight, R.C., *British Intelligence in the Second World War*, vol. 1 (London, HMSO, 1979), pp. 429–83.
22. A German infantry division in 1941 had 16,859 men, 5,375 draught horses, 930 motor vehicles and 530 motorcycles, so few rode to war. Damaskin, I. and Koshel', A. (eds), *Velikaya Otechestvennaya Voina* ('*The Great Fatherland War*') (Moscow, Olma-Press, 2001), p. 49.
23. Zhukov, *Vospominaniya i Razmyshleniya*, vol. 1, pp. 348–9.
24. Chuyev, F., *Sto sorok besed s Molotvym* ('*140 conversations with Molotov*') (Moscow, 1991), p. 31.
25. Cited in Murphy, D.E., *What Stalin Knew* (New Haven/London, Yale University Press, 2005), p. 249.
26. Mertsalov, A. and Mertsalova, L., *Tayny Istorii: Stalinizm i Voyna* ('*Secrets of History: Stalinism and the War*') (Moscow, Terra, 1998), p. 265.
27. Mertsalov and Mertsalova, *Tayny Istorii*, pp. 185–91.
28. Hinsley et al., *British Intelligence*, vol. 1, pp. 190–1.
29. General Halder's diary entry for 31 July 1940, cited in Bullock, *Hitler and Stalin*, p. 754.
30. In Heald, T. (ed), *The Best After-Dinner Stories*, by permission of the Beaverbrook Foundation (London, The Folio Society, 2003), pp. 151–2.
31. Temirov, Yu T. and Donets, A.S., *Entsiklopediia Zabluzhdenii: Voina* ('*Encyclopaedia of Errors: War*') (Moscow/Donetsk, Eksmo Grif, 2004), p. 188. The document can also be found on the Russian Battlefield website.
32. Korol'chenko, A., *Neistoviy Zhukov* (Rostov on Don, Feniks, 2007), pp. 33–8.
33. Gor'kov, Yu, *Kreml', Stavka, Gensthab* ('*Kremlin, Stavka, General Staff*') (Tver', Rif Ltd, 1995), p. 67.
34. Zhukov, *Vospominaniya i Razmyshleniya*, vol. 2, pp. 27–32.
35. Damaskin, I.A., *Stalin i Razvedka* ('*Stalin and Intelligence*') (Moscow, Veche, 2004), pp. 251–3.
36. Zhukov, *Vospominaniya i Razmyshleniya*, vol. 2, p. 345.
37. Suvenirov, O.F., *Tragediia RKKA* ('*The Tragedy of the Red Army*') (Moscow, Terra, 1998), p. 137.
38. Suvenirov, *Tragediia RKKA*, p. 311.
39. Suvenirov, *Tragediia RKKA;* Kul'kov, E., Myagkov, M. and Rzheshevskiy, O. (eds), *Voina* ('*War*'), *1941–1945, Fakty i Dokumenty* (Moscow, Olma-Press, 2001), pp. 313–16.
40. Suvenirov, *Tragediia RKKA*.
41. In the Russian edition of *The Great Terror* (St Petersburg, Neva, 1990), p. 132.
42. *Voiennye Arkhivy Rossii* ('*Military Archives of Russia*'), no. 1 (1993), p. 23.
43. Suvenirov, *Tragediia RKKA*, p. 138.
44. Kolpakidi and Prudnikova, *Dvoinoi Zagovor*, pp. 424–5.
45. Suvenirov, *Tragediia RKKA*, pp. 373–494.
46. Suvenirov, *Tragediia RKKA*, p. 312.
47. Ogonek, *Moscow*, 28/1987 and 25/1989.
48. Gor'kov, *Kreml', Stavka, Gensthab*, p. 50.
49. Zolotarev and Sevost'yanov (eds), *Velikaya Otechestvennaya Voyna*, vol. 1, p. 156.
50. Figures from *GSS*, pp. 164–5.

51. *Voyenno-Istoricheskiy Zhurnal* ('*Military-Historical Journal*'), vol. 8 (1991), pp. 45–7.

52. Knyshevskiy, K.N., Vasil'yeva, O. Yu, Vysotskiy, V.V., Solomatin, S.A., *Skrytaya Pravda Voyny: 1941 God* ('*Hidden Truth of War: Year 1941*') (Moscow, Russkaya Kniga, 1992), pp. 218–19.

53. Zhukov, *Vospominaniya i Razmyshleniya*, vol. 2, p. 338.

54. Knyshevskiy et al., *Skrytaya Pravda Voyny: 1941 God*, p. 218.

55. Kolpakidi and Prudnikova, *Dvoinoi Zagovor*, p. 426.

56. Portugalskiy, R., *Marshal Timoshenko* (Moscow, Yauza-Eksmo, 2007), pp. 116–17.

57. Mikoyan, A.I., *Tak Bylo* ('*Thus it was*') (Moscow, Vagrius, 1999), p. 386.

58. Zolotarev and Sevost'yanov (eds), *Velikaya Otechestvennaya Voyna*, vol. 1, p. 123.

59. Portugalskiy, *Marshal Timoshenko*, pp. 116–20.

60. Nikulin, L., *Tukhachevskiy* (Moscow, Voyenizdat, 1963), pp. 160–1.

61. At the XVII Party Congress, Voroshilov said: 'It is above all necessary to put an end once and for all to harmful "theories" about replacing the horse with the machine.' Portugalskiy, *Marshal Timoshenko*, p. 123.

62. *Voprosy Istorii* ('*Questions of History*'), Moscow, vol. 8 (1990), pp. 54–5.

63. Rokossovsky, *Soldatskiy Dolg*, p. 33.

64. Figures compiled by N.F. Kovalevskiy, table in *Voyenno-Istoricheskiy Zhurnal* ('*Military-Historical Journal*'), vol. 6 (2009), p. 8.

65. Suvenirov, *Tragediia RKKA*, p. 392.

66. Frunze, M.V., *Collected Works* (in Russian) (Moscow, Politizdat, 1929), vol. 1, p. 222.

67. *Voyenno-Istoricheskiy Zhurnal* ('*Military-Historical Journal*'), vol. 4 (1998), p. 46.

68. Temirov and Donets, *Entsiklopediia Zabluzhdenii: Voina*, pp. 190–1.

69. Temirov and Donets, *Entsiklopediia Zabluzhdenii: Voina*, pp. 190–1.

70. *Voprosy Istorii*, vol. 8 (1990), p. 245.

71. Kuznetsov, N.G., *Na Kanune* ('*On the Eve*'), 3rd edn (Moscow, 1989), pp. 366–7.

72. Karpov, V., *Generalissimus* (Moscow, Veche, 2003), vol. 1, pp. 316–17.

73. Zhukov, *Vospominaniya i Razmyshleniya*, vol. 2, p. 9.

74. Entries for 21–28 June are in Karpov, *Generalissimus*, vol. 1, pp. 326–31.

75. Temirov and Donets, *Entsiklopediia Zabluzhdenii: Voina*, pp. 234–5.

76. Mikoyan, *Tak Bylo*, p. 390.

77. Sudoplatov, P. and A., *Special Tasks; The memoirs of an unwanted witness – a Soviet spymaster* (London, Little Brown & Co., 1994), p. 149.

78. Kumanev, G.A., *Ryadom so Stalinym* ('*Alongside Stalin*') (Moscow, Bylina, 1999), pp. 28–31, and Mikoyan, *Tak Bylo*, pp. 389–92.

79. Zolotarev and Sevost'yanov (eds), *Velikaya Otechestvennaya Voyna*, vol. 1, pp. 390–1.

80. USSR State Statistical Committee, *Narodnoye Khozyaystvo SSSR za 70 let* ('*National Economy of the USSR after 70 years*') (Moscow, Finansy i Statistika, 1987), pp. 41–2.

81. Churchill, W.S., *The Second World War*, 3rd edn (London, Cassell, 1966), pp. 132, 135.

82. Kul'kov et al, *Voina 1941–45*, pp. 31–2, citing Bardoux, J., *Journal d'un temoin de la troisieme* (Paris, 1957), pp. 203–4.

83. Sipols, V., *Tayny Diplomaticheskiie* ('*Diplomatic Secrets*') (Moscow, Novina, 1997), pp. 168–74.

84. Sudoplatov, P., *Razvedka i Kreml'* (*'Intelligence and the Kremlin'*) (Moscow, Geya, 1996), p. 141.
85. Mertsalov and Mertsalova, *Tayny Istorii*, p.265.
86. Sudoplatov, *Razvedka i Kreml'*, pp. 256, 263.
87. A tank design specialist described Stalin's hostile reaction when he so addressed him at a meeting in 1939, and being told afterwards that Stalin disliked that form of address. *Novyy Mir*, no. 2 (1967), p. 85.
88. *Pravda*, 17 December 1953, p. 1.
89. Hinsley et al., *British Intelligence*, vol. 1, pp. 477–9.
90. Sokolov, B.V., *Stalin: Vlast' i Krov'* (*'Stalin, Power and Blood'*) (Moscow, AST-Press Kniga, 2004), p. 255.
91. Smirnov, S.S., et al., *Marshal Zhukov: kak my ego pomnim* (*'How we remember him'*) (Moscow, Politizdat, 1988), p. 121.
92. 'Afterword' by Professor B. Bonvech, Ruhr University, to Nevezhin, V.A., *Sindrom Nastupatel'noi Voiny* (*'Offensive War Syndrome'*) (Moscow, 1997), p. 260.
93. Rokossovsky, *Soldatskiy Dolg*, pp. 31–2.
94. Rokossovsky, *Soldatskiy Dolg*, p. 33.
95. To the extent of his ordering in 1945 a study (Operation 'Unthinkable', described later) of the possibility of attacking Soviet forces on 1 July of that year, with 47 British or American and 10 German divisions.
96. Churchill, *The Second World War*, vol. 10, pp. 17–26, 35–42.
97. *GSS*, pp. 202–6.
98. Seaton, A., *The Russo-German War, 1941–45* (London, Arthur Barker Ltd, 1971), p. 62, fn 29.
99. Zhukov, *Vospominaniya i Razmyshleniya*, vol. 2, pp. 28–9.
100. Knyshevskiy et al., *Skrytaya Pravda Voyny: 1941 God*, pp. 237, 242–3.
101. Knyshevskiy et al., *Skrytaya Pravda Voyny: 1941 God*, pp. 237–42.
102. *GSS*, p. 166.
103. Knyshevskiy et al., *Skrytaya Pravda Voyny: 1941 God*, pp. 263–5.
104. Prudnikova, E.A., *Beria: prestupleniya kotorykh ne bylo* (*'Crimes that were not'*) (St Petersburg, Neva, 2005), pp. 192–3.
105. Gorbachevskiy, B., *Rzhevskaya Myasorubka* (*'The Rzhev Mincer'*) (Moscow, Eksmo-Yauza, 2007), pp. 220–2.
106. *GSS*, pp. 236, 238, 240, 242.
107. *GSS*, pp. 234–64.
108. For example, Gorbachevskiy, *Rzhevskaya Myasorubka*, pp. 223–4.
109. Rokossovsky, *Soldatskiy Dolg*, pp. 34–6, 50.
110. Moscow, Defence Ministry Central Archive, f. 48a, Op. 3408, D.4, pp. 40–2. Hereafter TSAMO.
111. TSAMO, f. 48a, Op. 3763, D.102, pp. 1–2.
112. Knyshevskiy et al., *Skrytaya Pravda Voyny: 1941 God*, pp. 254–8.
113. Knyshevskiy et al., *Skrytaya Pravda Voyny: 1941 God*, pp. 258–60.
114. Temirov and Donets, *Entsiklopediia Zabluzhdenii: Voina*, p. 190.
115. Guderian, H., *Panzer Leader* (London, Michael Joseph, 1952).
116. Halder, F., *Kriegstagebuch* (Stuttgart, Kohlhammer, 1962), vol. 3, pp. 194–5.
117. Krasnov, V., *Zhukov: Marshal Velikoi Imperii* (*'Marshal of a Great Empire'*) (Moscow, Olma-Press 2005), p. 215.

118. Zhukov, *Vospominaniya i Razmyshleniya*, vol. 2, pp. 147–53.

119. *GSS*, pp. 164–6.

120. Knyshevskiy et al., *Skrytaya Pravda Voyny: 1941 God*, pp. 140–5.

121. Karpov, V., *Marshal Zhukov* (Moscow, Veche-Ast Press, 1994), p. 362.

122. *Kriegstagebuch des OKW* ('*War Diary of the Wehrmacht High Command*') (Frankfurt/Main, Bernard & Graefe Verlag, undated), vol. 1, p. 702.

123. *GSS*, p. 171.

124. Damaskin and Koshel, *Velikaya Otechestvennaya Voyna 1941–45*, p. 49.

125. Zhukov, *Vospominaniya i Razmyshleniya*, vol. 2, pp. 213–16.

126. Zhukov, *Vospominaniya i Razmyshleniya*, vol. 2, pp. 217–18.

127. Zhukov, *Vospominaniya i Razmyshleniya*, vol. 2, p. 226.

128. Rokossovsky, *Soldatskiy Dolg*, pp. 133–4.

129. Damaskin and Koshel, *Velikaya Otechestvennaya Voyna 1941–45*, p. 281.

130. According to Sudoplatov, a councillor of the Japanese embassy in Moscow and the Head of Military Police in the Kwantung Army were Soviet agents, and correspondence between the embassy and Tokyo was being deciphered (Sudoplatov, *Razvedka i Kreml'*, p. 167).

131. Zhukov, *Vospominaniya i Razmyshleniya*, vol. 2, pp. 254–62.

132. Zhukov, *Vospominaniya i Razmyshleniya*, vol. 2, p. 275.

133. *GSS*, pp. 143, 162–8.

134. Mertsalov and Mertsalova, *Tayny Istorii*, pp. 270–1.

135. *GSS*, pp. 175–7.

136. OKH, Qu IV, *Abt Fremde Heere Ost*, assessment of 4 November 1941.

137. Seaton, *The Russo-German War, 1941–45*, pp. 258–9.

138. Manstein, E. von, *Lost Victories* (London, Methuen, 1958), pp. 236–8. A post-Soviet source lists total losses as 'about 176,000'; that suggests only about 6,000 died before the rest surrendered. Rzheshevsky, O.A., *Kto byl Kto v Velikoi Otechestvennoi Voine* ('*Who was Who in the Great Fatherland War*') (Moscow, Respublika Press, 1995), p. 330.

139. Zhukov, *Vospominaniya i Razmyshleniya*, vol. 2, pp. 264–5, 276.

140. *GSS*, p. 166.

141. Zhukov, *Vospominaniya i Razmyshleniya*, vol. 2, p. 285.

142. Gor'kov, *Kreml', Stavka, Gensthab*, p. 111.

143. Mertsalov and Mertsalova, *Tayny Istorii*, pp. 291–2.

144. Zhukov, *Vospominaniya i Razmyshleniya*, vol. 2, p. 287.

145. Zhukov, *Vospominaniya i Razmyshleniya*, vol. 2, pp. 284–8.

146. Account by Mikoyan, who was present. Kumanev, *Ryadom so Stalinym*, p. 34.

147. Vasilevsky, A.M., *Delo vsey Zhizni* ('*A Whole Life's Cause*'), 6th edn (Moscow, Politizdat, 1989), vol. 1, p. 213.

148. Rzheshevsky, *Kto byl Kto v Velikoi Otechestvennoi Voine*, p. 330.

149. Chevela, P.P., in Zolotarev and Sevost'yanov (eds), *Velikaya Otechestvennaya Voyna*, vol. 1, pp. 319–21.

150. Trevor-Roper, H.R. (ed.), *Hitler's War Directives, 1939–45* (London, Pan Books, 1966), pp. 178–83.

151. Emel'yanov, Yu, *Marshal Stalin* (Moscow, Yauza-Eksmo, 2007), p. 246.

152. Zhukov, *Vospominaniya i Razmyshleniya*, vol. 2, pp. 67–8.

153. Portugalskiy, *Marshal Timoshenko*, p. 280.

154. Stalin, I.V., *Sochineniia*, vol. 15 (Moscow, 1997), pp. 110–11.
155. Zhukov, *Vospominaniya i Razmyshleniya*, vol. 2, pp. 298–9.
156. Yeremenko, A.I., *Stalingrad* (Moscow, Voyenizdat, 1961), pp. 131–2.
157. Yeremenko, *Stalingrad*, p. 306. According to the record of his movements in Korol'chenko, *Neistoviy Zhukov*, p. 225, Zhukov did not arrive there until 31 August.
158. Zhukov, *Vospominaniya i Razmyshleniya*, vol. 2, p. 306.
159. Zhukov, *Vospominaniya i Razmyshleniya*, vol. 2, p. 305.
160. Isayev, *Georgiy Zhukov*, pp. 352–3.
161. Zhukov, *Vospominaniya i Razmyshleniya*, vol. 2, p. 312.
162. Jones, *Stalingrad*, pp. 211–17.
163. Beevor, A., *Stalingrad* (London, Viking, 1998), p. 166.
164. Zhukov, *Vospominaniya i Razmyshleniya*, vol. 2, pp. 314–16.
165. Zhukov, *Vospominaniya i Razmyshleniya*, vol. 2, p. 349.
166. Zhukov, *Vospominaniya i Razmyshleniya*, vol. 2, p. 342.
167. Seaton, *The Russo-German War, 1941–45*, p. 309.
168. Glantz, *Zhukov's Greatest Defeat*, and Isayev, A., in preface to the Russian edition, Glants *sic*, D., *Krupneysheye Porazheniye Zhukova* (Moscow, Astrel, 2007), pp. 20–1.
169. Zhukov, *Vospominaniya i Razmyshleniya*, vol. 2, pp. 347–8.
170. Glantz, *Zhukov's Greatest Defeat*, p. 325.
171. TSAMO, f. 48a, Op. 3408, D.72, p. 262.
172. Sudoplatov, *Special Tasks*, pp. 152–60. See also Sudoplatov, *Razvedka i Kreml'*, pp. 180–8, and *Spetssluzhby. Pobeda v Taynoi Voyne, 1941–45* ('*Special Services; Victory in the Secret War*') (Moscow, Olma-Press, 2005), pp. 314–23.
173. Sudoplatov, *Razvedka i Kreml'*, pp. 180–8.
174. There was no body called the 'War Council', and Stalin's appointment book shows that he held no meetings with any senior military figures between 31 October and 5 November 1942. Gor'kov, *Kreml', Stavka, Gensthab*, p. 274.
175. Glantz, *Zhukov's Greatest Defeat*, p. 37.
176. Gehlen, R., *The Gehlen Memoirs* (London, Collins, 1972), p. 66.
177. Galitskiy, K.N., *Gody Surovykh Ispytanii* ('*Years of Severe Tests*') (Moscow, Voyenizdat, 1973), pp. 178–9.
178. Zolotarev and Sevost'yanov (eds), *Velikaya Otechestvennaya Voyna*, vol. 2, pp. 224–9.
179. Babadzhanyan, A., *Dorogi Pobedy* ('*Roads of Victory*') (Moscow, Molodaya Gvardiya, 1972), pp. 73–6.
180. Katukov, M.E., *Na ostrie glavnogo udara* ('*At the spearhead of the main blow*') (Moscow, Voyenizdat, 1974), pp. 236–7.
181. Gribkov, A.I., *Ispoved' Leitenanta/Vstrechi s Polkovodtsami* ('*Lieutenant's Confession/Meetings with Military Leaders*') (Moscow, Mysl', 1999), p. 118.
182. Glants *sic*, *Krupneysheye Porazheniye Zhukova*, pp. 20–1.
183. Glants *sic*, *Krupneysheye Porazheniye Zhukova*, pp. 22–3.
184. Newton, S., *Kursk: the German View* (Cambridge, Mass, Da Capo Press, 2000), p. 374.
185. Korol'chenko, *Neistoviy Zhukov*, pp. 225–6.
186. Glantz, *Zhukov's Greatest Defeat*.
187. *GSS*, p. 285.

188. Glantz, *Zhukov's Greatest Defeat*, pp. 20, 383 n26. Also see pp. 309 and 379 for casualty figures.
189. *GSS*, p. 228.
190. Zhukov, *Vospominaniya i Razmyshleniya*, p. 359.
191. Carell, P., *Scorched Earth: Hitler's War on Russia* (London, Harrap, 1970), vol. 2, pp. 266–74.
192. Seaton, *The Russo-German War, 1941–45*, p. 259.
193. Bialer, S. (ed.), *Stalin and his Generals* (New York, Pegasus, 1969), pp. 435–6.
194. *Izvestiia*, 29 September 2000.
195. Cited in *Voyenno-Istoricheskiy Arkhiv*, 3, 18 (2001), p. 96.
196. Bialer, *Stalin and his Generals*, p. 420.
197. Manstein, *Lost Victories*, pp. 318–24.
198. Sokolov, *Stalin: Vlast' i Krov'*, pp. 262–3.
199. Sokolov, *Stalin: Vlast' i Krov'*, pp. 262, 264.
200. Brown, D., Shores, C. and Macksey, K., *The Guinness History of Air Warfare* (London, Guinness Superlatives, 1976), p. 155.
201. Seaton, *The Russo-German War, 1941–45*, p. 332.
202. Zhukov in 1964 to V. Sokolov, in Smirnov, *Marshal Zhukov*, p. 245.
203. Cited in Anders, W. and Munoz, A., 'Russian Volunteers in the German Wehrmacht in WWII', http://feldgrau.com/rvol.html, accessed 12.04.09.
204. Smirnov, E.I., *Frontovoie Miloserdie ('Front Mercy')* (Moscow, Voyenizdat, 1991), p. 427.
205. *GSS*, p. 182.
206. *GSS*, pp. 178–82.
207. Kumanev, *Ryadom so Stalinym*, p. 37.
208. Carell, *Scorched Earth*, p. 203.
209. von Mellenthin, F.W., *German Generals of World War II* (Norman, University of Oklahoma Press, 1977), p. 104.
210. Seaton, *The Russo-German War, 1941–45*, pp. 246–8.
211. Jukes, G., *Hitler's Stalingrad Decisions* (Berkeley, University of California Press, 1985), p. 142.
212. Shtemenko, S.M., *The Soviet General Staff at War, 1941–45*, translated from Russian by Robert Daglish (Moscow, Progress Publishers, 1970), p. 99.
213. All figures are from *GSS*, pp. 171–5, 179–82, 187–90.
214. Evdokimov, R.B. (ed.), *Lyudskie poteri SSSR v Velikoi Otechestvennoi Voyne* (*'Human losses of the USSR in the Great Fatherland War'*) (St Petersburg, 'Blitz', 1995), p. 109.
215. Evdokimov, *Lyudskie poteri SSSR v Velikoi Otechestvennoi Voyne*, pp. 125–6.
216. Zolotarev and Sevost'yanov (eds), *Velikaya Otechestvennaya Voyna*, vol. 1, p. 518.
217. Data taken from *GSS*, pp. 143, 157, 391; and Zolotarev and Sevost'yanov (eds), *Velikaya Otechestvennaya Voyna*, vol. 1, pp. 516–18.
218. *GSS*, pp. 366–9.
219. *GSS*, p. 361.
220. Zolotarev and Sevost'yanov (eds), *Velikaya Otechestvennaya Voyna*, vol. 1, p. 519.
221. Zolotarev and Sevost'yanov (eds), *Velikaya Otechestvennaya Voyna*, vol. 1, p. 519.
222. Zolotarev and Sevost'yanov (eds), *Velikaya Otechestvennaya Voyna*, vol. 1, p. 520.
223. Bullock, *Hitler and Stalin*, p. 851.

224. Evdokimov, *Lyudskie poteri SSSR v Velikoi Otechestvennoi Voyne*, p. 126.
225. Evdokimov, *Lyudskie poteri SSSR v Velikoi Otechestvennoi Voyne*, pp. 166–7.
226. Evdokimov, *Lyudskie poteri SSSR v Velikoi Otechestvennoi Voyne*, pp. 167–8.
227. Evdokimov, *Lyudskie poteri SSSR v Velikoi Otechestvennoi Voyne*, pp. 170–2.
228. Evdokimov, *Lyudskie poteri SSSR v Velikoi Otechestvennoi Voyne*, pp. 124–7.
229. Shtemenko, *The Soviet General Staff at War, 1941–45*, p. 71.
230. Shtemenko, *The Soviet General Staff at War, 1941–45*, p. 71.
231. Carell, *Scorched Earth*, p. 126.
232. Shtemenko, S.M., *General'nyy Shtab v gody Voyny* (*'The General Staff in the War Years'*) (Moscow, Voyenizdat, 1981), vol. 1, p. 170.
233. Shtemenko, *General'nyy Shtab v gody Voyny*, vol. 1, p. 170.
234. Shtemenko, *General'nyy Shtab v gody Voyny*, vol. 1, p. 170.
235. TSAMO, f. 203, Op. 2843, D.323, pp. 1–4.
236. Zhukov, *Vospominaniya i Razmyshleniya*, vol. 1, pp. 231–4.
237. Carell, *Scorched Earth*, vol. 2, p. 270.
238. Rzheshevsky, *Kto byl Kto v Velikoi Otechestvennoi Voine*, p. 350.
239. Seaton, *The Russo-German War, 1941–45*, p. 588.
240. Mueller-Hillebrand, B., *Das Heer, 1933–45* (*'The Army'*) (Frankfurt/Main, E.S. Mitttler & Sohn, 1969), vol. 3, Tables 48–50.
241. Warlimont, W., *Inside Hitler's Headquarters* (London, Weidenfeld & Nicolson, 1964), p. 334.
242. Isayev, A., in preface to Glants *sic*, D., *Krupneysheye Porazheniye Zhukova*, pp. 24–5.
243. Point 12d of C-in-C Wehrmacht Operations Order no. 6 on the Plan for Operation 'Citadel' of 15 April 1943.
244. de Franceschi, C., de Vecchi, G. and Mantovani, F., *Le operazioni delle unita italiane al fronte russo, 1941–43* (Rome, 1977), p. 487.
245. Schreiber, G., in Foerster, J. (ed.), *Stalingrad, Sobitiie, Vozdeistviie, Simvol* (*'Events, Effect, Symbol'*) (Moscow, Progress-Akademiia, 1994), pp. 295–7.
246. *Kriegstagebuch des OKW*, vol. 3, p. 213.
247. Mannerheim, K.G., *Memoirs*, in Russian (Moscow, Vagrius, 1999), pp. 393–4.
248. Mannerheim, *Memoirs*, pp. 439–43.
249. Wegner, B., in Foerster, *Stalingrad, Sobitiie, Vozdeistviie, Simvol*, pp. 315–16.
250. Telegin, K.F., *Voyny Neschitanye Versty* (*'Countless miles of War'*) (Moscow, Voyenizdat, 1988), pp. 217–18.
251. Bartov, O., *The Eastern Front 1941–45: German Troops and the Barbarisation of Warfare* (Houndmills & London, MacMillan/St Antony's Series, 1985), p. 124.
252. Klink, E., *Das Gesetz des Handelns 'Zitadelle'* (Stuttgart, DVA, 1966), pp. 331–8.
253. Mueller-Hillebrand, *Das Heer, 1933–45*, Table 54, in Seaton, *The Russo-German War, 1941–45*, pp. 358–9, n.19.
254. Seaton, *The Russo-German War, 1941–45*, p. 356.
255. Korol'chenko, *Neistoviy Zhukov*, p. 228.
256. Zhukov, *Vospominaniya i Razmyshleniya*, vol. 3, p. 12.
257. Vasilevsky, *Delo vsey Zhizni*, vol. 2, p. 12.
258. Vasilevsky, *Delo vsey Zhizni*, vol. 2, p. 7.
259. Mikoyan, *Tak Bylo*, pp. 452–3.
260. Accoce, P. and Quet, P., *The Lucy Ring* (London, W.H. Allen, 1967), pp. 96–9.

261. Sudoplatov, *Razvedka i Kreml'*, p. 169. There are, however, some inaccuracies in his account.
262. Sokolov, B.V., *Razvedka, Tayny Vtoroi Mirovoi Voyny* (*'Intelligence: Secrets of the Second World War'*) (Moscow, AST-Press, 2001), pp. 145–6, 322–3.
263. Hinsley, F.H., Thomas, E.E., Ransom, G.F.E. and Knight, R.C. (eds), *British Intelligence in the Second World War*, vol. 2 (London, HMSO, 1981), p. 624.
264. Hinsley et al, *British Intelligence*, vol. 2, pp. 764–5.
265. Trubnikov, V.I. (ed), *Ocherki Istorii Rossiiskoi Vneshnei Razvedki* (*'Essays on the History of Russian External Intelligence'*), vol. 4 (Moscow, Mezhdunarodniie Otnosheniia, 2003), p. 246.
266. Trubnikov, *Ocherki Istorii Rossiiskoi Vneshnei Razvedki*, p. 184.
267. Trubnikov, *Ocherki Istorii Rossiiskoi Vneshnei Razvedki*, pp. 246–7, 280.
268. Sudoplatov, *Razvedka i Kreml'*, pp. 175, 178.
269. Trubnikov, *Ocherki Istorii Rossiiskoi Vneshnei Razvedki*, p. 185.
270. Hinsley et al, *British Intelligence*, vol. 3, pt 1, pp. 477–9.
271. Hinsley et al, *British Intelligence*, vol. 3, pt 1, pp. 479–82.
272. Ivanov, S.P., *Shtab Armeiskiy, Shtab Frontovoi* (*'Army Staff, Front Staff'*) (Moscow, Voyenizdat, 1990), pp. 428, 456–7.
273. Rokossovsky, *Soldatskiy Dolg*, p. 267.
274. *Kriegstagebuch des OKW*, entry for 5 July 1943.
275. *Russkiy Arkhiv: Velikaya Otechestvennaya. Tom 15 (4–4) Kurskaya Bitva. Dokumenty i Materialy 27 Marta–23 Avgusta 1943 goda* (*'Russian Archive: the Great Fatherland War. Volume 15 (4–4) The Battle of Kursk. Documents and Materials 27 March–23 August 1943'*) (Moscow, Terra, 1997), p. 32. Hereafter RA and volume number.
276. Hinsley et al, *British Intelligence*, vol. 3, pt 1, pp. 477–82.
277. Website: worldwar2aces.com/tiger-tank, accessed 20/01/08.
278. Sokolov, *Stalin: Vlast' i Krov'*, p. 259.
279. A history of the development of the T-34 can be found on website 'The Russian Battlefield T34 medium tank', accessed 10 January 2010.
280. Website: 'The Russian Battlefield T34 medium tank'.
281. Shtemenko, *General'nyy Shtab v gody Voyny*, vol. 1, p. 212.
282. Shtemenko, *General'nyy Shtab v gody Voyny*, vol. 1, p. 212.
283. Mikoyan, *Tak Bylo*, pp. 452–7.
284. Zamulin, *Prokhorovka*, pp. 126–7.
285. Kazakov, K.P., *Kogda Gremeli Pushki* (*'When the Guns Roared'*) (Moscow, Voyenizdat, 1986), pp. 92–5.
286. Isayev, A., *Anti-Suvorov* (Moscow, Yauza-Eksmo, 2005), p. 294.
287. Figures in the tables are from RA, vol. 4/4, pp. 407–9.
288. Rokossovsky, *Soldatskiy Dolg*, pp. 258–9.
289. Damaskin and Koshel, *Velikaya Otechestvennaya Voyna 1941–45*, p. 264
290. *GSS*, pp. 187–8.
291. The Central Front's divisions averaged 4.5–5 thousand, and only four had 6–7,000. Full strength was 10,400. Rokossovsky, *Soldatskiy Dolg*, p. 265.
292. Gor'kov, *Kreml', Stavka, Gensthab*, p. 114.
293. *GSS*, pp. 178–9.
294. RA, vol. 4/4, p. 417.

295. *GSS*, p. 188.
296. Kul'kov et al, *Voina 1941–45*, p. 101; converted from per kilometre data.
297. Rokossovsky, *Soldatskiy Dolg*, p. 267
298. Zhukov, *Vospominaniya i Razmyshleniya*, vol. 3, p. 47.
299. Lopukhovsky, L., *Prokhorovka Bez grifa Sekretnosti* ('*Prokhorovka without the stamp of Secrecy*') (Moscow, Yauza-Eksmo, 2007), p. 73.
300. Carell, *Scorched Earth*, p. 33.
301. Zhukov, *Vospominaniya i Razmyshleniya*, vol. 3, p. 47.
302. Lopukhovsky, *Prokhorovka Bez grifa Sekretnosti*, pp. 67–70.
303. Khazanov, D.B. and Gorbach, V.G., *Aviatsiia v bitve nad Orlovsko–Kurskoi Dygoi. Oboronitel'nyy Period* ('*Aviation in the battle over the Orel–Kursk salient: Defensive period*') (Moscow, Voyenizdat, 2004), pp. 100–4.
304. Rokossovsky, *Soldatskiy Dolg*, p. 269.
305. Antipenko, N.A., *Ryadom Zhukovym Rokossovskim* ('*Alongside Zhukov and Rokossovsky*') (Moscow, MBOF Pobeda-1945, 2001), p. 20.
306. Lopukhovsky, *Prokhorovka Bez grifa Sekretnosti*, p. 94.
307. Katukov, *Na ostrie glavnogo udara*, pp. 219–21.
308. Zetterling, N. and Frankson, A., *Kursk 1943: A Statistical Analysis* (London, F. Cass, 2000), pp. 179, 186.
309. Lopukhovsky, *Prokhorovka Bez grifa Sekretnosti*, pp. 92–3.
310. Lopukhovsky, *Prokhorovka Bez grifa Sekretnosti*, p. 93.
311. Zamulin, *Prokhorovka*, pp. 612–13.
312. Piven, V.A., in *Komsomolskaya Pravda* newspaper, 4 August 1993.
313. Zamulin, *Prokhorovka*, p. 657.
314. Zetterling and Frankson, *Kursk 1943*, pp. 102–9.
315. Zamulin, *Prokhorovka*, p. 657.
316. For example, Nipe, G.M., Jr, *Decision in the Ukraine* (Winnipeg, J.J. Fedorowicz, 1996), pp. 32, 60–1.
317. Korol'chenko, *Neistoviy Zhukov*, p. 231.
318. Lopukhovsky, *Prokhorovka Bez grifa Sekretnosti*, pp. 539–40.
319. Internet: militera.lib.ru/h/zamulin_yn2/18.html accessed 25 June 2009.
320. Lopukhovsky, *Prokhorovka Bez grifa Sekretnosti*, pp. 610–11.
321. Voyenno-Istoricheskiy Arkhiv (Military-Historical Archive), no. 3/2001, p. 89. Hereafter VIA.
322. Zamulin, *Prokhorovka*, pp. 477–8.
323. Safir, V.M., in VIA 1/1997, p. 110.
324. Safir, in VIA 1/1997, p. 110.
325. Zamulin, *Prokhorovka*, p. 598.
326. Zhukov, *Vospominaniya i Razmyshleniya*, vol. 3, p. 58.
327. *GSS*, p. 188.
328. Zhukov, *Vospominaniya i Razmyshleniya*, p. 59.
329. *GSS*, pp. 197–8.
330. *GSS*, pp. 181–2, 188–90.
331. *GSS*, pp. 181, 189, 190.
332. *GSS*, pp. 187–90.
333. TSAMO, f. 203, Op. 2843, D.427, L.17, in Lopukhovsky, *Prokhorovka Bez grifa Sekretnosti*, p. 516.

334. Website: The Russian Battlefield – T-34–85 Development History.mht.

335. Website: The Russian Battlefield, Table of Armour Penetration, F-34 gun.

336. Sebag-Montefiore, H., *Enigma* (London, Folio Society, 2005), pp. 259–60.

337. *GSS*, pp. 188–91.

338. *GSS*, pp. 146–7.

339. Figures from *GSS*, pp. 188–98.

340. Glantz, *Zhukov's Greatest Defeat*.

341. Hinsley, F.H. and Stripp, A. (eds), *Codebreakers* (Oxford, Oxford University Press, 1993), p. 91.

342. Golushko, I.M., *Shtab Tyla Krasnoi Armii v gody Voyny 1941–1945* (Moscow, Ekonomika i Informatika, 1998), p. 135.

343. VIA, 6/2001, p. 90.

344. Long, J., *Lend-Lease as a Function of the Soviet War Economy*. http://www.sturmvogel.orbat.com/SovLendLease.html, accessed 11 January 2010.

345. Emel'yanov, *Marshal Stalin*, p. 329.

346. Rubtsov, Yu V., *Marshaly Stalina ('Stalin's Marshals')* (Rostov-on-Don, Feniks, 2002), pp. 222–3.

347. Temirov and Donets, *Entsiklopediia Zabluzhdenii: Voina*, p. 212.

348. Zolotarev and Sevost'yanov (eds), *Velikaya Otechestvennaya Voyna*, vol. 1, pp. 391–9.

349. Evdokimov, *Lyudskiie Poteri SSSR v Velikoi Otechestvennoi Voyne*, pp. 40–2, 84.

350. Evdokimov, *Lyudskiie Poteri SSSR v Velikoi Otechestvennoi Voyne*, pp. 77–9.

351. *GSS*, pp. 360, 367.

352. All figures from *GSS*, pp. 351–60.

Index